Six Weeks in
SARATOGA

Saddlery

August 27, 2011

For Ralph,

Six Weeks in
SARATOGA

How Three-Year-Old Filly Rachel Alexandra
Beat the Boys and Became Horse of the Year

Enjoy the ride with
Alexandra the Great!

Happy Travers Day!

BRENDAN O'MEARA

Brendan O'Meara

excelsior editions

State University of New York Press
Albany, New York

Cover art: Rachel Alexandra and Calvin Borel courtesy of Nicholas Aquilino

Published by State University of New York Press, Albany

Excelsior Editions is an imprint of State University of New York Press

For information, contact State University of New York Press, Albany, NY
www.sunypress.edu

Production by Diane Ganeles
Marketing by Fran Keneston

Library of Congress Cataloging-in-Publication Data

O'Meara, Brendan.
  Six weeks in Saratoga : how three-year-old filly Rachel Alexandra beat
the boys and became horse of the year / Brendan O'Meara.
      p. cm.
  ISBN 978-1-4384-3941-9 (hardcover : alk. paper)
  1. Rachel Alexandra (Race horse) 2. Race horses—United States—Biography.
3. Thoroughbred horse—United States—Biography.   4. Horse racing—California—
Saratoga—History.   I. Title.

  SF355.R33O66 2011
  636.1'320922—dc22   2011004372

10 9 8 7 6 5 4 3 2 1

For Melanie

Contents

WEEK FOUR

WEEK FIVE

WEEK SIX

Acknowledgments

Whoever said writing is a solitary act had it all wrong. The author is every bit the pitcher: the center of attention, but nothing without the players behind him or her. And so because writing is a team sport, here's a thank-you to my lineup for making all the plays.

Thanks to Betsy Senior, Steve Duncker, Hal Handel, P. J. Campo, Don Lehr, Dan Silver (and his tireless staff), and the rest of the New York Racing Association Huddle; to Ed Lewi, Mark Bardack, Steven Crist, John Pricci, and John Scheinman; and to all the dozens of turf writers who were the foot soldiers that provided much of the muscle to this skeleton. Thanks also to Lisa Borel (Funk), Jerry Hissam, Robby Albarado, Shaun Bridgmohan, and Cecil Borel; to Amy Kearns (my Rachel Alexandra liaison), Scott Blasi, Hal Wiggins, Ed Dodwell, Dede McGhee, and Dolphus Morrison; to Tim Poole, Maxine Correa, Todd Pletcher, and D. Wayne Lukas; to Victoria Garlanda (from the Saratoga Room at the Saratoga Springs Public Library) who was a tremendous aid for my John Morrissey chapter (chapter 11); to Richard Hamilton, whose suggestions were priceless; to Donna Bates, who read the manuscript before its submission to SUNY Press; and to Marjorie Knechtel, who catalyzed the publication process, truly a stroke of luck.

The nonfictionist is nothing without characters, *willing* characters who allow you to be a partner in their lives and privacy. They withstand the most mundane questions (What did you eat that night? What was the weather like?). They also withstand the buzzing gnat that is the scribbling reporter always in their shadow, *is* their shadow. What do they have to gain by this? So it with heartfelt gratitude that I recognize my "A" threads in Charlie Hayward, Nicholas P. Zito, Calvin Borel, and Rachel Alexandra.

The greatest of all thanks, though, must extend to my wife Melanie. I worked on this book—the reporting and the writing—while on unemployment. And while my unemployment benefits weren't much less than what I was earning as a sports reporter for *The Saratogian*, Melanie felt the pressure of having to buy all our groceries and to be the rock while I continued to write.

So, Melanie, thank-you.

Prologue

The Answer

The Answer waited. It waited in the dimness of the Four Seasons Beverly Wilshire in Beverly Hills, California. Horse people in their best evening attire plucked hors d'oeuvres off of trays, trays that floated around the room. Their voices hummed. There was talk of the Answer: Who would win the 2009 Horse of the Year? Soon they found their seats and tuned their frequency to the stage for the start of the 39th Annual Eclipse Awards.

Zenyatta turned what was once unanimous into a debate. The 2009 Horse of the Year award had already been won—it was already Rachel Alexandra's award. Why did Zenyatta have to go and win the 2009 renewal of the Breeders' Cup Classic against male horses and look positively fantastic while in motion? She let the boys from America and Europe hold the door open long enough and unleashed her fury. Zenyatta, for those who don't know, was the unbeaten five-year-old mare who ran like a bulldozer on nitro down the middle of Santa Anita's synthetic surface to win the Classic. Perhaps race caller Trevor Denman said it best when Zenyatta struck the front in the Classic when he yelled, "This. Is. Un. Be. Lievable!"

It was supposed to be concrete.

Rachel Alexandra, the freakishly gifted three-year-old filly, had staved off older horses in the Woodward Stakes on closing weekend at Saratoga Race Course. She capped 2009 with her eighth consecutive victory—three against males, the latest against the older, more accomplished brand. Horse of the Year was hers. All she had to do was bask and smile for the camera. Then Zenyatta came running late.

The debating was virulent, the words venomous. Just read some of the forty-seven comments from *Horse Race Insider* editor and columnist John Pricci's Morning Line column, dated January 13, 2010, about the Rachel versus Zenyatta thread. Pricci wrote that it was best for Zenyatta fans if she lost the Horse of the Year vote, reasoning that Zenyatta would come back with her only loss to date being one handed out on paper, should the voters elect Rachel Alexandra over her.

What follows are actual comments, edited for clarity, from readers. Where no avatar was used, the full name has been abbreviated to simply the first or last name.

Jeff says:

My gut feeling is that RA will be retired if she wins HOTY and Zenyatta stays in training. RA can't hide in restricted 3yo races this year, and she wants no part of Zenyatta.

Freespirit says:

Nah, I don't think they will retire RA if she wins. Jackson won't do that, I don't think. However, even though I would love to see Zenyatta race again, not at the expense of her losing HOY. She so deserves it. RA is great too, but I think Zenyatta is better.

Anne says:

I do not understand all of you East Coast-voters' remarks always against Zenyatta. It is getting to be ridiculous and childish. Did that wine that Jess Jackson gave voters (that was announced) with her picture on it cloud your brains? We KNOW it clouded your votes. Stop it! RA can't run a 1¼. She beat a bunch of has-beens in the Woodward.

Zenyatta beat the best we and Europe had to offer in that BC Classic this year. She ran for the first time and proved she can handle it. She ran against the best males and beat them (why do it in 3 when you can beat a field like this in 1 race?). She always showed up and showed up in a fashion that we will NEVER see again. She has class, charm and determination (her own, not that brought on by 20+ whippings).

Give it a rest, Mr. Pricci.

Susan says:

Good Morning John,

I can tell you right now that this loyal Zenyatta fan is not rooting for her to lose. And if the Mosses are keeping her in training, and I hope they are, I don't think her running hinges on the outcome of HOTY. Of course she is going to win, BUT either way it appears that they may very well have a sound, fresh horse who has not been damaged by the rigors of a gut-wrenching campaign. That is the beauty and superiority of Zenyatta and ANOTHER testament to her greatness.

Ron says:

Ah, come on you guys touting RA for HOTY, can't you read a racing form's past performance or watch a race? Take a look at the older horses, horses that RA beat in NY. They certainly weren't the best or the same class that Zenyatta defeated in the classic plus the three-year-old-colt crop sure wasn't the best we ever had. Not taking anything away from RA—she was definitely an outstanding filly, but no Zenyatta.

Mike says:

RA is the HOY. Sorry Zenyat-iacs. Beating a few grass horses on plastic tracks in dumpy bankrupt, fire-ridden California can't compare to winning 8 races on 7 tracks. The only thing preventing RA from HOY honors is the anti-NY media bias.

Sheila says:

I love both horses. That being said, Zenyatta's race in the BC was great, a wow moment. Every time Rachel ran this past year was a WOW moment. You can't deny it! I think that's all that needs to be said!

ThePixiePoet says:

I'm from California, proving this is not an East Coast—West Coast thing: I think Rachel Alexandra is the better horse. She should (barring injuries) put a lid on all nay-sayers in this year's campaign.

When Rachel is given more time to rest, she is a powerhouse. For example, when Rachel was given 2 months off after the Preakness, in her next race alone she broke 2 stakes records (time and winning margin) and came within one second of the track record set by Secretariat, while being eased!

Mark says:

When you go 14-0 against the best in the world, win 2 Breeders' Cups and NOT win HOY, explain how there's NOT an East Coast bias?

Terlingua says:

The best horse of 2009 is quite simple. It's not that hard, people.

Question: Who won the most money with less starts?

Answer: Zenyatta.

Anne M. says:

HOY is simple—Rachel Alexandra.

Zenyatta had one really good race the whole year and people think she should be HOY??? NO WAY.

The room buzzed. Rachel Alexandra, as expected, won Champion Three-Year-Old Filly. Zenyatta, as expected, won her second consecutive Champion Older Mare. Then it was on to the big one, the Answer.

The video montage of Rachel Alexandra and Zenyatta's races called hairs to an about-face. The announcer recited the select few female horses that have also won Horse of the Year over the decades. It is a small sorority.

Rachel Alexandra soared through the fog; she launched for the wire. Zenyatta charged wide off the turns, straightened, and, yes, she somehow won. Fourteen races, fourteen wins, and fourteen photographs. The video's announcer, cognizant of the ongoing debate of who was best, said, "Tonight, we finally get the answer." The *Answer*.

The lights remained dim over the ballroom. Jess Jackson, dressed in a tuxedo with wide lapels, sat in his chair. Jerry Moss was nearby, equally dapper, his features sharp, his teeth gleaming, as if shined by Windex. His wife Ann sat beside him. All three felt confident that their horses would win. One would lose.

National Thoroughbred Racing Association president Alex Waldrop shook the envelope in his right hand like a Polaroid picture, drew a breath, and said, "The Eclipse Award for the 2009 Horse of the Year . . ."

Pre-Meet

1

Knock, Knock, Knockin' on 'Toga's Door

The bell screamed. The gate erupted.

Jockey Calvin Borel's grip on the reins was al dente as he toed his irons in the saddle of Rachel Alexandra, the lone girl in a race against boys, *colts and geldings*, the 2009 $1 million Preakness Stakes. She broke from the far outside and swerved to her right. Borel knew he had to hustle her. The ground was like quicksand under her as she struggled to center herself. Borel gave her a smooch, and she blitzed forward.

Rachel Alexandra cleared the field, felt comfortable. Borel told her, "That's enough," and she came back to him.

Twelve horses chased and drummed a war beat into the Pimlico Racecourse dirt. Behind her coasted the 2009 Kentucky Derby winner Mine That Bird, a gelding whose very jockey in *that* race sat chillingly still in the saddle of Rachel Alexandra. This had never been done, this abdication.

Rachel Alexandra's ears flicked to the outside, pivoting to absorb her surroundings, surroundings that included the fatigued exhalations of her pursuers. Her stride unfolded like a spool of ribbon. The colts' strides behind her shortened and chopped. And like a tide, most receded into the ocean of dirt, with maybe one more wave swelling from the rear.

The turn for home came quickly, and Borel went to work and let his filly uncork that near-thirty-foot long stride down the Pimlico homestretch. Borel's left arm chicken-winged while he let out more slack on the reins. He went to the stick and popped her twice. He switched arms and popped her again.

Mine That Bird was that final wave, the tsunami, the pregnant energy billowing from beneath the water. He took flight and split horses, gaining. Borel kept Rachel Alexandra to task as the wire drew near, its invisible laser waiting to break. Down the center of the track bombed the Kentucky Derby winner, and the question became: Will there be enough room to catch her?

Borel flattened his back and tucked his head into Rachel Alexandra's ribboned mane. His arms extended, his eyes peered to his right, he knew he had it. Rachel Alexandra's eye, ringed in fire, bore down her foe.

Race caller Tom Durkin trumpeted his words at the wire, "And the FILLY did it! Rachel Alexandra has defeated the Kentucky Derby winner Mine That Bird by three-quarters of a length. . . . A magnificent victory. An exquisite filly. And a THRILL to see!"

Borel wagged his right index finger in the air and gave Rachel Alexandra one congratulatory clap on her neck as the pair continued to glide around that oval.

She became the first filly since 1924 to win the Preakness, this after she handed her own sex a 20¼-length sock-to-the-stomach in the Kentucky Oaks, a race for three-year-old fillies run the day before the Kentucky Derby.

The rumble of hooves and the effort with which Rachel Alexandra crushed her feet into the dirt signaled that someone new was at the door, an equine figure trampolining her profile to the pages of every racing periodical in North America.

She banged, she knocked, no, she smashed down the door, this very door.

⌁

Snow blankets Saratoga Springs, New York, and Saratoga Race Course. It buries memories to create geologic striations, each layer an epoch, each a season of racing. Plows leave banks of crusted snow trash as tall as a high school point guard. Salted streets smear with sludge, an unappetizing, slushy gathering by the curbs and on the hidden yellow line dividing lanes of traffic on Union Avenue. Trucks spray sand and salt in fans, like the expanding V behind a swimming duck. Cars purr by with snow tires clicking on the exposed tar.

An afternoon walk in the skin-cracking weather reveals a barren landscape, as if an apocalyptical event took place on Saratoga Race Course. Lone trees that withstood the blast sway but are no less daunted. The wind is eye-squinting sharp. Saratoga Race Course, first erected in 1864, creeks and moans as it endures yet another winter, weathering an off-season of forty-six weeks. There is still time to thaw and have this track perform its calisthenics, to cast off the crust of ice and age.

Snow and ice weigh down the barns' roofs. Plastic window insulation— or something similar—partitions the track's grandstand from the elements. Some of it is torn and frayed, as if it quit and let the air have its way. The fans that circulate air for patrons hang like icicles, barely moving, still months away from work.

The track is indiscernible. It looks like a desert, a tundra, images of racing's past hibernating somewhere below. Now with winter fully upon Upstate

New York, when racing seems as distant a thought as Benedict Arnold's battle against the British here in 1777, one wonders what 2009's meet will bring and what 2009's Travers Stakes—Saratoga's feature race—will leave in one's memory for years to come. Perhaps the Travers will play bridesmaid to the 56th running of the Woodward Stakes. It was a year ago that 2008 Horse of the Year, Curlin, charged like a locomotive down the track in the Woodward, adding to his bankroll and legacy. The city of Saratoga Springs celebrated this horse like Funny Cide before him, lining its streets with maroon-and-gold banners brandishing the name CURLIN up, down, and around Broadway. To match his feat would be spectacular: the thought of surpassing was positively ludicrous! But this is, after all, Saratoga.

Now, skin turns pink, limbs go numb, and you ask yourself, "How is this so wonderful a place for six weeks from the end of July to Labor Day?"

But the winter visions fade. The snow drifts and moguls of slush shrink, and the once-smothered grass stretches to the sky. The rivers roar, fierce with mountain snow. The days lengthen, and the air forgives. Picnic tables of previous seasons rest in stacks of three or four and wait to be scattered like seeds all over the property.

The trees remain skeletal, branches clicking and chattering like shivering teeth. Soon the red oaks start teething buds, which blossom into leaves, feathering together in a hushing swish. The weeping willows cry and moan again.

Soon after the Oklahoma Training Track, opposite the main track across Union Avenue, opens for training, weeks before Season 141 readies to etch its name alongside its 140 predecessors. That horsemen's cologne of hay, feed, and manure wafts through the air as truck after truck buses in body upon body of horseflesh.

Downtown, motorists hurdle from traffic light to traffic light at a slug's pace. The horse statues come out of storage, showing off their designs of jazz musicians or the local leading realtor. Restaurateurs power drill their patios into the sidewalks for the summer.

The shops put their horse paintings on the sidewalks, Putnam Wine Shop's glugs wine for free tastings, and when one looks down at one's watch and sees that it is 9:00 p.m. and the sky is still bright, one says, "Yep, track season is right around the corner."

∽

She looks positively stunning, turning this way and that, ceding to *Vogue* photographer Steven Klein's whims and commands. Her legs are roped in muscle, her gaze both haunting and inviting. She stood in size 6 Silver Queen shoes with white socks on two of her feet. The shutter to his camera purrs and clicks, and his lamps cast a shine on his model. She turns her head; her ears, oddly enough, fan out in a surfer's "hang loose" hand signal. Then, there it is, the winning shot exposed when she cranes her neck over her right shoulder, as if annoyed, putting down an all-too-eager chap who might have been checking her out for too long at a bar, slaying him down almost as if to say, "You?" It's quite the attitude for a three-year-old.

Rachel Alexandra, a filly as brown as dark chocolate, stood, her knees locked, in the gravel outside her barn at Churchill Downs. Just days prior to her photo spread in a female-style magazine for humans, this horse defeated three-year-old colts—including the Kentucky Derby winner, Mine That Bird—in the Preakness Stakes, the second of three Triple Crown races usually reserved for males.

Up until this point she had proven much, but she would need to do more still in America's "What have you done for me lately?" landscape. In these terms, she hadn't done anything, save pose for a magazine. It's safe to say that even with her celebrity and her magnetic pull, she would not find herself taking hits from a bong like Olympic champion Michael Phelps, or philandering like Tiger Woods. All she could be guilty of was spirited bucking in a round pen or eating her fill—four quarts of sweet feed for breakfast, six for lunch, and ten for dinner, with four quarts of cooked oats stirred in. For the remainder of this year, though, she'd have to do more if she wanted to be more than just a flash in the pan, a one-hit wonder. Scott Blasi, assistant trainer to Steve Asmussen, who trained Rachel Alexandra, said, "After all, they call it Horse of the Year, not Horse of the Six Months."

This being, as Blasi said, just halfway through the year, they had a long stretch ahead, many furlongs, where anything could happen, both good and bad, leaving Rachel Alexandra, and the sport of horse racing, shy of goals and heroes. And with his words it became clear that the goals this horse and her connections sought were not unlike the fruits of Tantalus, impossibly far away, but then again, Rachel Alexandra was no Tantalus, and she just might reach the grapes.

She certainly would if the man in the irons had his way.

◦◦◦

Calvin Borel won the Kentucky Oaks on Friday and the Kentucky Derby on Saturday. Everyone wanted a piece of Calvin Borel—*The Tonight Show*, *The Late Show*, and *Pardon the Interruption*, not to mention all the print outlets that gave his phone insomnia. It had yet to reach the point of nausea, though that would come. Borel was the rock star of a dying sport.

Back when Rachel Alexandra was simply an impressive female horse lacking the crossover appeal that turned the filly into an icon, Borel rode her to five straight victories at a slew of tracks in Arkansas, Louisiana, and Kentucky.

Rachel Alexandra was so good, so swift and fast, that Borel would often showboat on her back, much to the chagrin of her owner, as well as of those who hate basketball players who flex after a dunk, football players who dance excessively after a touchdown, and baseball sluggers who stare too long at that magnificent parabola. The consensus is, "Act like you've been there before." He had, and he hadn't.

When he won the Fair Grounds Oaks, Borel peeked back at the field, steered Rachel Alexandra in a hand ride, and celebrated from the sixteenth pole, indicating that they were a sixteenth of a mile from the finish line. Dolphus Morrisson, then the owner of Rachel Alexandra, clouded more by rage than jubilation, roared up to his jockey, and said, "Borel, if I ever catch you doing anything like this on a horse of this caliber, anything at all that would've caused her to swerve a little bit, you would've been face first in that mud out there."

Borel was no stranger to the winner's circle, and at the time Rachel Alexandra's first trainer, Hal Wiggins, was giving Borel a leg up on her back, Borel was near five thousand wins. In horsemen's circles Borel was well known, a jock who woke in the mornings to darkness, whose early days on the Louisiana bush tracks hardened his ethic and calloused his hands while he mucked stalls and rubbed horses. But with a near last-to-first ride on Street Sense in the 2007 Kentucky Derby, the world soon met Calvin Borel and, it seemed, was better for it. So it was, in this instance, that yes, he had been there before.

Out of his near-five thousand wins, he had never been on a horse as good as Rachel Alexandra, and until a jockey has sat on a chest of buried treasure like her, he'd best keep his tongue tied about at-the-wire antics. Already comparisons had been made to Ruffian, regarded as the greatest filly in the history of horse racing. Ruffian's only defeat came when she catastrophically broke down in a match race against Kentucky Derby winner Foolish Pleasure. Comparisons have been made to the late-great Secretariat, namely because he and Rachel Alexandra have such long strides, freakishly long. When in full gallop, Secretariat could cover nearly half the distance between home plate and a major league pitcher's mound. Rachel Alexandra possessed that stride, the way a certain measure of afflatus is dolloped on the most fortunate of athletic specimens. She was in that company.

Which is why Borel, who normally takes the summer off, turned the ignition, shifted into "D," and motored east to Saratoga Springs to ensure that she wouldn't get away. His fear was that if he was out of sight, then out of mind would follow, and he'd be damned if he were both. Not with this filly. Not ever.

∽

Trainer Nick Zito finally made it, at least in his mind. Until 2005 his struggles and his grind were ubiquitous, they were everywhere and anywhere, and until

2005 Zito would never admit to anyone or to himself that he had made it in this game of thoroughbred horse racing. In 2005 Zito was inducted into the National Horse Racing Hall of Fame, just across the street from Saratoga Race Course.

Sure, he admitted, being elected into the Hall of Fame after winning two Kentucky Derbys with Strike the Gold and Go for Gin, a Preakness with Louis Quatorze, and two Belmonts with Birdstone and Da'Tara was the moment he had felt like he had made it. But those visions faded. The old New Yorker in him, his voice crackling like radio static between frequencies, never settles into himself, never rests. This game kills the complacent, so he entered the 2009 Triple Crown season with a handful of sophomores that were far from brilliant. Yes, 2009 for Nick Zito was going to be a long-shot year, and with the horses he had coming to Saratoga, a long-shot meet. "But that's why they run the races," he said.

Coming out of the spring and into the mid-summer, Zito had a smattering of three-year-olds that one may have noticed, at least on the surface, as his contenders for the Saratoga meet and the Travers Stakes. They were horses like Nowhere to Hide, Miner's Escape, and Brave Victory. He was also quick to say, "Or some horse you don't know yet." A late bloomer, no doubt, and there the colt galloped around the Oklahoma Training Track. He breezed by with a red-haired exercise rider mother of one straddling his bay back with that distinctive Nicholas P. Zito saddlecloth, NPZ. A long shot, yes, but the old New Yorker seemed to have an ace up his sleeve if the events-that-be should work in his favor.

Also not to be ignored was the George Foreman of horses, Commentator. This gelded son of Distorted Humor had been racing for five years now, something unheard of in racing at this level. He possessed no shortage of speed, and younger horses around the barn should be so lucky as to pop off the quarter mile fractions he still registered from pole to pole. He won the Whitney in 2008, going right to the front, never looking back. This was after he won the same race in 2005, defeating eventual Horse of the Year, Saint Liam. Zito inked him in for this third Whitney. Should Commentator win, there was a good shot that he would retire a winner, like John Elway, or Michael Jordan . . . the second time.

To hear Zito talk about Commentator is to hear a father talk about his most accomplished son. To Zito, his horses, and he has quite a bunch, are more than just race muscle. He'd point down to his horses getting their hooves treated and say, "That's old school." He appreciates their sacrifice and respects them fully as athletes and as colleagues. Under the NPZ banner, they are all a team, and Commentator would be the captain, the one with the most stripes, the most wins, the most moxie, and the most money, over $2 million earned.

The two look at each other, warped reflections emblazoned on each other's corneas. Zito may also love Commentator the way he does because he may see himself in him, a horse who works hard, loves the grind, whose efforts in this unforgiving game have seen its share of reward, but only after struggle and pain. To see Commentator off may be to see a part of himself forever gone.

Not yet. In the meantime there was one more race and one more crack at history with a legacy written in ink still wet.

∾

After yet another long and barren winter at Aqueduct, the New York Racing Association chief executive officer (CEO) and president, Charlie Hayward, leaned back in his leather recliner in his office, as he was wont to do, and eyed the calendar. In spring the air still had bouts of temper lashing at outsiders who so dared to tempt the elements. Still some three months away from the start of the 141st running of the Saratoga meet, Hayward took note that Labor Day would fall late this year, September 7, 2009. This, he thought, could be devastating. The last week and the last weekend were always ravaged by people who stayed home for Labor Day cookouts, choosing instead to wear white for the final time in backyards under the banner of grill smoke and sizzle. Not to mention that children would be going back to school, buying supplies, new shoes, and new outfits. *Monies were responsibly going elsewhere instead of the late Pick 4.* This, after all, was understandable, but with the meet diving deep into September, Hayward's apprehensions were further exacerbated. It also signified his one day off during the meet, a day where he would cast aside his silken noose, buttoned shirts, pleated pants, and matching suit jacket for shorts, a polo shirt, a cap, a beer, and a *Daily Racing Form*—the same form he helped resuscitate some ten years prior. Handicapping was always an escape, but whenever he threw his traditional garb into the flames for this one day, it took on new meaning, recharging his battery and basking in the near six weeks of racing and the months of preparation that went into that final brushstroke.

Now it was late May 2009, and Hayward left his office at Belmont Park, his black shoes clicking on the pavement. Next he slid into his car for a trip north to Saratoga Springs for what he thought would be a breath of fresh air.

∾

With the 141st running of the Saratoga meet still two months away, much was anticipated when Charlie Hayward planned on being the special guest at the Parting Glass Pub and Restaurant. Tom Gallo, racing manager for Parting

Glass Racing, hosts monthly meetings for his clients who buy shares of horses in partnerships and provides them and others with this gathering, free for all.

Like most of Saratoga Springs, the Parting Glass pays homage to the thoroughbred racehorse, an animal rooted in the Upstate New York economy: just drive through the farms here where countless horses run and graze, grow and race. The Parting Glass's walls are tattooed with framed photographs of winner's circle triumphs and newspaper clips from champions past and paintings of jockeys standing with arms folded. Fresh pictures rest there too: photographs of Mine That Bird winning the Kentucky Derby and Rachel Alexandra throwing down the hammer in the Kentucky Oaks. All this was further evidence, as if one needed more, that racing is embedded like cabinet inlays in the culture of Saratoga Springs.

These meetings garnered the same clientele, owners of various percentages, some in their golden years, others fresh from work, still in suits with suspenders and tie knots loosened just so. But this meeting was different. Voices hummed in the cavernous backroom punctuated with the familiar sound of forks and knives tapping and scraping on plates once filled with salad, shepherd's pie, burgers, and fries.

The backroom became stuffy as the recesses of its cavity swelled and swarmed with more people. Tom Gallo paced around the stage, giving handshakes to clients, making sure the LCD television was in good order so that he could replay races of two Parting Glass horses hitting the wire first downstate at Belmont Park.

Outside the sun still shone like burning magnesium while it remained dark in the pub. Any moment now people expected to see Charlie Hayward walk by outside, framed by the windows, a motion picture show highlighting the sun shimmering on his white hair. The windows, however, failed to broadcast this image: instead, it was just advertisements, the static picture of Henry Street and the Tiznow restaurant across the way.

Light rudely reflected off the buildings and glass across Henry Street, highlighting the placard that rested on every table:

Parting Glass Racing invites you to our:
MONTHLY MEETING
THURSDAY, MAY 28
CHARLIE HAYWARD
NYRA President & CEO, will discuss NYRA plans for the 2009 meet
and take your questions.
7:00 p.m. at The Parting Glass Pub
FREE & OPEN TO THE PUBLIC—
PLEASE JOIN US!
SARATOGA!
Don't just watch it . . . be part of it!

Dinner plates emptied and Guinness, Smithwicks, Killians, and Coors Light refilled glasses. It was already past 7:00 p.m. Reporters from several local newspapers, the Glens Falls *Post Star*, the Albany *Times Union*, and the *Saratogian*, stood in the back, swaying impatiently, deadlines creeping ever closer. When will this meeting get under way? And, more importantly, where was Charlie Hayward?

❧

The day had started off just fine, typical work for Charlie Hayward downstate on Long Island. Spirits were high as he and Hal Handel, New York Racing Association's (NYRA's) vice president and chief operating officer (COO), had a meeting with the soon-to-be-named chair of the New York City Off-Track Betting, Meyer "Sandy" Frucher. The meeting went as well as it possibly could have, with both parties walking away feeling like they had accomplished something, walking away energized, something that is hard to say and feel in horse racing circles.

Before Hayward could think about heading north to Saratoga Springs for his prescribed meeting with horse owners at the Parting Glass, there were still some administrative matters to tend to. He met with the NYRA franchise oversight board, and this had not gone as well as the previous meeting. Up until this point, his afternoon was book-ended with feelings of joy and the typical frustrations of politics. At this point what he needed was to feel rejuvenated by racing fans, passionate people waiting for him in Saratoga Springs, planning their evenings around pub food and horses.

At 1:15 p.m. Hayward got inside his 2008 Volvo S80 and headed north toward the Thruway and Northway, Interstate Route 87, a road that runs like a spine the entire length of New York's eastern border, connecting New York City to Montreal.

Hayward flicked the dial of his radio to WFAN and listened to New York sports talk with Mike Francesa, gibbering on about the Mets' or the Yankees' early struggles without Alex Rodriguez. Hayward's Red Sox still had a solid grasp on the American League East division and were still unbeaten against the Yankees this season. The hope would be that the Sox could hold off a Yankee lineup that was soon to be re-energized by the return of Rodriguez, thus cutting loose the newly signed Mark Texeira, the same Texeira who had previously balked at signing with the Red Sox. Before long, Hayward was on the Tappan Zee Bridge, traffic busy but moving at sixty-five miles per hour.

A stone-fisted uppercut—something blindsided him from the southbound traffic on the other side of the median. Hayward was shocked and startled, jarred by an object that smashed into the hood of his car, peeling back a strip of metal as if it were a piece of string cheese. *Was it a rock? A brick?* Whatever it was, it ricocheted off the left side of his hood and tumbled into the median. Had Hayward seen the projectile, he might have swerved his car into another, creating a wreck in the afternoon traffic. Or, worse, in swerving to the right he could have put himself in the crosshairs of the missile. Even his days as a competitive downhill skier could not have prepared him to move from the projectile's belligerence.

Hayward steered to the right and off Exit 9. He cut the engine and stepped outside to assess the damage. Since the car had been running without a sputter, he figured he could peel down the hood, make his appointment at the Parting Glass, and worry about getting his Volvo fixed once home. He folded down the strip, but when he looked under the hood, the computer box with its Chiclets circuitry had absorbed most of the shock from the impact, its pieces scattered like Legos. Hayward knew then that this little computer deflected the object. He didn't want to think about what could have happened.

Hayward thought to give the car a try, but despite his urgings, it wouldn't start. After seeing the scattered remnants of computer bits, he understood that he had to arrange to have the car and himself brought downstate, away from Saratoga Springs.

After his latest meeting with the franchise oversight board, it would have been nice to greet racing fans "who have some skin in the game." He was deeply interested in their inquiries and insights, a fresh and passionate outlook on this game that he has come to love in all his years, and certainly in his nearly five years since he was hired to run the New York Racing Association.

At first Hayward had his assistant, Maria Diaz, phone Tom Gallo at the Parting Glass to clue him in. After some time had passed, Hayward realized he had time to call Gallo himself and to prepare an announcement for the people eager to attend this gathering.

He promised to reschedule, but he would have to wait until sometime after the 141st Saratoga meet or until another window might open up elsewhere. For now there were other matters to tend to, most notably his Volvo.

༄

Tom Gallo, in a tan blazer, his mood ever light, given that his star guest would not be arriving, took the mike.

There was a collective groan when the audience heard the news, as many racing fans had eagerly awaited Hayward's talk. They tossed their heads in a way that illustrated disappointment and frustration, another public figure letting down the audience, the headliner skipping out on the main act.

It was only a year ago, at about this time, that Hayward came to the Parting Glass for a meeting and spoke about the video lottery terminals (VLTs)—slot machines—that promised to give the state millions and to bolster the purses of all of New York racing at Aqueduct in Ozone Park, Belmont

Park in Elmont, and Saratoga Race Course in Saratoga Springs. He also spoke of track safety and how he thought that Big Brown would probably win the Triple Crown. The jury is out on racetrack safety, and Big Brown laid an egg.

Afterward, having satisfied the crowds, Hayward hung in the back and spoke with fans one on one, answering their questions and appeasing their concerns. One such man went up to a reporter, put his finger on his chest, and said, "Hayward's an honest man. He tells it how it is. I better not read a bad story tomorrow."

So naturally it was with much disappointment that Hayward was stuck downstate, but he made sure to pass along a press release of sorts to Tom Gallo. Gallo stood before the crowd, some still eating, most slamming back pints, and read from Hayward's statement, where he touched upon Saratoga's horse population (strong) and VLTs (stalemate).

Gallo continued reading, projecting his voice as best he could since the mike was no longer working. Of course, those privy to the VLT debacle have heard the word "delay" so often that some may wonder which will happen first: the end of the war in Afghanistan or the installation of slots at Aqueduct.

The kicker and the moment all people waited for was Hayward's words on the Saratoga meet itself, an entity that is every bit Saratoga Springs as Fenway Park is every bit Boston.

Horses are the culture, with restaurants named the Grey Gelding and the Tiznow. Horse statues stand tall down Broadway. Every shop has paintings and photographs of horses running and images of past Travers Stakes winners, often called the Mid-Summer Derby, the feature race of North America's premier racing meet.

The wait staff cleared away the plates and pint glasses and hustled into the kitchen. Patrons stood up and left the Parting Glass. Perhaps this statement by Hayward appeased the crowd, perhaps not. Given the unsteady nature of horse racing in other jurisdictions, it was a warm thought for patrons to know that their treasure would remain rooted to its tradition, unstained and untainted. Still, with two months to go, there was an incredible amount of work to do.

2

Health, History, Horses

Saratoga Springs is a city of many cross sections, all of which have their own charms, such as the devotion to the local public high school teams, the Saratoga Springs High School Blue Streaks. The bleachers clang and roar during football games. The cheerleaders have both boys and girls stirring rallies with their calls and handsprings.

One night on the field in 2008, close to ten coaches barked out commands and, much to the chagrin of those in attendance, saw their Blue Streaks lose a pivotal sectional play-off game to LaSalle (Troy) after being up by three touchdowns at halftime. After the game there were more tears and fallen athletes than one would ever imagine from adolescent boys. A sour headline from the local newspaper garnered dozens of e-mails and phone calls of the "How could you?" variety.

As much as the Blue Streaks are beloved, their rival, the Shenendehowa Plainsmen (Clifton Park), is hated. Separated by eighteen miles of Interstate 87, the two schools are like the Union and the Confederacy, the Red Sox and the Yankees, and Coke and Pepsi. In Saratoga Springs, a Shenendehowa loss is as big as a Saratoga win. After the Blue Streaks won their homecoming game in 2008, the front page of *The Saratogian*—front page as in A1—ran a picture above the fold with the headline, "Go 'Toga!," impartiality be damned.

There is also the private school, Saratoga Central Catholic—Spa Catholic in some circles—located on Broadway, south of the attractions. The Saints have sent pitcher Tim Staufer to the major leagues. Scott Cherry, now a Division I basketball head coach for the High Point University Panthers, was a star guard for the Saints before joining legendary coach Dean Smith at the University of North Carolina at Chapel Hill, winning a national championship.

Spa Catholic rests at the bottom of Broadway, the main drag through town. At the corner of Ballston Ave and Broadway, fifty yards south of Saratoga Central, a politically charged minivan of a local chimney sweep opines on the endless corruption of US government. The rear window is an Orwellian telescreen that broadcasts messages like: "Should greedy corporations run

Congress?"; "Should Congress run us?"; "For Christmas Consume Less"; "For Our Children Consume Less"; or "Should corporations run health care?" There is no telling what will be the topic of this window. Call it the glazed donut that gives the south end of Broadway an activist flavor to accompany one's morning joe.

Heading north, Broadway gives the impression that its inhabitants must be sleepy, groggy, and lethargic. Not far from the chimney sweep's van lie a Dunkin' Donuts and a Stewart's, followed by a Starbucks, an Uncommon Grounds, Saratoga Coffee Traders, The Cupcake Lab, and another Stewart's, all within six furlongs of each other. This, one might think, makes Broadway the most caffeinated stretch of road in the area.

One may also gather that not a single person within the city limits enjoys a home-cooked meal. The restaurants are, by far, the most prevalent proprietorships along Broadway. Such is the case that you may be seated on the patio of Circus Café and get a whiff of something delectable, only to have your server tell you that that is a meal from Brindisi's an arm's length away. Or is that Char Koon? Lillian's? Ravenous? Stadium Café? Hattie's? Irish Times? Bailey's? Cantina? Chianti? Il Forno? Grey Gelding?

Putnam Wines boasts daily wine tastings—dry or sweet, white or red, bottled or boxed, Italian or French, American or Australian. Its sign out front says, "Wine Flu: No Cure Yet, More Cases Every Day," in a delicious pun.

Coming to the main intersection at the corner of Broadway and Church Street/Lake Avenue, you could have behind you a Jaguar, to your left a Ford 150, and in front of you a high school junker. At this intersection you are confronted with any number of routes to take, from Route 50 to I-87, Route 9, Route 9N, and Route 9P. Should you want to head north to Glens Falls, take Route 9. Should you want travel to Lake George and Bolton Landing, take 9N. And if all you want to do is drive around the white-capped Saratoga Lake, take the narrow stretch of pavement that is 9P.

Broadway is as chic as it is working class, with not one but two dog boutique shops, Dawgdom and Sloppy Kisses. This is just down the road from where motorcyclists congregate, their hogs penned in geometrically fine hash marks in front of Uncommon Grounds for a cup of Kingsford charcoal-black coffee to match the leather of their jackets and chaps.

One teenage girl took to straddling one of these bikes and triumphantly raised her arms. With the coils of the bike's suspension barely depressed, the bike's owner bolted toward her and barked her off the bike, inspecting for any damages. She, along with her friends, who were basking in her bravery, scurried away as the hog teetered ever so dangerously, the first domino in a line of stalwart sentinels in no mood to move. The bike stood tall, and all the men tied to the fate of that one bike dabbed their brows and stroked their beards, realizing that danger had been averted.

A McDonald's radio commercial pays homage to the area with its own "regional" blend of Newman's Own organic coffee:

Man One: Got your coffee.

Man Two: Cream and sugar?

Man One: That all depends. The five-one-eight?

Man Two: Albany.

Man One: Mohawk?

Man Two: River.

Man One: Four to six inches of snow?

Man Two: A dusting.

Man One: April showers bring May . . . ?

Man Two: Potholes?

Man One: Okay, you earned it.

Political activists tout posters and signs at the corner of the post office or city hall. Some call for peace and an end to the wars in Iraq and Afghanistan. Other protests surround local contractors, those who have been marginalized and undermined, and protesters hand out fluorescent fliers asking for support from the public. The flyer reads "AREA STANDARDS VIOLATED IN SARATOGA!" and states that the subcontractors who were hired for carpentry work in the High Rock Condominiums are being paid a less-than-fair wage, "below area standard wages."

But there is something to chuckle at amidst such turmoil involving the injury of a horse. Let it be known that the horse, the victim, was never alive to begin with, at least not in a literal sense. After a wedding, or some other event where men donned tuxedos, and under the influence of, perhaps, an open bar, said men set their crosshairs on the Roohan Realty fiberglass horse statue, bolted to the ground between two benches. The images are fuzzy due to the low light and low resolution of the camera tucked in the corner above Roohan's window-paned façade. For an unexplainable reason, people feel compelled to climb atop static fixtures, this horse being no exception. The horse was jumped upon by one man who had a running start. The horse's side was slammed into. The horse swayed, and the man fell to the concrete. Not to be outdone, another man took a similar path, with similar results. After several more jumps, the horse's legs gave out from underneath and broke down, tumbling to the earth in a heap. The men fled the scene, but alas, in a bout of equine brilliance, the horse did not have to be put down; rather, it lived to see the light of day.

Let this be a lesson that if a horse should throw its rider, it may be best to scratch the horse rather than risk further injury. Or is it best to gamble?

～

So how do you explain why a store like Saratoga Saddlery would open on Broadway centuries after Saratoga Springs' founding? And why this store would have a gravestone-size photograph of Rachel Alexandra in its window? Rachel Alexandra's massive head is illuminated, golden in the 6:00 a.m. sun, her amber eyes like a solar eclipse, the whites of her eyes a ring of light flecked pink by blood, her head bowed, and her mouth crunching hard on the bit. For without a racetrack and a culture, this store would not exist, and neither would this fire-breathing photograph of Rachel Alexandra.

After the Revolutionary War, America did its best to depart from the ideals and habits of the Mother Country, and horse racing was cast aside. A "Sport of Kings" would not be tolerated in a new country that fought to squash monarchy. So in 1802 racing was banned in New York State. Edward Hotaling, author of *They're Off: Horse Racing at Saratoga*, wrote that racing was defined as gambling and that the law prohibited "any bet or stakes, in money, goods or chattels, or other valuable thing." Still, Maryland formed its jockey club in 1783, followed soon by the District of Columbia in 1798, and even the third president of the United States, Thomas Jefferson, frequented the National Course.

Eventually Saratoga Springs leaned into the bit, though not in the form racing fans have become used to in the past 150 years. The day was July 4, 1843, at Beacon Course in Hoboken, New Jersey, and Lady Suffolk, a ten-year-old mare, smashed the mile-record of two minutes and thirty-eight seconds for a trotter, a barrier considered "mystical." In that race she defeated a bay gelding by the name of Beppo. Turf historian John Hervey called it "the most sensational exhibition of speed by trotting horses that had yet been seen." She then became the subject of Stephen Foster's old folk song "The Old Gray Mare" ("she ain't what she used to be")

Saratoga had to have her. Lady Suffolk christened the first official day of organized racing in Saratoga Springs on August 14, 1847, as a fourteen-year-old, towing a seventy-four-pound skeleton wagon with her owner, David Bryan, in the back. Seidler's Band gave the packed crowd milling around Congress Park music to move to, a variety that included opera, waltzes, and polkas. The concert began just after sunup, at 6:00 a.m., and made the event every bit a carnival. The band's set lasted nearly three hours, interrupted only by the ring of the breakfast bell at 8:00 a.m.

The road to the track later that afternoon, a soggy afternoon due to the rain from the prior night, was estimated to be filled with thousands of people. Many of the spectators were women from the South, whose interest outweighed those of their male counterparts. Perhaps the Southern women were drawn to the track on this day to witness a girl take on a boy. His name was Moscow, a bay gelding with ivory legs and a bald face, a big, "raw-boned horse, sixteen hands high, a hard puller," as Hotaling noted.

Hiram Woodruff of the *Spirit of the Times* newspaper, as quoted in Landon Manning's *The Noble Animals*, took a kind eye to Lady Suffolk: "When young, Lady Suffolk was an iron grey, rather dark than light but in her old age she became almost white. She was in my judgment little, if any, above fifteen hands and an inch high. She was well made: long in body; back a little roached, powerful long quarters; hocks let down low; short cannon bones and long fetlocks. She had good shoulders, a light and slim yet muscular neck; a large, long, bony head, and big ears. In trotting she went with her head low, and nose thrust out."

At last, the two horses, Moscow with a seventy-five-pound sulky, and Lady Suffolk, with her seventy-four-pound skeleton wagon, were set to race, to kick off what would turn out to be a tradition the city would latch onto indefinitely.

∾

The time was 4:00 p.m.

The horses cantered to the stand. As was typical for racing at the time, they would run one-mile heats in a best-of-five series. The two got in line. Moscow jumped the flag in a moment of anticipation, broke early, and had to be called back. After the second offering the race launched and, despite taking the early lead, Moscow broke—a term when a trotter breaks into an illegal gallop—several times, thus allowing the sure-footed Lady Suffolk to take to the front. She defeated Moscow in the first-mile heat, laboring home in 2:52. In the second-mile heat, she staggered ahead, winning in 2:54. This tied her slowest time in her career at this distance.

The connections for Moscow cried that he was sick. The owner, Gen. A. C. Dunham of Troy, called on the judges to withdraw his horse because he appeared "extremely distressed," and to award Lady Suffolk the purse money. Driven and trained by James Whelpley, he said he paid the entrance, so Dunham had no right to withdraw Moscow. The judges consulted with one another and chose in favor of Whelpley and did not award the money to Lady Suffolk until she had won outright.

After much time, the third heat was under way, and both horses came to run. A *Herald* reporter writes, "The horses moved at a rate which I have never seen equaled." Lady Suffolk was in front, with Moscow gaining, and at the last quarter he was in front of Lady Suffolk. The crowd roared, and Lady Suffolk broke, giving Moscow an even greater advantage. It seemed that it was his race, his heat, but a terrible break occurred within fifteen rods of the stand. Moscow broke stride. The Old Gray Mare got her nose to the finish first, winning by a neck, her head low, her nose thrust out. This time was respectable, at 2:44, defeating yet another gelding, this time for $250.

Years later, in 1851, John Hervey writes about a visit Lady Suffolk took to St. Louis, where her presence drew thousands of eyes to witness this fading specter.

> It was one of those moments which occasionally give a touch of morning splendor to the afterglow of a champion, possibly only to such a champion; to those of a minor order they never come. How it affected the good city of St. Louis itself may be gathered from the flowing item.
>
> When it was known that "the lady" was to start for the East on the fine packet Pennsylvania, Capt. W. Fuller, thousands gathered on the wharf to take a last look at the best piece of horseflesh known. Capt. Fuller ran his boat up the river about a mile, and returned under full steam, the Lady, with Charley Ellis on her back, standing between the capstan and Jack-staff, and when opposite the city, the national flag on the Jack-staff was lowered within about two yards of Ellis' head, streaming out as if proud of its position. Words can hardly describe the scene, and the enthusiasm that was displayed. Even the housetops were crowded on account of the high water; the wharf could not hold the people.
>
> Half way on her journey up the Ohio, Lady Suffolk was taken off the steam at Louisville, and there at the stable of Henry Duncan, she held a regular reception, her presence in the city producing a sensation. And on her arrival at Cincinnati she was received with public honors, and Ellis (Bryan had recently died suddenly on the trip) presented her bridle to the gallant Captain Fuller, who hung it in the grand saloon of the boat as a memorial to its most distinguished passenger. (quoted in Manning, *The Noble Animals*, pp. 12–13)

Theo Marsden, in his painting, illustrates Lady Suffolk in the foreground of a pasture, just in front of a carbon-colored stallion named Black Hawk. If this was a photograph, one would say she looked washed out and overexposed. But that was just her: a specter. In her later years it was said that the old gray mare was getting lighter, nearly transparent, almost as if she made the transference, a friendly ghost meant to haunt the flats, or to bless them.

Throughout history men have plundered most of the fame and infamy, as it were. Still there were the matriarchs who had every bit a role in shaping the generations that would follow, from as early as Egypt's Queen Nefertiti to Russia's Catherine the Great, from Queen Elizabeth, who thwarted the Spanish Armada, to the ill-fated Marie Antoinette.

Why not a racehorse?

∿

Though not connected to Lady Suffolk, an imported sire named Glencoe was to become a great sire of fillies (and, as a result, a great sire of sire of sire of fillies), some of whom ran at Saratoga. Glencoe bridges the past to the present. It was his everlasting legacy that launched into orbit 2009's most charismatic filly. Evidence to the contrary would be hard to argue, since he gave way, in a biblical sense, to the mare Pocahontas, who was bred to The Baron, who beget Stockwell, who beget Doncaster, who beget Bend Or, who beget Bona Vista, who beget Cyllene, who beget Polymelus, who beget Phalaris, who beget Pharos, who beget Nearco, who beget Nearctic, who beget Northern Dancer, who beget Sadlers Wells, who beget El Prado, who beget Medaglia d'Oro, who beget *Rachel Alexandra*.

3

Is She the One?

The June sky was a radiant blue with suspended marshmallow clouds. Underneath this sky Rachel Alexandra, upon the urging of her jockey, Calvin Borel, saw a seam between the two fillies before her, and she split them like firewood. All Borel had to do was stay in the saddle as Rachel Alexandra opened up and up on this field in the Grade 1 1 1/8 miles $300,000 Mother Goose. The track camera panned out, yet still lacked the range to capture the other two horses. The gap between Rachel Alexandra and the field was nineteen and a half lengths by the time her flared nostrils hit the wire, an equally brilliant performance that brought back memories of the Kentucky Oaks, just less than two months ago. She soared over the dirt, bounding close to thirty feet per stride.

It was the first time Rachel Alexandra set foot in the state of New York, and she set a stakes record. Her skin gleamed with sweat, and the veins on her withers throbbed. A promotional poster leading up to the Mother Goose asked, "Is She the One?" Time would tell, but it felt that way. She would need to keep extending her boundaries and conquer more land, to slash the Gordian Knot, as Alexander the Great once did.

For this reason, for the remainder of 2009, she would not run against fillies.

∽

In the weeks leading up to the Mother Goose, the speculation for her next start caused a stir. Her Kentucky Oaks win was greeted with questions about whether or not she should have been running the following day in the Kentucky Derby. But after her goose-bump-inducing win against the boys in the Preakness Stakes, she then became a drumming pulse not just on the racing scene but on the sports scene.

For Borel this trip with Rachel Alexandra to New York and to Belmont Park would be his second, his first since the disaster that was the Belmont Stakes. That experience grated at him and his agent, Jerry Hissam. Borel was chastised for not taking any mounts prior to the Belmont Stakes: instead he was seen walking the streets of New York with his fiancée, Lisa Funk. Perhaps Borel, a Kentucky jockey, was not refusing mounts but, rather, was not offered any. So the mile-and-a-half Belmont Stakes saw him aboard Mine That Bird, the Kentucky Derby winner.

The trainer of Mine That Bird, Bennie "Chip" Woolley, took Borel back. The two do share a diamond-crusted Derby ring that will forever bind them. But in this Belmont Stakes, Borel moved Mine That Bird sooner than most expected, and by the end dueled with Dunkirk and finished third. Now the jockey whom everyone adored was being whipped. *He moved too early! He should have had more mounts!* Had they forgotten that just three weeks earlier Borel had left the Kentucky Derby with white paint on his left boot when he sliced up the rail on Mine That Bird to win? It was the day after he won the Kentucky Oaks by twenty and a quarter lengths aboard Rachel Alexandra.

Mine That Bird aimed for the Preakness. But what would happen to Rachel Alexandra, and who would Borel choose should both go to Maryland for the Preakness? For Borel there was no choice; he would ride Rachel Alexandra, but first it had to be determined whether Rachel Alexandra would run against the boys in the first place.

Dolphus Morrisson, the breeder and owner of Rachel Alexandra for her Oaks win, entertained dozens of phone calls. Then, when wine magnate Jess Jackson called him on Wednesday, May 6, 2009, well, Morrisson threw out a number, an egregious number, and Jackson said it was too much, no deal. Morrisson knew it was too big a price, but he saw Rachel Alexandra as a once-in-lifetime horse, one he wanted to hang onto, and should she be taken from his hands, it had better be for a lot of clams. After a time, Jackson got back on the phone, and said, reluctantly, that they had a deal. Though confidentiality agreements were signed by both parties, that number was said to be as high as $5 million . . . for a filly.

What prompted the deal was what Morrisson said following the Kentucky Oaks: that the Triple Crown races were for future stallions, and that fillies should not run against colts and geldings. This was perceived as chauvinistic, narrow-minded, and even maddening, because he was sitting on Rachel Alexandra when she could be the fastest horse—male or female—in North America, but who would know? Jackson, revered as a gamesman, willing to keep horses in training, and willing to take chances with his horses by putting them in unconventional spots, put his money where his head was. What he saw in Rachel Alexandra was a generational horse, one for the ages, and there was no price too high to see whether he was right or wrong.

∾

So Calvin Borel did the unthinkable. He took himself off the Kentucky Derby winner for Rachel Alexandra. Borel became the first jockey to take off the Derby winner for another horse in the Preakness. This, he knew, would be met with criticisms and darts, because it seemed that, on the surface, he kicked up sand and mud in the face of Mine That Bird and his connections, namely, trainer Chip Woolley. But just like Jess Jackson, he put his money where his head was, because even Borel saw that Rachel Alexandra was a generational horse, one for the ages, and it seemed there was no price too high to see whether he was right or wrong.

∾

This brought Borel to Belmont Park, since Jackson and new trainer Steve Asmussen decided to rest Rachel Alexandra for a race farther downstream. Woolley welcomed Borel back on Mine That Bird, a gelding with a Derby win and a Preakness runner-up in a five-week span, to try and tackle the Triple Crown from the jockey's angle. No, Borel failed in the Belmont Stakes, but he knew he would be back, and beneath that perennial smile in the creases of his forty-two-year-old face burned a need to show just who was boss and who held pocket aces.

∾

On Wednesday, June 24, 2009, the New York Racing Association hosted a national teleconference with Jess Jackson and Calvin Borel leading up to the Mother Goose, which was to be her first race since the Preakness. Of course this followed Borel's gaffe, if one wants to call it that, in the Belmont Stakes. Naturally all the reporters were eager to hear how Rachel Alexandra was doing and how she might do in her first race against fillies since she embarrassed them in the Kentucky Oaks. And the elephant in the room was whether or not Borel would take any mounts on the day of the Mother Goose. This, Borel felt, came with the turf.

"And first to Calvin," Mike Ingram of BlackAthleteSports.net asked, "I'd like to know if you're going to accept any mounts prior to getting on board Rachel in the Mother Goose at Belmont."

This question, were it possible, should have been directed at Borel's agent, Hissam, but Borel fielded it all the same. Borel just gets on them—he lets Hissam go ahead and book the mounts, as he had done in their previous nineteen years of business, business that went all the way back to the Bayou.

"I really don't know yet, sir," Borel said. "I think my agent said I had a couple maybe to ride the day before. But it really doesn't matter. You know,

I know the track and I know my filly and I know what she wants and where we're going to be. It really doesn't matter. But I think I'm going to ride one other, two other horses actually for Ian Wilkes, I think."

Wilkes, a Kentucky trainer, books Borel for many of his horses and he ships to New York for marquee race days his stock from barns eight hundred miles away. This idea that Borel rode only the big horses, like a diva jockey, was a myth. If Borel had his druthers, he would ride a number of horses every day, especially on a race day where the stakes are higher than just money. Borel gets out on the track and feels how his horse sinks into the dirt, how his horse gets over the ground, whether the rail is sticky, or if it is best to pilot his horse wider. Such details travel in a sort of osmosis into the psyche of the rider over the course for the day. Would Borel need this for a projected three-horse field in the Mother Goose against fillies that constituted junior varsity competition? The answer, in this case, was probably no, but reporters and fans alike would have circled like vultures should Borel err, ready to point straight to the fact that he had not been on a horse leading up to the race of merit.

Winning puts animosity to bed, and this was the case when Borel rode Rachel Alexandra in the Mother Goose. Gone were the questions of whether or not he should be riding more horses or not. Perhaps he would be vindicated on this front should he be a regular rider for an entire meet when surrounded by all things New York—jocks, trainers, and horses. He'd be given that chance, or at least that was his hope, for when he was asked whether or not he would be riding at Saratoga he said, "Yes, sir. I sure am. Yes, sir."

And the reason, the only reason, was because of Rachel Alexandra.

After the Mother Goose, Rachel Alexandra scarfed down her food as if she had been starved all day. This training-by-the-feed tub is a good sign that after she set a stakes record her appetite was every bit as strong as it was the morning of the race. Even the next day, she ate every last bit of grain, an indicator that she was a happy horse ready for the next challenge.

Barely twelve hours after her record-setting win in the Mother Goose, Rachel Alexandra was on a van heading north to Saratoga Springs, accompanied by the thirty-five-year-old Scott Blasi, assistant trainer to Steve Asmussen. The van grumbled out of Gotham and onto the Northway in the late-June air. Some four or five hours later, Blasi led her off the van and into Stall No. 1, next to his office, the same stall that was occupied by two-time Horse of the Year Curlin, owned by the same man, Jess Jackson, and conditioned by the same trainer, Steve Asmussen. Naturally the hope was that Curlin's greatness would rub off on her, though that may not be necessary. Rachel Alexandra, at this point, was her own name, her own brand, and great by any stretch. Comparisons to Curlin may be unfair to Curlin. No matter, this was where she would take residence for the summer and, presumably, into the fall.

A number of races were tossed like angel hair, such as the Coaching Club American Oaks for fillies, the Jim Dandy on opening weekend at Saratoga, the $1 million Haskell Invitational at Monmouth Park, the Alabama Stakes at Saratoga, the Travers Stakes at Saratoga, or Rachel Alexandra's first test against older fillies and mares in a try against the unbeaten mare Zenyatta in the Personal Ensign, also at Saratoga. Principal owner Jess Jackson knows well the rivalries in the sport of horse racing, being a part of one in 2008 with Curlin and the Big Brown camp. Words were traded like jabs and uppercuts, but Big Brown came down with a foot injury prior to the Breeders' Cup, and the two never met. Now Jackson had Rachel Alexandra, and Jerry and Ann Moss had Zenyatta out West.

In North America, in 2009, it was said that the two best horses in the country were females, so what more could racing want than to see two competitive females squaring off, taking the spotlight away from the colts and geldings? Over the coming weeks and months, no subject in racing would be talked about more than Rachel Alexandra and Zenyatta. Jackson's camp was well versed in the Curlin–Big Brown sparring of a year ago. Their worry, if there was any, was the health of their champion filly. There would be time for that later, but it was evident that Jackson wanted a third consecutive Horse of the Year title, and that his only shot at it in 2009 was on the back of Rachel Alexandra. The feeling was that a meeting with Zenyatta would determine Horse of the Year honors come January 18, 2010, the date of the Eclipse Awards. Still, perhaps Jackson would have an ace up his sleeve that could trump all. Yes, the Zenyatta–Rachel talk percolated, but these horses are Fabergé eggs or the freshly frozen film of ice on a lake. No one could be more disappointed than the person who has expectations in a game so full of uncertainty.

As the van taxiing Rachel Alexandra neared Exit 12 on the Northway, the median was blanketed with a sheet of black-eyed Susans, the simply elegant flower that looks like *oro*, a golden propeller in constant motion. Normally it would have been just a pretty sight along a highway's scenery that becomes mundane in the rippling summer heat, but this median carried an extra bout of meaning, as if whoever planted those flowers knew who was coming. Black-eyed Susans are the flower of choice for the Preakness Stakes, the race that made Rachel Alexandra a superstar and put her in *Vogue* magazine, and now before her it unrolled like a carpet, a yellow-brick road, on the way to the track that would be her home for the next 111 days.

4

Lunch with Trophy

On Monday, a muggy and cloudy June 29, 2009, Charlie Hayward was back on the horse. Just a few weeks after his Volvo was wrecked by an errant projectile while driving near the Tappan Zee Bridge, he traveled back to the Capital Region for a press conference at the Desmond Hotel in Albany, by Albany International Airport, just off Exit 4 on the Northway. High above, fighter jets tore grooves across the horizon, leaving a Doppler-type roar in their wake.

This was Hayward's official kickoff to the Saratoga meet, where he would sit in front of throngs of media people who were starved more for the free food than for any information Hayward could shower upon them.

In the main room, a theater with elevated tiers, stood a stage with name tags for Dan Silver, director of communications and media relations, Charlie Hayward, president and CEO, P. J. Campo, vice president and director of racing, and Hal Handel, executive vice president and COO. They planned to entertain and welcome an estimated 111 people.

Candies mingled in bowls and pitchers of water sweat. Up front were folded "Saratoga" banners waiting for a human touch and pushpin. Classical music was piped in through speakers, a symphony of woodwinds, strings, and horns.

A "Saratoga" tile was stuck to the lectern with duct tape, the backdrop the 2009 Saratoga logo draped behind the main table. Also decorating the stage were framed Saratoga 2009 logos and a Samsung flat-screen television.

Saratoga icon Sam the Bugler, in his red jacket with a painting of Street Sense and Calvin Borel by Frankie Flores on his back, white pants, and ink-black boots, entered the hall. Sam even signs his name Sam the Bugler, as if future Social Security checks will be made out in this moniker. He rested a case on a table and pulled out the mouthpiece to his bugle and motioned to Ed Lewi, a compact, well-dressed man with a Rudolph nose and inviting smile and founder of the public relations firm Ed Lewi Associates. "I've got something new," Sam said, and he pulled out his bugle with a red Saratoga flag hanging down from the neck and held it up like he had caught a marlin.

Lewi smiled and gestured that Sam was crazy, certifiably crazy. Sam told Lewi that he was to pick up his fiancée from the airport. "I'll welcome her like this," he winked, and put the bugle to his mouth, "and play here comes the bride. I gave her the ring weeks ago, so it's a done deal. I found Mrs. Bugler No. 2."

All Lewi could do was laugh. "This is going to be a good summer, Ed," Sam said. "Good golly, there's Molly!" and with that he exited the hall for a moment's time before he returned to the back of the hall to rehearse and warm up with high notes and low notes. He descended the steps with the mouthpiece detached, blowing muffled notes. Sam relayed a story about his celebrity, which, it must be said, is quite broad: "They said, 'You're gonna be on the cover of the *Times*.' I said, 'Great!' I get the *New York Times* and I'm not on the cover. He said he meant the *Times Union*. 'That's not the *Times*.' I've been doing this long enough where any newspaper is great."

Behind Sam, workers wrestled with getting the backdrop just right, bringing in different poles and flags to cover up blank space since, as it turned out, the Saratoga backdrop was too small. "As long as the poles are covered, she doesn't care about the green," someone said.

Just outside the hall, brochures and media kits were fanned out like a deck of cards. Lewi, Dan Silver, and Mark Bardack, who works for Ed Lewi Associates, conversed in a huddle.

On the morning of June 15, 2009, two weeks before Rachel Alexandra's win in the Mother Goose Stakes, workers at Saratoga Race Course labored to prepare the grounds for the 141st thoroughbred meeting. As horses cantered around the backstretch of the Oklahoma Training Track and poked their muzzles at their hay nets, another hoofed animal lurched about the main grounds. A moose with pogo-stick legs clopped onto the tar where bands would soon play and dancers would soon swing. The moose halted in front of a NYRA help booth with a sign above that read, "May I Help You?" A man shot the moose with a camera before an Environmental Conservation official shot it with a tranquilizer dart. The moose was moved elsewhere, as far away from the racetrack as possible. Still, a moose on the grounds?

Lewi, Silver, and Bardack discussed this moose sighting because the photographer who took the picture would be in the audience as the guest of honor.

A young man sipped his cup of coffee while Bardack instructed him about his mission—to dress in a moose costume for prescribed theatrics. "If you're comfortable with a high five, do a high five," Bardack told the young man. "I wouldn't do a moose kick. That could be dangerous. This won't be until the very end. You're gonna be in the bathroom and I'll look for you. Have the outfit on and the head off. Come in, walk down here. I don't think you can talk, but you can shake hands." "All right," the young man said. "Terrific." Silver came over to Bardack after the moose left. "The moose," Bardack said, gesturing to his BlackBerry, "I'll call him." "I'll be down here and he'll be able to walk in and come in front," Silver said. "As you say that I'll call the moose in." "Make sure the cameras know what's going on."

And with that the journalists filed into the room with hunger in their bellies and their arms full of handouts, taking their seats before the stage, armed with verbal darts and lightning bolts. At 11:45 a.m., Handel, Campo, and Silver were ready, but the show had to wait for Hayward, whom no one had seen. Handel, a man who often greets a friend by taking a firm hold of a forearm, stood in the doorway in his suit, making small talk in a voice so soothing and strong it would be better suited for audio books. Of course there was talk of Rachel Alexandra and what she had done in the Mother Goose Stakes just two days earlier.

"Real racing is coming back," he said. "She's something else."

At 11:50 a.m., Silver stood at the lectern, ready to start the press conference. Handel sat at the far end of the table with his arms folded, and to his right stood Campo at the front, leaning in toward Handel. At last Hayward, keeping all those present waiting, entered in a navy-blue suit, a white shirt, and a blue tie adorned with horses in full stride. He took his seat and leaned into Silver, and they exchanged words. Hayward's glasses balanced atop his head of wizard-silver hair. Five television cameras framed Hayward and the camerapeople pressed their "record" buttons.

Out from the hall came Sam the Bugler in his full regalia, and he stood stage left. He took a deep breath, pressed his bugle to his lips, leveled it like he were preparing to blow a poison dart, and shrilled "The Call to the Post," as is so often heard prior to post every day of racing for every race.

"Thank you, Sam," Silver said from behind the microphone of the lectern, "We are certainly looking forward to hearing much more of that coming up in July and August and September. I would like to thank everyone for coming to the Saratoga news conference and for taking the time to join us today. From what I've been told, this may be the biggest turnout we've ever had, hopefully a good indicator for the upcoming meet."

A year ago, the 2008 Saratoga meet did not meet expectations, especially the expectations set by 2007's race meeting that saw only six races get rained off the turf in thirty-six days. Infinite rain defined 2008. Just when they thought it wouldn't rain, it would. And when they thought it would only rain a little, the rain was torrential. So, yes, if this turnout was an indicator that the 141st meeting at Saratoga would exceed expectations, then enthusiasm could be welcomed, albeit tempered, because of the state of the economy.

Silver, a twenty-eight-year-old graduate of the University of Arizona's racetrack industry program, was new to the scene, just a newborn pup who drove to Saratoga the moment he got his driver's license over ten years ago. He considered Saratoga the most beautiful track in the country, and though he worked for NYRA, which operates Aqueduct, Belmont Park, and Saratoga race courses, it wasn't posturing. Prior to taking his post at NYRA he was director of media for the Missouri River Otters, a AA minor league hockey team, a far cry from Upstate New York.

"So without further ado," continued Silver, "I would like to introduce to you a person who was recently named one of the Top Ten most influential and powerful leaders in racing by the *Thoroughbred Times*, NYRA president and CEO, Charles Hayward." Then Hayward stood and walked to the podium as if being pulled to a mountain summit, a frosted cone of rock, as was the case time and time again in his youth.

～

The ski lift's stuttering motion swung the chairs like dangling earrings. Charlie Hayward stood static on top of the mountain and fixed his goggles, poles anchored.

A push, a calculated dismount from a position of potential energy, now riding gravity, he sloshed, digging his skis into the crust with that grind of directional change between flags, left, right, left, right. Hayward was a competitive skier of many tastes: jumps, cross-country, slalom, and giant slalom. He took the Ski Meister Award for the best overall score in all four events for three out of his four years as a history major at Bowdoin College. He was undefeated his last two years in his best event—cross-country. At the time he ran cross-country, which grounded in him a sense of endurance, building a foundation to glide over hills and take unexpected turns at a whim. His mind, his compass, was calibrated for skiing and for becoming the most dominant skier against schools such as the University of Maine, Bates, and Colby.

Born on the southeastern coast of Massachusetts near the cranberry capital of the world, Middleboro, where there are more bogs than Red Sox fans, he emigrated north to Bridgton, Maine, where his father, H. John Hayward, a ski patrolman, made a skier out of him. He took his fandom for the Red Sox over state borders and weathered the eternal bludgeoning that came with being a Red Sox fan through the sixties, seventies, and eighties, with loyalty at last rewarded in 2004 and 2007.

Hayward was the second of four siblings—two brothers and the youngest, a sister, Barbara. The four would play touch football in the neighborhood and while they protected their sister, they also hazed her and treated her like she was one of the boys. "Get beat up, bloody noses, I wanted to be part [of it], even though I was younger," Barbara recalled.

Hayward and his older brother shared an "orderly" room, according to Barbara. They led a humble life in Bridgton, Maine, where everybody knew everybody. The Haywards were a close family and skied every winter spending Christmas mornings unwrapping new skiing gear. Everyone skied until Mrs. Hayward broke her leg and decided to spend her time working in the lodge while the others shredded the trails. Barbara said that while they were growing up they were encouraged to "be your own person." Hayward, the skinny, scrawny adolescent, proved this by filling up his days working on Nantucket as a paperboy, a milkman, a bank teller, or a piano player.

The Haywards would visit their grandparents in Duxbury, Massachusetts, and go water skiing and swimming and barbeque by the lakes.

High school for Hayward was a stage where he was the leading man. He was the president of his class of sixty-nine students, president of the student council, captain of the football team, captain of the baseball team, and captain of the ski team. In addition, he was quarterback of the football team and shortstop of the baseball team. He joked, "You're talking about not a particularly big fish, but a small pond."

Given the nature of his type A accolades, his peers dubbed him "Trophy," because he was always being presented with a memento of yet another triumph over those who lacked his talent and drive. Hayward also graduated number three in his class. "So I did okay," he said. "I was just a highly motivated, decent kid."

He had his senior portrait taken at the Wendell White Studio in Portland, Maine, where he wore a dark suit and tie with a white shirt. His hair shone and his face brimmed with a confident smile. Handsome with a right-slanting part in his blonde hair, he signed a card to his friends, Bruce and Sandy, which read:

> Thanks ever so much for all the help you've given me; it certainly is appreciated. I only hope some day I can repay you for the faith and trust you've had in me.
>
> Charlie

When Hayward searched for colleges, his principal and guidance counselors directed him and others to the University of Maine at Orono. Children from small towns weren't encouraged to enroll at the private colleges. Hayward applied for early acceptance at Bowdoin College, a private school, and was admitted.

When Barbara readied herself for college she sought advice from Hayward. When she wanted to take a year off, he listened to her and told her he supported her decision. He eased her apprehensions. *Be your own person.*

Meanwhile, he had his own challenges. College provided another set of obstacles. Most of his classmates at Bowdoin attended prep schools, so in their files they had papers on King Lear tucked away should they ever need to regurgitate it like a mother bird nursing its chicks. While in high school—a rural public high school—Hayward, to the best of his recollection, wrote only one paper. At Bowdoin, he had to write one paper a week for English and two papers for history. While his buddies changed the date of their King Lear papers, he was left in his dorm or at the library scratching his head trying to figure out what to do.

Cold turkey.

That was how it had to be done. Not that skiing made Hayward worse at anything else, or was a detriment to his ability to get his work done, to write that English paper and the two history papers, but it had been an obsession since his childhood, and that was where he felt it belonged, in the past.

After college he moved to Boston, the home of his Red Sox, to sell books. While the mountains, in a sense, were still in sight, his job necessitated a move to the Midwest, Chicago to be precise. He was far from skiing, far from the mountains and the bite of Arctic air turning his fair skin into the color of raw pork chops.

Here he began to make his imprint on the publishing world, eventually scaling the heights of Simon and Schuster and Little, Brown.

And while he was at it, in 1980 he also ran the New York City Marathon.

When in New York in the late spring of 1980, Hayward and four or five of his friends wanted to go to the Belmont Stakes. None had been to the races and thought it a lively way to waste an afternoon. They knew nothing and placed bets solely on the colors of the silks, gray horses, birthdays, and names. Then Hayward took notice of a man sitting in front of him reading what Hayward called a "funny newspaper." This was before Andrew Beyer's Beyer Speed Figure was popularized and sold to *Daily Racing Form*, and this man—in the mad scientist lab of his own creation—made his own speed figure and told Hayward that this horse ran a 94. Hayward ran to the window with the tip and placed the bet. He lost. But suddenly Hayward saw the logic in the numbers, of the fractions run by each horse, that out of that type on that page of that "funny newspaper" was a puzzle to decode. "Whoa! There's analytics. I love numbers," he recalled. He picked up the paper and started to read it.

Hayward boarded a plane later that week to see a girlfriend who lived in Washington, D.C. She worked for *Equus* magazine, so naturally she had a knowledge of horses. She picked Hayward up at 5:00 p.m. since the pair had reservations at a restaurant in Georgetown. He started talking about his experience at Belmont Park, about this new passion. It turned out she too loved the racetrack and she said that at nearby Charles Town in West Virginia, just an hour away, they could make the first post. They went to Charles Town Thursday night, Friday night, and Saturday. She taught Hayward how to handicap, and that was it—he was hooked.

Hayward's first trip to Saratoga occurred when Ronald Reagan was the president of the United States, the summer of 1981. And there was a sense that "Yes, this is what racing is about." It was the idea that racing still had a place in the sardine tin of North American athletics. It was crammed in with football and baseball, but it proved that though its arena was the size of an anchovy, it could still swim in the same pool. Saratoga was a carnival then as it is now, with candy cane-colored tents and booths, picnic tables, and cotton candy. It was the place to be, and the hope was that it would always be the place where all the focus would turn.

But like an ant under a magnifying glass in the sun, it gets the light but also the magnification, not to mention the increased heat of being between the ground and a concentrated beam of light.

∾

It was a scene similar to this press conference, with hundreds of eyes staring down and stabbing Hayward in the face. Hayward stood on the apron of Belmont Park before venomous horsemen.

Hayward had just taken the job as president of the New York Racing Association in November 2004 and was met by the ire of racing media and horsemen. Who is the man? A publishing executive? What makes him think he can arrive and operate racetracks? Hayward wasted little time.

On July 14, 2005, Hayward overhauled some of the NYRA's upper management, sending the chief examining veterinarian and the vice president for human resources and labor relations packing. He also fired long-time NYRA racing secretary Mike Lakow and replaced him with his assistant, P. J. Campo, which was why Hayward was met by the steely gaze of trainers. "I felt we needed to make changes to make our racing program a little more progressive and dynamic," Hayward told the *New York Times*.

The late Hall of Fame trainer Bobby Frankel soon organized a caucus of horsemen and arranged a meeting with Hayward. Frankel's words razored in a July 15, 2005, article: "This is a guy (Lakow) who worked his butt off. I think he lost 40 pounds since he took the job. This is a disgrace; it's just terrible."

Todd Pletcher, a five-time Eclipse-winning trainer, while not at the meeting because he was at his brother-in-law's wedding, felt a reason for the firing was merited. "It wouldn't be one of the decisions that I necessarily agree with," said Pletcher. "I think the biggest question mark was, 'Why?' " As much as they wanted an explanation, it was more a gesture to illustrate how upset they were with their status quo having been upended by this Book Man. "Everyone back here," Pletcher continued, "understood how hard he worked and how good of a job he did. I don't think there was a proper explanation. I think he did a phenomenal job, cared a lot about the quality of New York racing." This wasn't to say that Pletcher thought poorly of Hayward. He liked that Hayward was easy to communicate with and that he was a horseplayer, so he understood the needs of the bettor: "Those are the people we need to keep happy," said Pletcher. But the termination of Lakow still rubbed him raw.

Nick Zito received word of this meeting and wanted nothing to do with it. "I've got respect for those trainers. I don't think trainers, in my opinion, should be that tight with a racing secretary. That's a conflict of interest. In other words, Todd and Frankel are looking to help themselves. Let's say if I'm friends with P. J. Campo and tomorrow he's fired. I'm not supposed to go to Hayward and organize something. If the new guy comes in, then you should have a meeting with the new guy. If Charlie Hayward let him go, he had a reason for it. That's none of my business. If P. J. Campo gets fired, I'm not supposed to get trainers. 'What do you think, Gary Contessa? What do you think, Bill Mott?' Can't do that. Am I right or wrong?"

Zito had a revelatory moment while discussing this because it was his thought that there ought to be a separation between the racing secretary and the trainer. "Nobody should be allowed in the racing office. In other words, there should be a sign: TRAINERS. NOT. ALLOWED. IN. UNTIL. AFTER THE RACES ARE DRAWN.

"Why not? In other words, after the races are drawn then, Nick, you are allowed to say hello to P. J. 'Don't come near that fuckin' office until I'm done with my business.' "

Unlike others who were at once skeptical upon Hayward's arrival, Zito held him in high esteem, noting that, "He just loves the game. I'm not the guy to judge him, but I know people. I know that guy genuinely loves the game and he gets my vote. So, for me, he's OK, that's why I endorsed the guy when I first met the guy."

And that wasn't always the case with other horsemen. Frankel and Pletcher felt they needed reasons as to why Lakow was shown the door. So too did trainer Rick Violette. He heard Hayward use innuendo; that Lakow's firing was grounded in impropriety, that there were facts to back it up. Violette said the facts never came.

Violette backed Lakow. He thought Lakow put on the best possible show, realizing, of course, that the job of a racing secretary is a tough job. Violette figured if the racing secretary made 50 percent of the people happy, then he did good work. Violette liked Lakow's accessibility, that he didn't hide, that he was a straight shooter, that you could disagree but still have a cup of coffee.

Violette's first impressions of Hayward, on the other hand, were unfavorable. But, he admitted, he himself is very issue oriented. If you're on his side, in agreement, then you're best friends. Disagreement will meet a different side. He is civil. For the past two years he's worked closely with Hayward as Hayward has grown into the job. Violette and the rest of the horsemen simply wanted to be included because they were players and not pawns, not offspring relegated to the children's table, which was why he, and others, supported Empire Racing Associates in the NYRA franchise war.

Hayward, meanwhile, brushed off the trainers who ripped him, how they stoked him like pulsing embers for reason. He had a franchise to run. And, he thought as he addressed them on the Belmont apron, it was none of their business.

∽

"Thanks, Dan, and thanks to everyone for showing up today," said Hayward at the 2009 luncheon. "This is really the kickoff of the Saratoga meet just around the corner and we're really, really excited."

And so he took the mike, thanking a number of people, eyeing the crowd while tilting his glasses atop his head, to his nose, and then back atop his head. He acknowledged chairman of the State Racing and Wagering Board, John Sabini. "It's been about a year since he's been appointed, and he started just before Saratoga. John's been to the track many, many, many times and I know it's an easy job to come to Saratoga, which a lot of political leaders do. It's a less easy job to get out to Belmont, but I've seen John many times at *Aqueduct*."

Much of Hayward's job is this sort of posturing, and he knows it, and as a man as assertive as he is, standing before people and acting like a politician makes his stomach turn since, like most everyone in this room, he dislikes politicians. Such has been the case since Hayward was hired as NYRA's president in November 2004. The state of New York has always balked on VLTs. Hayward knows, and so do many others, that there is no other place the state can get $300–$400 million worth of money—$1 million a day—than with VLTs, yet they have come and gone since before Hayward's time. The significance is that the sport will get millions for capital improvements and millions to increase purses and incentives, thus keeping New York mares in state and bringing the best possible equine athletes to New York time and time again to race for more and more money. Slot machines would make that possible and ensure a stable racing product. "On the VLT front, I started this job on November 4, 2004. I was asked at that time when we thought VLTs would be operating," Hayward said. "I've been opining on that topic consistently, and I've been wrong every time. All I can tell you is that we've been told by the governor that he is going to make a selection by August 1. It's an interesting assertion, which I hope comes true. But as you probably know, the selection of the VLT vendor has to be a consensus among the governor, the head of the [state] assembly, and the head of the [state] senate . . . whoever that might be." This last statement filled the room with laughter, as Albany politics is so apt to do.

But ineptitude isn't and wasn't a uniquely Albany idea. The horse racing industry finds itself in an ever-souring mood for those who try to love it and for those who are still married to the idea of Secretariat. "As you know, the industry has some challenging times around the country," Hayward continued. "Churchill Downs announced the elimination of Wednesday racing. They are now racing four days a week. Hollywood Park announced the elimination of Wednesday racing. Even Del Mar, which is sort of the minor league Saratoga of the west . . . um [chuckles and guffaws] has gone from six days of racing to five days of racing. I'm here to tell you that we will be continuing to race six days a week at Saratoga."

This, of course, was welcome news but, as Hayward knew, not enough to keep questions totally at bay.

∼

The closer to New York, the grouchier the racing press gets. Hayward thought that award-winning columnist Paul Moran, formerly of *Newsday*, used to puncture him. Moran sliced into NYRA after the 2005 Belmont Stakes that NYRA "almost gleefully picks the pockets of those who remain interested in actually attending the races on days when they sense a demand."

Hayward said, "We are always reluctant to raise our prices."

To which Moran continued, "Can NYRA completely mess up Saratoga, too? Tough assignment, but not out of the realm of possibility."

∼

Dan Silver got back on the mike. Stomachs grumbled a bit longer. "There was a different species of animal that was trying to strut its stuff at Saratoga two weeks ago," he said. "On Monday, June 15, a moose wandered onto the Saratoga grounds, presumably to get its starting gate card. As you can see on the PowerPoint that we have to the left, we have a great photo of the moose which was taken by NYRA employee Lynn Drew, who is here today. Lynn, where are you?"

Drew, sitting in the front row, was an honorary guest for the afternoon, and sat on the aisle seat perhaps thinking that his part in this function was nothing more than ceremonial and, well, goofy. "Please stand up so that everyone can see you," Silver said.

Mark Bardack was in contact with the moose and the moose had, at last, put his head on straight and surfaced from the bathroom and put his phone somewhere out of sight, because what could be less professional than a moose carrying a cell phone?

With his antlers on straight, he waited with Bardack just outside the hall.

"I also heard rumors that there is someone else here who wants to thank Lynn for his photography skills," Silver continued as Bardack stepped aside. "Oh! The moose is here today."

Incredulous looks, smiles, snickers, and even some laughs, though sparse, were witnessed as the moose skipped down the left aisle and by the front row, waving his swollen, fuzzy brown hand. The moose stuck out his hand and gave a flaccid high five to Lynn Drew before scampering out from where he came.

∾

Nick Kling, a cigar aficionado, avid Frank Sinatra fan, handicapper, and columnist for the *Troy Record*, had the floor. "Charlie, given the dysfunctional nature of New York politics, is it time for NYRA to acknowledge that you may never get VLT money, and do you have plans if that happens?"

"We don't have plans," Hayward said. "If you look at the VLT money— let me just restate that: the VLTs will yield over $300 million a year to the state, and that's a lot more important to the state than it will yield to racing. So I think that the VLT as a public policy matter is much more important to the state than what it will be for racing. Having said that, the yield for racing will be significant."

While at Bowdoin College, Hayward studied the futile efforts of charismatic leaders of the past and how hubris had resulted in millions spent and spilt blood. Louis XIV, while on his deathbed, said he loved war too much. Napoléon Bonaparte, in his attempt to take over the world, buried his chances by invading Russia, freezing his "People's Army." Adolf Hitler, in his attempt to take over the world, buried his chances by invading Russia, freezing his goose-stepping army of bigotry. Past presidents clamored for universal health care. And it would seem that in 2009 the issue of VLTs would be the unraveling of another person in power, Albany politics adopting the scorched-earth policy of the Russians to ensure that what was coveted came at a suicidal price. The illustration should not be misconstrued; to whisper Hayward's name in the breath of hedonistic Visigoths is merely to establish that men of power are apt to chase lost causes, no matter how sour or noble the intentions.

"I've been stupid enough to opine on that topic, but it's a long-winded way that I've still got to believe that the VLTs will be forthcoming in this state, but we never choose to wager on when that might happen," Hayward added.

"You could have said the same thing three or four years ago, Charlie, and you still don't have them," Kling said.

"Listen, I completely agree with you. The VLTs were authorized in 2001, at eight harness tracks and one other thoroughbred track. Aqueduct would dwarf the total sum of monies that are currently being produced by the eight harness tracks and the other track. So we tried our best. We had what we thought was the best. The MGM deal that we had on the table during the Pataki administration turned us back on; it was far superior to any deal that the state is now willing to have. You can't blame that on the current political leaders. We just need to get this resolved, not only for the state, but also for racing."

Reporter Paul Post of *The Saratogian* asked, "Why would that have been better than anything being offered now?"

"Because MGM and NYRA were going to put up all the money to build the facility so that the state would have to put up no upfront money to receive considerably more. But again, that's water over the dam, and we just need to move forward on the existing bill," Hayward said.

Water over the dam was a fitting choice of words that would imply that this subject had boiled over and, by its absence of a solution, would wipe out the city in the valley, whatever the city and wherever the valley.

∼

The retirement of Curlin, the 2007 and 2008 Horse of the Year, left the older division of horses about as lifeless as overcooked spaghetti. The focus has traditionally been on the male division, and perhaps that is more cultural than anything else.

Still, a female whose athletic gifts are great crosses over. For example, Michelle Wie and Annika Sorenstam made their presence felt on the "men's pitch." And eyeballs lock. A culture that pushes female athletes to the fringe is at the same time one that is intrigued, to the point of fanaticism.

∼

"Will NYRA actively try to get Zenyatta to Saratoga for a race against Rachel, and if so, would you change the purse structure in the Go For Wand or the Personal Ensign?" asked Tim Wilkin of the Albany *Times Union*.

For Hayward this was, most certainly, a magnetic question. Yes, he thought, to get Zenyatta, the unbeaten five-year-old mare, to Saratoga against

Rachel Alexandra could be the race of the year. But to get them to Saratoga might compromise his stance on purse structure. Tracks across the country that lack Saratoga's prestige toss money around to lure connections into choosing their tracks and their races. Hayward had always said, "Saratoga should be enough incentive to run." Add to that the fact that Saratoga's purses are the highest in the country and he felt that to raise them for one or two horses would compromise his integrity as an executive. "It's interesting," Hayward said, "I spent some time in January with John Shirreffs, who is the trainer for the Mosses, and actually had dinner with Mr. and Mrs. Moss the night before the Eclipse Awards, and they already talked about possibly coming east, not with Zenyatta, but in general. They liked the idea of racing on the East Coast. They are still doing what the Jacksons are doing, which is looking at all of their options and trying to decide where they might go. The health and physical state of the mare and the filly . . . I could have my partner here, Mr. Campo, talk about his thoughts on the likelihood of that scenario."

∾

P. J. Campo was, at one time, awkward in front of cameras and reporters, but like a muscle, he strengthened his camera savvy. His answers, while not rude, were terse, short, and lacking.

As racing secretary he writes the condition book: weeks of races that he expects to fill with the names of horses to structure a race card with as many as thirteen races a day. He spends sunless mornings on the backside speaking with trainers about the condition of the track and fields questions about why this race was absent from the condition book or why that stakes race moved to this date, or anything track related, short of being blamed for the weather. He gets blamed and prodded for race cards that are lackluster, so one might as well blame the weather on him too.

"What Tim is referring to is that some tracks provide incentives for horses to come and race," Campo said. "NYRA has never really done that. I'm not sure in the case of Mr. Moss and Mr. Jackson that they necessarily need the money, but I think they're both really good owners to work with, and they both really want what's best for their horses. So I think that it is part of the discussion. Could that possibly enter the discussion? I think the answer is probably yes, but it would be done in a manner that would be appropriate for NYRA as well as both the parties and for other horses, both fillies and mares."

After a momentary pause, a question was asked about the dismal economy. Hal Handel delivered a Handel-ian response: "Sure, that's a wonderful question to ask me, and I'd be thrilled to answer."

∽

Many of the reporters filed out of the room and upstairs to the buffet tables and loaded their plates with meats and sides. Hayward remained behind in his chair, his hands folded, sweat beaded on his forehead like morning dew. Hayward liked this part of the job—talking to reporters, conveying a message, and talking racing. When asked what he would get excited about, he blurted what he deemed most important: "Sunshine!"

But so too was Rachel Alexandra. She was True North, with all compass needles pivoting to her home in Barn 65. "That race on Saturday was spine tingling," Hayward said, recalling her Mother Goose performance. "She broke the stakes record, just off the track record by Secretariat. I would really like to see Zenyatta and Rachel Alexandra. The Travers is going to take care of itself."

Soon the lights dimmed, but Hayward remained, speaking to whomever requested his audience. The Rachel questions were numerous, and through his years of being a fan and an executive, he realized that she was no ordinary horse, that she was above and beyond the game. Her magnetism would only grow, her gravity ever stronger. "We're a pop, splint, or a tendon away from taking a horse out of the race, that's why the entry box is drawn on the Wednesday—then we'll know who is running."

∽

At last Dan Silver took Charlie Hayward out to the parking lot for one more interview, a television interview. Silver looked like a Secret Service agent standing in Hayward's orbit. Hayward said, "My guys at Del Mar are gonna kill me. 'My Triple A affiliate.'" To this he laughed, showing off his slanted, overlapping bottom teeth. "They come spontaneously, unfortunately. It can be a little problem. You've got to have fun and laugh a little."

After the interview Silver and Hayward marched inside and up the stairs, hoping to get some scraps for lunch. "That moose was a nice touch," Hayward said.

∽

Later that same day off North Broadway in Saratoga Springs the sky divided its clouds like a black and white cookie—to the west aqua, to the east gray. Rain came down in sheets, with almond-shaped gems of water breaking on the tar like clamshells. The western sun cast a golden light that spotlighted the raindrops like chandelier crystals. It was bizarre, these flashes, these stars shimmering. It was the beauty of unexpected things.

5

No Fear

Calvin Borel's head spun. Though he had been through a media blitz before in 2007, 2009 was a mutant hybrid in comparison. In 2007 Borel won the Kentucky Derby aboard Street Sense and he was catapulted into a celebrity he never saw coming.

Trainer Carl Nafzger, whom Borel calls Mr. Carl, believed in Borel. He believed that the horse would tell him what rider it would want and Street Sense needed Borel, a ground-saving specialist. In 2006, when they won the Breeders' Cup Juvenile at Churchill Downs, both horse and rider were relative unknowns. *Who's that coming up the rail?*

In 2000, prior to Street Sense, Borel had a horse with freakish talent named Dollar Bill. Dallas Stewart trained the colt that he felt was on his way to the Kentucky Derby. Borel had figured this quirky horse out, had won stakes races when Dollar Bill was a two-year-old baby. When Dollar Bill turned three in 2001, Stewart pulled the colt out from under Borel like a tablecloth and put Hall of Famer Pat Day in the irons.

Lisa Funk, Borel's fiancée, watched Day ride Dollar Bill poorly. She maintained that Day was a fantastic jockey, but that he just didn't have the rapport that Borel had with Dollar Bill. It saddened Funk to see a horse that possessed ability, ability that Borel helped coax out, slip from Borel's aging hands. The feeling was that had Borel stayed aboard, then maybe they would have won the Derby that year.

Borel smiled, his eyes ever youthful. Don't be fooled, it stung. Sometimes it felt like *it* would never happen. He just had to imagine that if he were aboard he could have lived up to his name.

They call him Bo-Rail. Saying it aloud elicits a Southern enunciation, a Bayou-type brogue. Borel sees no move too grand and no slot too small for him to thread a horse. Give him a hole the width of a smiling jack-o'-lantern and he'll muscle a horse through and by.

Borel's brother Cecil, a horse trainer, always told him, "The shortest way around a track is on the fence." Such was the lesson he taught Borel when most teenagers are getting their learner's permits. Borel took one of Cecil's horses wide in a race and lost. Afterward Cecil made Borel walk the horse in circles around the barn. There, Cecil placed barrels, and on each lap he moved the barrels farther away from the barn's center. He kept telling his brother to walk the horse around the barrels.

See how much farther you're traveling? You see? "It's a little bit farther than going to the inside," Cecil coached.

◊

Blimp shots reveal Borel's talent. The blimp shot of his 2007 Derby win illustrated his patience aboard Street Sense. While nineteen other horses slowed to a canter, Borel and Street Sense picked them off one by one, from twentieth place to nineteenth, and then to eighteenth. Borel and Street Sense peeled the paint off the rail in such a sleek manner. Borel guided the horse as if following a predetermined path, a river of dirt that pulled them—and only them. They struck the front and hit the wire first. Borel threw his arm into the air, tossing his victory high into the heavens.

◊

Two years later they put Calvin Borel on a rat, a gelding whose stature was reminiscent of a pony at a petting zoo. The horse's name was Mine That Bird and he was 50-1 heading into the post parade for the 135th running of the Kentucky Derby. A *Daily Racing Form* handicapper wrote the following:

> 4 wins on synthetic surfaces, he was unable to last at a shorter distance test in 2009; an ambitious placement to say the least; 5.40 Dosage Index is the highest in the field; sire captured the Belmont Stakes and Travers; new rider won the Derby in 2007 with Street Sense; could be a pace factor, but is hard to recommend.

Mine That Bird had nothing going for him, no bettor confidence, no signature wins in months, just a trainer, Bennie "Chip" Woolley, who was glued to a pair of silver crutches and down on his luck with one win in thirty-two starts to date. Woolley shadowed his face behind a broad Stetson hat, matching sunglasses, and a handlebar mustache reminiscent of a Chinese emperor.

Perhaps all that Mine That Bird had in his favor was the 111-pound Cajun on his back.

◊

From the rail in the winner's circle at Churchill Downs, one saw the field of nineteen three-year-old colts and geldings march in the parade on a muddy surface. Mine That Bird looked so small, so outmatched. But there atop was Calvin Borel, his face creased in a smile, the folds of his forty-two-year-old face concealing the confidence that could have, and should have, swayed the betting public into his corner. This was Borel's home track, and he was about to make Mine That Bird just as comfortable.

∿

The gate blasted open and Borel, with an oxymoronic relaxed immediacy, steered Mine That Bird to the rail, content to watch the rumps of eighteen other horses gallop ahead. Mine That Bird was Rocky Balboa, a compact, tightly muscled commoner. The other horses, all the other horses, were Apollo Creed, Clubber Lang, and Ivan Drago combined.

∿

A few weeks later, Calvin Borel was a guest on the *Late Show with David Letterman*. Borel strode out in jeans and blazer. He swelled with a benign swagger. Letterman, a towering figure, literally looked down upon Borel from his gargoyle's perch and said, "Now let's talk about the Kentucky Derby. There's a lot I don't understand. Mine That Bird, 50-1, you start essentially dead last out of the gate, is that right? Then we see you moving along the fence there, what do they call it? The rail? I think we have some video here, is that what we're looking at?"

Cut to a shot of the Kentucky Derby, the blimp shot—there went Borel and Mine That Bird, picking off every horse. As he passed the first ten horses there was not a single doubt that he would win this race, *if he could just slip through on the rail.*

Letterman continued, "Oh, sloppy track too. Look at that, that's a thing of beauty, there you go," and as they both watched the replay, they relived Borel slipping his horse through a slit of daylight, scraping the rail with his left boot, before going on to win by over six lengths. Once in the clear Borel stood up and pointed his whip to his fiancée, Lisa Funk, sitting in the grandstand. "Holy cow!" Letterman said. "Did you know that animal had that kind of speed before?"

"Yes, sir, I did get on him a couple times," Borel said. "The trainer, Chip, told me to ride him with a lot of confidence. He tried to explain to other riders. When he'd run, he'd have them a little too close early. He had a turn of foot, but they were using it a little early."

"But you hadn't really met this horse until the Monday before the race?" asked Letterman.

"No, I got on him about three weeks before," Borel replied.

∽

Funk recalls a moment when Dallas Stewart mused with Borel, "You've won two Derbys and you could've won three."

So it was just a matter of marrying the two to bring out Mine That Bird's true running style, an unsung horse with an unlikely hero in the irons.

∽

Calvin Borel, the youngest in a tribe of Borels, grew up on a sugar cane farm in St. Martin Parish, Louisiana. Down in the Bayou it was, as one would imagine, sweltering. The humidity hangs on one's shoulders like a lead jacket and stays on day and night. But that was no excuse, no excuse to check work and work ethic at the door. The farm needed tending, the animals needed to be fed, and all else was secondary. So the Borels stabbed pitchforks into the straw and flicked the manure aside.

Cecil took Borel under his wing. He was there when his younger brother sat on his first horse at age two. In a thick Southern drawl, Cecil recalled his time on the farm with his mite-size brother. "Bad, very bad, *bad*," Cecil said. "He wanted to get into everything, didn't know what 'no' was. He was a good kid, but just bad. I don't know how you say that in Uptown [*sic*] New York, but where we're from, sometimes bad is good. He was just a kid who was into everything, and there was nothing that he couldn't do, that he didn't think he could do. That's what made him a good kid, but he was a *bad* kid."

Borel was always willing to put his word against another's, and in so doing, words were eaten and Borel stood atop a pile of spoils. And once he sat upon the back of a horse that was it, that was all, that was his life. English classes, math classes, and science classes were cast aside in the name of racing. It was only a matter of time.

"He didn't go to much schoolin'," Cecil said. "I didn't go, his three older brothers didn't go much to schoolin'. We don't have much schoolin', but we work hard and horses were what we did and that was about it. There wasn't much else. We did sugar cane, we did corn. But when it came down to me and my little brother, we left home to do the horse business. I left home and went to Kentucky [and] then I went to Chicago. Calvin followed me around, and the next thing you know he was doing the same thing. So it's just one of those things that all we had was horses."

So Borel, like his older brothers, cast aside the shackles of traditional education. His lessons were not bound by books but in the fields, under the unrelenting sun. He studied by means of morning gallops, with "exams" on the track in the afternoon. Homework was sweat, and grades were measured by the calluses on the folds of his hands, tested by action, by the yield of the harvest.

"Calvin was good at that, he would love to get into something," Cecil said. "If you told him he couldn't do this, he'd try to do it, and so that was what I meant by bad. I don't mean bad by an ugly way. He grew up with my girls. He was very polite, but if you told him not to go ride this horse right here, he was going to ride him just to show you that he could ride him, and he would ride him and sometimes he'd get hurt, and he would just bide his time and start again. He was just that kind of person; he worked hard all his life. He worked hard when he was small. He come to live with us when he was seven or eight, with me and my wife, but like I said, he was kind of hardheaded, but hardheaded in a good way."

Their mother, Ella Borel, was the strong, quiet type but a hard worker. Their father, Clovis, whom Borel takes after, spoke no English but would get rowdy depending on the circumstance.

"My little brother is quiet in front of the people in New York," said Cecil, "but he can get a little rowdy. I'd say he takes after my Daddy. My Mama wouldn't get rowdy, but my Daddy would get a little rowdy. I'd say he takes after my Daddy, cuz Mama was awful quiet."

When Borel was a little boy, back when he was nicknamed Boo Boo, since he was born thirteen years after Cecil, and when he still attended school, he would hunt and do other things that boys do, but if it wasn't a horse, it got in the way, it was a distraction. "It was always, horses, horses, horses, horses," Cecil said. They had horses at the house, so on Saturdays and Sundays Borel would ride in match races and in between the weeks when he was in school, he'd skip. These were races where a chicken was tied to the tail of a horse so the horse would have a rider. At the end of such races, the jockey would just jump off the horse and roll in the dirt until he came to a dusty halt. For the rest of the week Borel would come back to Cecil and slog away at the barn and the racetrack. "It was mainly horses," Cecil said. "Where we come from, it was mainly horses."

Horses—and loyalty, to their fellow man, to their neighbors, even if that meant telling them a searing truth, whether they were upset by the action of a neighbor or felt slighted by a friend. Such were the times growing up on the farm. Cecil doesn't romanticize those early days; rather, he says they were troubling. But, "We didn't owe nobody, we had food on the table seven days a week. It was real good. It's kind of hard."

Cecil maintains that people will try and stab you in the back, "Back home there was none of that shit. Back home, where we come from, everybody did their thing, paid attention to their thing, did the work, and went to church on Sundays, [and] after that we did our thing chore-wise. We went crawfishing on Sundays most of the time. We'd chill a lot of the stuff that we ate."

Not only that, but it was communal; they were all brothers and sisters. Should one family slaughter a hog, many more would come over for a feast. Cecil, surely echoing the sentiment of the Borels on the whole, has found the mood in the North to be callous, cold, and even seclusive.

"It's not the same, it's not the same, not to me." Cecil said. "To me, we were raised to say it like it is. I don't know if you quite understand that. Like if we tell somebody off and they don't like it, that didn't mean that we didn't have to be friends. If you say something and I would disagree with you, that don't mean you gotta get mad and not be friends. That's how we were raised up."

∾

Calvin Borel, on the cover of *Sports Illustrated (SI)*, has his right arm extended, his hand balled up in a fist, choking his whip like it were a venomous snake. The *SI* headline reads: " 'Miracle in the Mud' 50–1, Derby Long-Shot Winner Energizes Horse Racing." In moments he would pluck a rose from Mine That Bird's blanket and throw it up to his parents. The rose flew, its redness in stark contrast to the grayness of the skyline; its thorns and stem and folded petals spun and fluttered at the peak of its ascent. Gravity threw it down, as if his parents caught it and gave it back and said, "No, this belongs to you, Boo Boo."

Open the *SI* cover to the early pages and you'll find a bird's-eye view of Borel committing to that most unthinkable slit of daylight. You can almost see Borel take his horse and slide through with near-reckless insanity. The track is pockmarked with hoof prints. Only four horses are ahead of him, and they have already lost, they just don't know it yet. There is no thinking; thinking could kill him. "They always drift out when they're tired," Borel would later say. "My brother always told me, inside is the shortest way around. It's not as bad as it looks. I've been thrown over the rail, but if you're afraid, you're in the wrong game."

In that *SI* photograph, Mine That Bird is smeared with mud. His muscles twist in folds like a basket full of garlic knots. Borel's toes keep him steady in the stirrups, with four pairs of goggles hanging from his neck like Olympic medals. His eyes are as wide as dinner plates through his last pair of goggles. The mud stains both long shots, and Borel's face is a dam of emotion on the verge of bursting and flooding the village in the valley.

∾

After Calvin Borel and Rachel Alexandra won the Preakness Stakes, two weeks after his Derby win on Mine That Bird, making history in the process and elevating the profile of both horse and rider, Borel found his exposure erupting. With the backdrop of Churchill Down's twin spires behind him, Borel was on television yet again for ESPN's *Pardon the Interruption*, with Michael Wilbon and Tony Kornheiser.

Borel sat humbly, like a student ready for a lecture. It was just another stop on the media blitz that found so interesting this uneducated man, who went from a dropout to a sport's apex with sweat and heartbreak, and the nominal triumphs granted to those who endure. Perhaps it was because of the time he surfaced from devastating injury. A mount he had at Evangeline Downs, Miss Touchdown, clipped heels with the horse in front and launched Borel into unconsciousness. Borel hit a light post, smashing his ribs, puncturing a lung, and damaging his spleen in such a manner that it had to be removed. How cruel it was for a man who saw no limits to his work ethic, his mucking of stalls, his grooming of horses, his walking hots. When he came out of the coma and was fully rehabilitated, Cecil, trainer of Miss Touchdown, put his brother right back on her. It was a test on the limits of courage and fear.

It was also a time when he struggled with his weight. Borel is relatively tall and would take to heaving or flipping—induced vomiting—to expel the calories. He'd even roast his body in the hot box. These days he consults with a nutritionist and traded the hot box for a whirlpool and the occasional rubdown. He relaxes, often staring off into the clouds while other jockeys play basketball, ping-pong, or pool. In some cases he sits patiently during interviews.

"The last time you won the Kentucky Derby, Calvin, you met the Queen of England. Is there anybody in the whole world you would like to meet now?" Kornheiser said.

"Huh, no, I can't say that," Borel said, in that "aw shucks" way he has. "I wish I could talk to my mom and dad so they could see me right now and see what I accomplished in my life. I know they're watching me from upstairs. I'm very blessed."

"Horse racing is maybe not as grand a sport as it once was, but you're becoming the most famous man in it—do you welcome that?" asked Komheiser.

"Yes, sir, I'm a real humble guy," answered Borel. "I try to go out of my way to help anybody, autographing, doing things for the racing. I've been through it all. I've been a groom, walker, my brother taught me the right way. I went to the eighth grade and I left home. Like he told my mama, I wasn't going to be a doctor or a lawyer. I was a natural. When I first started on the bush tracks when I was eight years old, I was just a natural. My brother told my mom and dad, 'It's him, he's a natural.' I lived with him, he kept me straight, kept me away from drugs, kept me on the right road, taught me to work hard, get on good horses, bad horses, I wasn't scared. I had no fear. I think I gotta give my brother a lot of credit because he kind of raised me, kept me together in good and bad situations and made me a stronger person, and to never, never forget where you come from."

"What a nice story," Kornheiser said, and he squinted his eyes, looked into that camera, and was positively moved by what he had heard in five good minutes with Calvin BO-Rail. "Thank you so much, Calvin."

∽

Rachel Alexandra stood in her stall in Steve Asmussen's Barn 65 tugging at her hay net. Nailed above her stall, atop the threshold, was a souvenir New York State license plate with her name in caps: RACHEL. Her security guards stood at ease.

Borel waited for a decision on her next start. He knew she was situated in Saratoga Springs, in Stall No. 1 at Barn No. 65 on the Oklahoma Training Track backside. It was July 2009 and the 141st Saratoga meet was just weeks away.

Soon enough Borel and Lisa Funk would pack up their belongings and begin the eastward trek from Louisville, Kentucky, their home, where Borel made a name for himself, where Borel became a star.

Borel historically vacationed this time of year, electing to unwind from the Triple Crown season, but as dog tired as he was with the interviews, the television appearances, the newspapers, the magazine pieces, the autographs, and everything else that comes with being Calvin Borel, being Bo-Rail, his vacation would have to wait. The fear was that if he should sit on his haunches that maybe the horse of his life would slip through the cracks. Of course this horse was Rachel Alexandra, the best horse he'd ever ridden and will likely ever ride. Such were the thoughts as their truck purred across Ohio and into New York. Soon, Borel and Funk unpacked their belongings into their summer apartment just behind the Saratoga Springs Police Department.

6

Christmas Eve

Nick Zito pressed his cell phone to his ear, always pressed to his ear. It was a flip phone, but he seldom had the chance to let it rest like an unsteamed mussel. One call bled into the next, and after one call ended he looked down and dialed another number. This he did every morning, every afternoon.

He paced by his barn, a stretch of twenty-four stalls where the dirt is grooved by rakes, and sat in his throne-like wicker chair by the patio table outside his office. Bug lamps hung like Chinese lanterns the length of the shed row. Saddles draped over sawhorses, while his staff, an ethnic blend of men and women, washed the tack and kicked mud off their boots. The mood was reminiscent of a family-run operation, light and loyal. Smiles. Tension, despite the pressure of Saratoga, dissipated from his barn, vaporized by the rising sun. His barn faces east to the volcanic summer, just beyond the trees and bushes, before turning its back to it twelve hours later. As Zito looked to that eastern meridian he saw a blue jay feather through the shrubs. "There's a beautiful bird," he said.

Zito conducted much of his face-to-face business here by this patio table. Owners would visit to see their horse or horses and hope to greet their trainer, their horse consultant. Jockey agents are not welcome.

His barn is an island, and he likes it that way. "You know me," said Zito. "I stay by myself, what do I give a fuck? Mike Lakow, P. J. Campo, they're all the fuckin' same to me. I have a lot—with the grace of God," he said, now knocking on wood, "of fans locally and around the country. One of the reasons I think it is: just leave me alone. I'll leave you alone. You treat me with respect. I'll treat you with respect. You try to forgive me. I'll try to forgive you. I don't want to be in any clique. I have not been in any clique. With agents? You never see an agent hanging out here, because we don't believe in it. This is our fort. My barn is like this at Belmont. My barn is like this at Churchill. Palm Meadows is a fort. This is our thing. We do things the way we do. We treat people the right way. That's it. We're no-nonsense people, but we try to be nice too. The best thing is always just be myself and respect everybody."

Nick Zito's 2009 Triple Crown horses fluttered like a butterfly, but if they had the heart and developed late, then maybe he would have another shot at winning his second-career Travers Stakes in late August.

He won it five years ago with Birdstone, who would go on to sire 2009 Kentucky Derby winner Mine That Bird and 2009 Belmont Stakes winner Summer Bird. On that 2004 afternoon the skies turned to tar and the rains came with thunderclaps and jagged spikes of lightning. The sky cracked with light, and Zito stood up tall, silhouetted against the strobe-like sky, pumped his fist, and punched the air while his colt split raindrops.

Zito won that race for Saratoga Springs socialite Marylou Whitney, and the two of them, along with jockey Edgar Prado, got their picture taken. Zito said he felt like Gene Kelly, "singin' in the rain," as the group stood in calf-high mud.

For the time, in 2009, it seemed as though Zito might be shut out of the Travers, since his three-year-olds failed to show enough progress. There were twenty-four stalls in this eastward-facing barn. Not all of the horses were known, not all were yet in the public's consciousness. Zito was quick to mention, the way a magician holds suspense, "Or a horse you may not have heard of yet."

∿

Zito saw it on television, choosing instead to be by his string in Saratoga Springs, but he tuned in to Delaware Park for the Grade 3 Barbaro Stakes. He had a speedy horse equipped with bar shoes, a protective and heavy shoe for his front hooves. His name was Our Edge.

Our Edge took to the front and led all the way around the oval. Zito, while watching, was excited. If all went well for the next five weeks, Zito had his Travers horse, the horse no one had heard of—until now.

∿

Nick Zito parked his Mercedes SUV under the tree by his barn. His dashboard was cluttered with papers, and parking tags hung like mistletoe from his rearview mirror. Inclined to wear a navy-blue vest, shirt, tie, and blazer to the races, his vehicle had become his wardrobe closet. Zito pre-knotted his ties and draped his shirts from hangers inside the cabin.

One morning, eight days before the start of the meet, Zito took out a white cylinder, spritzed his mouth with breath freshener, and reflected on Our Edge's win in the Barbaro. He was matter of fact, harboring excitement, because he knew the relentless nature of horse racing, how dire the fate was of someone foolish enough to be hopeful. "We're having ups and downs, just like any barn," he said. "It's disappointing to have a horse ready and then get hurt. We have a nice filly with a foot bruise. The X-rays came clean. Thank God. But we were going to run her once before. Now she'll run at Saratoga, but it would've been nice to have run her once."

Such is the nature of horse racing and running under the banner of Nicholas P. Zito at Saratoga. He is a brand, a New York staple. He grew up on Long Island and longed to be an athlete of some kind. He played three sports—baseball, football, and basketball—basketball being his best, or if not his best, his favorite. But one day his father took him to the racetrack. "I was very, very young," he recalled. "I saw the horses walking around the paddock and I saw the trainer and the owners and I knew that's where I wanted to be. That was it. I was sixteen or seventeen. That's what I wanted to be."

He lacked the background many trainers have; horses were not in his blood. He plunged into the culture and learned on the job. He reflected on playing infield on the diamond, flanker in football, and guard in basketball, but "once I got hooked with horses, that was it. Once I saw them walking around the paddock, the owners and the trainers, that was it."

∾

He and his neighbor on the Oklahoma backside, fellow Hall of Famer D. Wayne Lukas, have been friends and rivals for decades. Lukas, a four-time Kentucky Derby-winning trainer and winner of six straight Triple Crown races (with different horses), has butted heads with Zito on the track. After all, Zito started to come to power when Lukas dominated the racing headlines. They've been next to each other on the Saratoga backside for twenty years. "He's a typical horseman, a New York horseman," Lukas said. "A lot of my friends come from the Southwest and the South, and Nick is New York all the way, from his expressions to his mannerisms, to everything else. I think he typifies the New York trainer in every sense of the word. He's not only successful and so forth, but he's got the mentality as well."

The two men are like water and oil in terms of style. Zito wears a baseball cap. Lukas wears a ten-gallon hat. "I think that would be the way I would typify him," Lukas said. "There's different ways to get different places, like, for example, I'm adamant about being on a saddle horse and Nick is going to pull up in a golf cart and watch them from the rail. That's the way the New York trainers always were. There's different ways to go about this and all of them successful."

Both men have reached the pinnacle of the game, further proof that the variety of forks and tributaries can be funneled toward the same goal. "I think that what happens to all of us, and Nick is no exception, is that early on in your career when you're trying to get to the Classics, winning races is one thing, but the recognition and the rewards are greater when you can establish yourself as a Classics trainer."

Lukas, Zito, and the entire culture wake up with the sun to prove that they belong in that elite circle. Lukas relayed that Zito has felt that pressure, dealt with it, and has come out successful, "And I think now that he has accomplished that and is in the Hall of Fame and won his share, been to the Classics. I think he's a lot more comfortable in his position and his legacy is more in shape."

Different roads, same destination. Zito's assistant trainer, Tim Poole, said, "The main difference between Nick and I is I was born on the racetrack and Nick used to jump the fence to get in."

∾

Seated at his patio table, Zito unloaded a plastic bag with a number of newspapers: a *Saratogian*, a *New York Post*, and a *Daily Racing Form*. He unfolded *The Saratogian* and asked, "What does this mean?" He read the second paragraph of the story first, pointing his finger to the page, reading aloud, "The 15-member group was created under state legislation that granted New York Racing Association a new 25-year franchise to run Saratoga, Belmont Park and Aqueduct." Then he read the lead, "Joseph Torani of Saratoga Springs has been named chairman of a Saratoga Race Course Local Advisory Board that held its first-ever meeting on Monday." And, finally, the headline: "Chairman named to Saratoga Race Course Advisory Board."

Zito skimmed over other sentences and paragraphs in varying order, internalizing them with scattered logic. He cast *The Saratogian* aside like a dirty napkin and looked at the cover of the *Post*, which exposed ESPN's sideline reporter, Erin Andrews, through a peephole camera. "This is the lowest of the low. With all that's going on in the world, this is on the front page?"

∾

Three days before the start of the meet, Saratoga Race Course opened its gates for its annual open house, an appetizer, a cocktail hour, if you will. Cotton shirts clung to the skin. Moody was the sky with a bullying threat of thunderstorms. Flowers gyrated to the wind's subtle exhalations.

Charlie Hayward had yet to arrive into his all-mahogany office. The administrative building, the heart of the entire property, still had file cabinets in its hallways that had arrived from Belmont Park. His office was naked, with just his desk and a television stand. A painting, titled "Amber Morn," hung from the wall. Another showed in powerful gallop the great filly Ruffian. The office also was filled with stacks of newspapers, a phonebook, a *Daily Racing Form*, and printouts of Opening Day entries.

Hanging on the walls of the administration building are photographs of a different era. Jockeys sit atop their horses in a post parade with hats (not helmets) and no eye protection. A clock hangs by a wire, its arms pointing to 3:30 for the next race. A photograph by H. C. Ashby captures a 1929 clubhouse scene of dining patrons. The caption reads: "Two months before stock market crashed."

Even the king of India, along with his wife, visited on July 31, 1893. A shot from 1919 shows all of the men in hats, a sea of bottle caps, with grass covering the apron where the benches of modern-day Saratoga Race Course sit.

The photos are a window into the past, revealing that while much has changed, much has also stayed the same.

The 2009 track, largely, was still stretching its joints, still waking from hibernation, as televisions remained gutted from consoles with wires splayed out like frayed spaghetti. Burnt-orange pine needles insulated the shingles of buildings in the core of the property. Trees were lush and pregnant against a blue canvas layered with menacing cumulus clouds.

The scent of popcorn wafted through the air. Burgers sizzled and sold for $2, hot dogs for $1.50. A man walked by in a pinwheel hat, an orange shirt, comic-book pants, suspenders, with scarlet Chuck Taylors on his feet. By 11:00 a.m., the air cooled, became more aggressive, while air conditioners hummed, hard at work. Outside the administrative building, Mark Bardack, a media advisor with Ed Lewi Associates, met Charlie Hayward—both were waiting for an interview that should have started five minutes earlier. "Good sign," Bardack said. "They're stuck in traffic."

"I guess," Hayward said.

Instead of waiting in the humidity, both trucked inside. "Might need some water before the day's over," Bardack said. "Maybe more than water."

∼

The treetops swayed above, as if fanning the players below. "Hi, Jess, how are you?" Hayward said to the interviewer. "We spend most of the time on the weather, but we're generally excited. Racing's down about 10 percent; Saratoga is a little bulletproof when it comes to that. We had 3,400 stall applications for only 1,800 stalls. The Wednesday and Thursday cards have 134 entries and are oversubscribed."

Hayward's gray hair danced in the wind and his body swayed in step as he listened to the reporter. Hayward realized that these are the times that, no matter what the question, he can broadcast NYRA's message. He talked about the cement washing areas on the backside so that the horses could stay cleaner after their baths. He talked about how the track drainage is better so that they won't lose a day of racing after a deluge, like they did in 2008. And he touted the new plumbing, new floors, general maintenance, and long-term developments, "but we'll talk about that when the VLTs are installed."

Hayward, to a fault, has always been optimistic with regard to the slot machines that are supposed to be installed at Aqueduct. He knew that the state would never find another vein that could funnel $300–$400 million for New York. "The government said they're selecting a vendor by August 1," Hayward said. "I think that's optimistic. By selecting a VLT operator next year, it will be big for racing and breeding."

As this date got pushed farther and farther back, it seemed less likely that it would ever get done. When the 2009 Saratoga meet would be a distant landmark in the rearview mirror, VLTs would still be an issue, before, at last, ground would be broken on October 28, 2010. But, alas, the conversation turned to brighter matters—to the track and to Rachel Alexandra, and whether or not they would see her at this meeting.

"You can see Rachel Alexandra. She's in her stall!" Hayward said. "She's owned by Jess Jackson, who owned Curlin. They've been big supporters of NYRA. We know she's going to the Haskell this Sunday. That leaves three logical options for her. She can run back in three weeks in our best three-year-old race for fillies, the Alabama. She could run back in four weeks in the Travers, or she could the following day in the Personal Ensign against older fillies and mares. We're getting Summer Bird, who's running in the Haskell, to run here in the Travers. Mine That Bird, who was disappointing in the Belmont, but ran great in the Kentucky Derby, is running in the West Virginia Derby. If we can get Mine That Bird, winner of the Kentucky Derby, the filly Rachel Alexandra, who won the Preakness, and Summer Bird, the Belmont winner, it will be the first time since 1982 that all three Triple Crown race winners will be in the Travers. It's really exciting. It could be huge. This week we solidify where we are in five weeks."

༄

Back in his office, where the air was crisp like aluminum foil, Hayward pulled the entries for Opening Day and smiled, as if grading them with an A+. Hayward also reflected on the people at Nassau Off-Track Betting (OTB), namely, its president, Dino Amoroso, who reportedly pirated NYRA's satellite feed and failed to pay for over two months.

Hayward controls the rights, and his motive was to get them to admit that they had control of that pirated feed. Hayward refused to believe that

Nassau OTB lacked any knowledge of the theft. NYRA gave them a forty-five day notice to write a letter to confirm that they did what they did. A few days earlier, on a Thursday, Hayward was in his Belmont Park office when Jerry Bossert of the *Daily News* and Dave Grening of *Daily Racing Form* burst into his office. They read the lead from the *Post*, "Amoroso called you a liar and a thief."

Hayward said, "That doesn't seem like a smart thing to do."

If this nonsense kept up any longer, Hayward would be forced into action.

∽

But most of that was poison, paralyzing the energy that comes with a fresh Saratoga meet. Underneath the awnings near the At the Rail Pavilion, Hayward sat with his public relations man, Don Lehr, a coffin-shaped man with slicked hair, glasses, and a thin mustache the shape of a pyramid's capstone. His speech and sense of humor are drier than a martini. Hayward and Lehr ironed out logistics for the remainder of the television interviews for the rest of the day.

"Racing's down 10 percent," Lehr said, "so is NYRA. Saratoga always outperforms the rest of the industry."

"It was unexpected last year because of the rain," Hayward said. "Number one, we have the highest live attendance in the country, the highest on-track handle, the highest all-source handle."

"The on-track wagering is a substantial part of the all-source handle," Lehr said.

"No, only a racing person will understand that," Hayward said.

"Can we talk about the place? Saratoga? In the general economy, the entire world, upstate, my idea is we want people to feel good and have fun and that you don't have to spend a lot of money. It's the new normal. Gas is $1.50 cheaper, and consumer spending is up. Some people are doing well in Saratoga. I'm just saying to spin as positive as we can."

Don Lehr, in many ways, is the consigliere to Charlie Hayward. He is the after-picture of the scarecrow from *The Wizard of Oz*: all brains. He walks with deliberate heel-striking strides in his black, laceless leather shoes. His spiral notebook, containing all of his figures, pats his hip from within his blazer's side pocket.

Lehr's connection to Hayward goes back twenty-five years to Hayward's days in publishing at Simon and Schuster. Lehr has been a career public relations man, organizing the numbers and spewing them out. Lehr puts out fires. He also threads the company message into the public fabric.

Lehr fixes NYRA's communications department and, when not working for NYRA, allots his other energies to environmental summits and clients.

"I'm the eyes and ears of Charlie," Lehr said. "I'm also diplomatic, make sure he's not pissed off while trying to do things right. I had Charlie's ear and slowly I had Steve Duncker's ear. I am a media consultant at NYRA. I know the business. I'm a horseplayer. I know PR, and the last two years I've been brought into various situations to be dealt with. People know I'm Charlie's guy."

So when Lehr and Hayward sat down to map out a media strategy just days before the Saratoga meet opened, it was no wonder Hayward had Lehr sitting across from him.

"You can take a family of five to the track for $15 and you can bring your own food and drink," Hayward said.

"The Capital Region is hurting less and a lot of the industry is okay," said Lehr. "People are staying here and gas is $1.50 cheaper."

"What we should try to do is manage expectations. That way when the end of the meet comes . . . Talk about positive things like stall applications."

"One hundred and thirty horses on Wednesday's card."

"One thirty-four. And if we have a nice day Wednesday, we could be up 15 percent. And the nice thing about math is that if you're down 20 percent from 100, you're at 80 percent. But to get back up to 100, you're up 25 percent. They play in our favor. If we stay on the turf, we could be 30 percent over last year."

"Some people may say, 'Sure, I'll get to Saratoga a few more times. We're entitled to it and lucky we have it.'"

"No question, and our customers—big or small—are more careful whether they wager or not."

"What's great about the game is that it's a big equalizer. Thoroughbred racing is an international sport and this is the absolute pinnacle of thoroughbred racing in the world. The big stars—equine and human. It doesn't get any better. This is the best thing. For thoroughbred racing, this is the top of the sport, the best venue in the world. We make history every day."

"Sure, the stars come here, but what this place does is make stars. Look at Big Brown. Go into the paddock for the two-year-old races and there's a $4 million yearling, or a homebred to a $10,000 stud fee.

"You don't know."

"You don't know. What you do know is that a colt or filly in a two-year-old race you see will be one of the tops. The Sanford [Stakes] this year has nine, last year we had four. So . . . acknowledge the economy which is real and here is why it's good."

"Things get better," Lehr said.

Hayward paused as if to signify that the discussion had come to a close. "All right," Hayward said, "make it happen."

Hayward filled his plate with a cheeseburger and two hot dogs, grabbed a lemonade, and ate with world-conquering vigor. Out on the track, a mascot race was about to take place between the Skidmore Thoroughbred and the Albany Firebird, among others. Hayward stood by the window in the At the Rail Pavilion, his image warped in the reflection of a convex television screen. "Here we go," he said. "The ones without the big heads have an advantage. They're going to actually use the gate?"

The mascots stood in line. They stumbled from the gate, fifty yards to go. Their high-stepping, stuffed feet kicked up dirt, and though it was a photo finish, the Skidmore Thoroughbred won. Hayward's head shook at the goofball display, but his warped reflection showed that he was smiling, even laughing at the mascot race.

It came to Hayward's attention that the parking lots were full, which translates into about twenty thousand people, this on a day that featured four steeplechase, or hurdle, races, where jumpers have to clear a number of hedges, and *no gambling*. But the sky looked angry, and the fear was that people would be coming home to blinking clocks.

∾

Should that be the case, it wouldn't happen for many hours, and Hayward still had to meet with television reporters. "The open house is great to shake the place out. The economy hurts, but the weather is a much bigger deal. The economy seems to be turning the corner. The handle in July was stronger than in May and June. We have 1,800 stalls and 3,400 applications. A family of five can come in for $15 and bring food and bring beer and soda, get a picnic table for a stay-at-home vacation. We have a lot of places to sit and enjoy."

It was the usual stuff, talking about VLTs, the economy, and the weather. He spoke of Calvin Borel, how he is a great human being, how his celebrity hasn't changed his demeanor. With his last interview done, he took his hand and pinched his shirt to ventilate his suit, puffing an air current over his torso. "Phew, I've never sweat so much . . . other than with a girlfriend or two," he said.

Don Lehr leaned against a fence smoking a cigarette as Hayward passed by, "Family of five, baby," Lehr said, "family of five."

So Hayward walked in quick chicken steps back to his office. Up above, the wind tipped the treetops and scattered raindrops on the asphalt. The water splatted and darkened the surface. The latent heat vaporized the liquid into the air. Hayward noted the crowd in the grandstand and said that he was impressed by the shear numbers. "This is pretty cool."

But back at his office, he sat down into the air-conditioned limits of his all-mahogany office. Outside, the faintest drops of rain spotted the ground, staining the asphalt a deeper shade of blue-gray. Sure, it was light rain, but rain is rain, and Hayward has seen what havoc it can wreak.

∽

At 5:00 a.m., on Monday, July 27, Dominic Terry, Rachel Alexandra's exercise rider, stretched in the dark with a foot up on a railing, bent over at the waist, working his hamstrings outside of Barn 65. Twenty minutes later, a photographer arrived.

Terry kept loosening up his muscles. On the ground rested a tossed Granny Smith apple, half eaten, rotting in the dirt. Bags of ice leaned against the wall of the barn that would eventually be wrapped around the shins of sore horses.

Scott Blasi, Steve Asmussen's top assistant trainer, walked out of his office with the screen door slamming. "How's it goin' guys?" he said to a television reporter.

The stress that came with training a horse like Rachel Alexandra was immense. Imagine the opportunity to train the best and most popular horse in North America. Imagine how great and how terrible that is, which is why Blasi was apt to be short, apt to wear a frown, apt to snap. "A special motherfucker you are," he barked one morning at a groom. It belied his emotionless façade, his normally benign, kind persona. Underneath rested a bulldog. And that ferocity was channeled into his work and then released in moments of triumph.

There is a photograph where Blasi, in a brown suit and Windsor-knotted tie, walks on the dirt of Pimlico's track after the 2009 Preakness. He grips the leather lead shank in his left hand. The shank attaches to the drooling muzzle of Rachel Alexandra. Calvin Borel, still on top of the filly, leans forward and wraps his left around Blasi's neck and pulls him close. Blasi's eyes squint into the creases of his smiling face. In that photograph lies the reason he gets up in the morning.

∽

Calvin Borel arrived at Saratoga. In fact, he was at the Oklahoma Training Track with striped polo shirt tucked into his jeans. He wore a Rachel Alexandra ball cap pulled over his eyes. He stood by Blasi's office, as in indicator to let them know that, *Hey, I'm here if you need me. We are a team.* By 5:40 a.m., Rachel Alexandra was under tack and walked briskly around the trees by her hot walker, Juan Gonzalez. Overhead a flock of Canadian geese traversed the sky.

At 5:50 a.m., Asmussen grumbled his Escalade up to his barn, sipping coffee from a Styrofoam cup. At 5:54 a.m., he and Borel followed Rachel Alexandra to the track. The pair stared ahead, noticing the throngs of people lining the rail to watch Rachel Alexandra breeze over the Oklahoma Training Track. Borel walked in lockstep with Asmussen, his elbows bigger than his biceps.

"There is a crowd no matter what she does," Asmussen said. "I was enjoying the solace of home." "Home" was Texas.

The sunrise was electric, with clouds ribbing across in erratic patterns. Rachel Alexandra galloped around the near turn. Terry straightened her out and then lengthened her stride. She might as well have been tethered to the rail by a mechanical arm pulling them counterclockwise around this oval. They swept around the turn, stopping traffic, drawing eyes. Rachel Alexandra whispered over the brown-sugar surface.

The spectators' necks craned to the right, following Rachel Alexandra's liquid canter into the morning sun, watching her bend away from the clockers. The $1 million Haskell Invitational at Monmouth Park against the colts was her next race. So much for getting her to run at Saratoga now, but that was acceptable. The hope was that she was in the middle of writing her legacy, that her end days were far from now. Whenever that day should come, it did not seem to matter to her jockey, whose eyes still locked on the best horse he had ever ridden. She whipped by the wire. The corners of Calvin Borel's mouth nearly touched his earlobes.

∽

Later that evening, the National Thoroughbred Hall of Fame bustled with racing fans eager for the meet to kick off, so that they could carve out their experiences at Saratoga Race Course. The theater of the Hall of Fame is lined with the silks of famous owners. The walls are tiled with the plaques of the immortalized greats of the sport. Tonight the doors opened for a roundtable that featured Charlie Hayward, Calvin Borel, Saratoga's defending leading trainer, Kiaran McLaughlin, and NYRA racing secretary, P. J. Campo.

The room was so full that to keep the attendance in the room was like pinching off a water balloon. Mike Kane, director of communications for the Hall of Fame, led the proceedings and took to the lectern. "We have Charlie Hayward. He said he marked us down in indelible ink. I didn't know you could get indelible ink anymore. Calvin Borel, probably did not recognize him four years ago, but in the last four years his profile went up dramatically. Add the success he had in 2007 with Street Sense and this year with Rachel Alexandra. I guess he's an old friend, Calvin Borel.

"P. J. Campo, he's well known to all of you as the racing secretary for the last five years. He brings you those turf sprints. If you like them, he's the guy to thank. If you don't, he's the guy to complain to."

Kane, relaxed and leaning on the lectern, reminded the audience that this function was about them, that if they wanted to ask questions to do so, but he started it off. "Let's start with Calvin Borel. Mine That Bird, he proved himself, give him a lot of credit, but the filly is just unbelievable."

"Yes, sir," Borel said. "It was me and my agent talking. He didn't say much. I've never been on a horse as good as her. She's awesome. She's had a five-week vacation. I remember her as a two-year-old. She was a very big filly; in the meantime, something happened to her."

Charlie Hayward hopped on the mike, "First of all, I'd like to welcome you. It's kind of like the night before Christmas." Hayward recounted some of his favorite races, and certainly his first experience at Saratoga in 1981, when Pleasant Colony lost the Travers Stakes to Willow Hour. In an allusion to some of the great female races, the hope being that Rachel Alexandra may face Zenyatta, he said how much he loved the Breeders' Cup Distaff between Personal Ensign and Winning Colors, trained by D. Wayne Lukas, in 1988. Kane sprung to life, "I remember saying, 'Beat Lukas! Beat Lukas!' "

"Hey, hey, hey!" interjected Kiaran McLaughlin. "I worked for him at the time!"

"If you've seen that shot of what Calvin Borel and Mine That Bird did," Hayward said, "you look and it seemed all the horses were moving backwards. There's no other rider that could've got the job done that day other than Calvin Borel."

The audience applauded Borel, and he gave them a bashful nod. His move on Mine That Bird was as fearless a move on a horse that a rider can make without the consequences turning catastrophic. With five mounts on Opening Day, someone asked him if riding was always his goal. "That's all I wanted to do. I knew I couldn't be a doctor or a lawyer. I was born to race that way. If a child has a dream, you've gotta let them fulfill it. Yes, sir, I knew I wanted to ride."

As was natural and expected, the talk turned to Rachel Alexandra and whether or not Saratoga would see her. Hayward, who never tired of this question, knew that Saratoga could live without her but would rather prosper with her. He said, "The way the racing schedule sets up, there are interesting options for the filly. I have no inside information, but if she's run so well against three-year-old colts, what about the Woodward? I think that the owners have a great sense of history."

If Hayward was about managing expectations for the meet, then this was about building anticipation, of generating an engine that could drive the public conscience. The more talk of Rachel Alexandra, the bigger she grew, like William Wallace. *She's ten feet tall and shoots lightning bolts from her eyes and thunder from her arse.* Borel leaned back in his chair and relaxed, absorbing the Rachel Alexandra banter as if she were his crown of laurels.

"Prior to the Preakness, did Steve Asmussen give you any advice?" Kane said to Borel.

"None," answered Borel. "He said, 'Go get it done.' When you ride them kind of horses, if I don't get to the lead, just lay off them. Oh, yeah. She run the race. I knew she wasn't getting a hold of the track. I knew Mine That Bird was comin'. When you eyeball her—not that she's been eyeballed lately—it's unbelievable."

"Has life changed much?" Kane asked.

"Life hasn't changed much," Borel said. "It's been a little easier. I take everything as it comes. I dream of winning the Derby, not going to the White House or going on *Jay Leno.*"

"What are you dreaming of now?" inquired Kane.

"I don't know," replied Borel. "Gonna have to ask my fiancée."

Week One

7

Opening Day

The sun lagged its way up the eastern horizon, hesitating just enough so that a caterpillar of light glowed. The air forecasted oppression. Discerning where the morning fog ended and the haze began was next to impossible. Racing fans sat on their coolers outside the main gate waiting to enter and mark their territory for the first day of the 141st race meeting at Saratoga Race Course. They mimicked galloping horses, whipping their backsides with rolled up newspapers.

At home, Charlie Hayward had already set the coffee for his wife, Betsy Senior, and fed his two cats, Nomar Garciapurra, named after the former Red Sox shortstop, and Black Minnaloushe, the cat named after a horse that was named after a cat in a William Yeats poem. But now, shortly before six in the morning, Hayward readied for an onslaught of interviews for print, radio, and television, and if he was lucky, maybe some time to place a bet or two. At the track, the lamps in Hayward's office were the only ones on, squares of light that tiled a building loaded with dark and empty caves.

Out on the main track, hundreds of horses were training, galloping, and breezing in all directions. Hayward arrived on the apron in a striped shirt and blue pinstripe suit, black shoes, and a tie adorned with horses. He cupped his coffee and turned to Maureen Lewi, Ed Lewi's wife and partner with Ed Lewi Associates, and said: "I may lose my coat, what do you think?" He then took his coat off and draped it over the fence of the winner's circle. Sweat started to blotch his cotton shirt.

NBC 13 was his first of nearly thirty interviews that day as the sun yawned over the horizon at the top of the home stretch, an orb as rich as an egg yolk. "Beautiful scene as we open the meet," the reporter said.

"It's like Christmas Day at Saratoga," Hayward said. "I'm thankful that the weather is great. By this time last year, it was rain all the way around. The big stars are coming and we're making stars too."

Hal Handel, NYRA's vice president and COO, and P. J. Campo, vice president and racing secretary, scurried from interview to interview themselves.

Campo walked by Hayward with a shirt with two buttons undone, no tie. "You've already been?" Hayward asked.

"I've been everywhere," Campo said, a smile stamped on his face.

"See you later," returned Hayward.

Hayward was ushered with haste to the flower box for another interview, while a siren blared over the PA system. "Loose horse!" Hayward yelled. "Is it gorgeous here at Saratoga?" It wasn't so much a question. And perhaps that has much to do with having the franchise in place and the company out of bankruptcy. What Charlie Hayward did, dating back to his hiring in November 2004, was run the Saratoga meet with a piano on his back. Discussions with the franchise contract date back to 2006 with then-governor George Pataki. When Eliot Spitzer took office, further discussions ensued with his aides in the fall of 2007. After seven months of negotiations to create the formal franchise documentation, in September 2008 a deal was at last inked. Hayward was, in every way, tied to the drafts, meetings, conference calls, and compromises. But that was just the beginning, because NYRA ran out of money and filed for Chapter 11 reorganization.

To avoid bankruptcy, NYRA agreed to sell its land—Belmont Park, Aqueduct, and Saratoga Race Course—a net value of $2 billion, in exchange for a twenty-five year franchise agreement. While NYRA competed with other factions for the franchise deal, it always had the upper hand: it always had the land.

If Hayward's hair wasn't already the color of sea foam, then the process would have driven any color out. Betsy Senior, his wife, saw it in him, how maddening the process was. Here he was, trying to put on a meet at Saratoga, and the bidders for the franchise circled the grounds like turkey vultures about carrion. To Senior, it was crazy. To Hayward, it was frustrating. The thought of losing the franchise was horrifying for all involved. The first franchise talks for NYRA began in 2006; a nightmare, as Hayward put it. Hayward and his team submitted a 1,400-page document, most of it written while at Saratoga, Hayward having written some of the executive summary. He admitted that, in some ways, it was a fool's errand. Bankruptcy followed shortly, in November 2006, and the franchise process was forced to start over before, at last, getting the deal done in 2008. To run a Saratoga meet with NYRA's future in shambles was a huge distraction.

The state ranked the bidders for the franchise: it was Empire Racing Associates, Excelsior Racing Associates, and NYRA, NYRA being a distant third in the selection process. Excelsior possessed a weak resume in the face of NYRA. Empire's was better, since it had the Magna tracks, Churchill Downs, and the support of the New York Thoroughbred Horsemen Association. Hayward was relieved that none of this reached the patrons, but it did get to the employees. It made it hard to hire people, but it made the people who worked for NYRA—pari-mutuel clerks, peace officers, ushers—apprehensive.

So when, at last, Charlie Hayward and NYRA won the franchise, he was flooded with letters and e-mails. Senior remembered one letter from a woman who thought she was going to lose her job but didn't because Hayward kept the franchise. Senior remembers it as very affecting, that those who fill the fundamental positions of NYRA, those whose garb is free of Windsor knots, power suits, and BlackBerries, felt connected to the hierarchy. All sorts of people who were making peanuts down on the ground floor expressed their affection, even devotion, the way a serf may respect his king. "It makes him a very beloved manager," Senior said.

∽

Which was why in 2009 Charlie Hayward had a bounce to his step, a quickened pace to his cadence. This meet was the first in his five years as NYRA's president and CEO that the franchise was no longer an issue. He hustled up the chained-off stairs and into the flower box, a segment of the grandstand's roof where CBS 6 made camp.

"Here's the No. 1 fan of Saratoga, Ed O'Brien," Hayward said to the CBS 6 reporter.

"I thought you were going to say the No. 1 fan of the Big A inner," O'Brien joked, referring to the oft-chided winter Aqueduct inner-track meet. "You know, just to get my fifty bucks . . . ," he continued, jabbing at his dysfunctional OTB account, "it's better to lose."

"I wouldn't do that," Hayward said.

The red light of the camera flashed and O'Brien switched to television reporter mode and turned to face Hayward.

"The horses are working," O'Brien said, "fans don't understand, they're animals, not machines."

"To be here in the mornings, say for breakfast time," Hayward said, "you see Todd Pletcher, a potential Hall of Famer."

"There's a lot of irons in the fire."

"When we get the VLTs up and running and get the capital—I think they'll get it done in August, hopefully by September 2010—we'll be spending money."

"You're not going to put in some grand attraction like Churchill Downs did? The luxury boxes dwarfed the attraction in the Twin Spires."

"We have a lot of temporary structures, the club house and the grandstand that need work."

"It is now 6:14," O'Brien concluded, sending it back to the studio."

Hayward, still making small talk, unclipped his mike and followed Maureen Lewi. A sliver of water, black against the soft-tar shingling the roof, was camouflaged like a predator. Maureen led Hayward to the stairs.

Then she slipped in the puddle and hit the ground. "Maureen!" Hayward exclaimed. "I'll get in big trouble from Mr. Lewi. It's a slippery surface and you have slippery shoes."

Passing through the restaurant, fans greeted Hayward with handshakes, like a campaigning politician. It made him question whether he knew the person or not. He always thought, *Did I meet that person, or did they just recognize me from TV? They know me, but I don't know them.* He sat down with Fritz Hauck with WCSS Radio.

"Rachel Alexandra, ridden by the popular jockey, Calvin Borel, is there talk of her and the unbeaten Zenyatta?" Hauck asked.

"At this point there is a low probability Zenyatta will run at Saratoga," said Hayward. "She's going to stay on the West Coast. We're focused and hoping that Rachel Alexandra comes out of the Haskell well. She could run in the Alabama, Travers, or the Personal Ensign. If she really wants to take on the boys and go for Horse of the Year, she could run in the Woodward."

"What about dirt versus synthetics?" inquired Hauck.

"I think there was a rush to judgment with Keeneland, Arlington, Woodbine. They thought it would be safer and that has not necessarily been the case. They thought it would be less expensive to maintain. There's no underlying science. We've got good old fashioned-dirt here. We'll be sticking with dirt here," Hayward answered.

"In effect, on WFAN, Robert Zimmerman with Nassau OTB," Hauck said, changing the subject, "well, I'll give you the Reader's Digest version: Nassau OTB basically illegally took control of the signal for forty-five days or so, so you stopped the signal?"

Liar and a thief? Dino Amoroso's negligence? His arrogance? Undoubtedly Hayward rolled these thoughts through his mind.

"They were, without our permission, taking our video signal and putting it on the Internet," said Hayward. "They continued streaming our own races for forty-five race days, which is seventy actual days. The fans, since June 5, have been without racing. Hopefully some time today we can proceed. I'd like to turn the signal back on."

Hauck replied, "There's been a lot of name calling from Nassau OTB."

"It's a unique situation. It's hard to imagine. The OTBs get 40 percent of the revenue bet on NYRA racetracks. It's hard to believe they had no idea what was going on," Hayward concluded.

∾

"You hear about the Red Sox? They had a 7–4 lead heading into the ninth," Mark Bardack said.

"Pap blew it?" Hayward said, referring to Red Sox closer Jonathan Papelbon, before turning his back to go on camera.

"Yeah . . . not a good idea to put him in a bad mood before he goes on," said Bardack.

❧

The sun's color had yet to pale, and Hayward bumped into Hal Handel. Sweat beaded and spotted like surfacing islands on the lower back of Hayward's cotton shirt. They huddled close, separated by steaming waves crawling from their coffee cups, "You're the man, talk about anything you want," Hayward said.

Then Hayward ran into one of his favorite reporters, a lively female with a toothy smile, from Capital News 9. "My main man!" she said.

"MY main man!" said Hayward.

"It's good to see you!" she replied.

Hayward was on his third cup of coffee.

❧

Hayward now headed to his ninth interview of the morning, gabbing with Rich Becker, a television sports reporter. Hayward, who owns a horse named Radical Sabbatical as part of a syndicate, was selling the idea to Becker, who flirted with getting into the game. "Whether you own 2 percent or 100 percent, it's your horse," Becker said.

"I'm in a small syndicate, I don't know," Hayward said.

"Jerry Bossert said at the Hall of Fame, the most important female at Saratoga is not Rachel Alexandra, it's Mother Nature," replied Becker.

After they went on the air, Becker added, "I may bet a few bucks, make my donation to NYRA."

"We appreciate it," said Hayward.

❧

Fourth cup of coffee, tenth interview, this one with Paul Vandenburgh. Every Wednesday for the rest of the meet, Hayward would meet with Vandenburgh, a radio host who favors Albany politics. Vandenburgh sat at the same table in the restaurant and kept his receipt out for Hayward to sign.

"I'm getting to the point where I come here because of you," Vandenburgh said. "This is five years now. I thought it was three. A lot of it was the franchise, those morons in Albany. Now you have the twenty-five year lease, so racing is stabilized. What's going on in your head?"

"I wish I could say racing," replied Hayward. "We're trying to resolve this situation with Nassau OTB. Hopefully we'll make an announcement today and turn the signal back on."

"You've resolved that?"

"No. Basically what happened, we have our own website, and you can't stream our races. They started streaming races in January and we wrote them a letter to cease and desist and tell us that that won't do it again. They said no one in the organization knew. The reason it's important is because we charge a lot of money to stream. That allowed them to get the best price. It's an economic decision, not just pride."

"But there is some pride, not just economics. The OTB people think that they can do whatever they want. You've got backstretch people. You've got to fix toilets. NOT. THEM. The OTB legislation is separate from NYRA. The only thing the OTBs do is take bets, pay winners, and pay the counties. Did I miss something?"

"You can't put them all together; we need some kind of consolidation."

"Tell me about those guys."

"I'm not sure. I don't want to make this personal. Let's move on."

"Everyone knows you're right and they're wrong. Get it done."

"If Nassau doesn't care about their customers, we care about ours. The OTBs are outdated."

"There was a time," continued Vandenburgh, "this was in the 70s, to go to a place in a branch, you couldn't get in. Now this is commonplace, you can watch in your house. These OTBs can't reach in and take what they want. It's an intellectual property, you have that, you can't take the logo, that's yours. It's important now to look at the business plan, there are a lot of changes coming."

"I think you're referring to the VLTs," said Hayward. "When they get up and running we'll get about $25 million a year. I'm passionate about racing. That's why I'm here. I'm talking in the late 90s, NYRA wanted to change Saratoga's gate. That was a huge problem. The sad part is it's beautiful. You've seen what they did at Churchill Downs and at Gulfstream. People have a right to get angry."

"You've got this thing, the people at Delaware North screwed you. You don't want to use that term. I will."

"The history, in fairness to them," Hayward said as Vandenburgh tried to interject, "Listen up for one second. In 2006-2007, the bid process, the bids were done in May. The state couldn't decide until October 2008. You and I both know the credit markets changed. No one could have seen it drop 40 percent."

"I've got a problem watching you get beat up."

"Where the state is, they seem competent with the governor's plans. He's down to earth, pragmatic, and the one thing he understands is that nowhere can the state get $300 million a year. The governor said they will get somebody by August 1. I think by the time we leave here September 7, we'll have one."

"Charlie, you seem already to get down to it and with these yo-yos, people want to see races. How about this guy from Nassau not coming in?"

"Mr. Amoroso came on at 3:05 on the YES network, Zimmerman comes on for a bait and switch. Mike Francesa was pissed. Those folks want to talk Yanks and Mets. They don't want to hear me."

"They are kicking dirt in the faces of horsemen."

Hayward then took off his headphones and shook people's hands, while a few tables away, Sam the Bugler played the Call to the Post. He serenaded a woman whose cheeks became as red as Sam's jacket. He then posed for a picture, one of hundreds over the course of the next thirty-six days.

Vandenburgh slid his receipt across the table, and Hayward signed for it.

$$\sim$$

Charlie Hayward came up on a break, but first he finished his fifth cup of coffee before heading to PYX Radio with Wolfman, sort of like a Howard Stern team with multiethnic cohosts. Hayward knew this was the "fun" interview, one not as serious or stuffy, no VLTs, no OTBs. It was in Hayward's body language, leaning back with one leg extended to the heel.

Asked Hayward: "Hey Wolfman, baby, how ya doin'?"

Wolfman replied: "Charlie, he's all right too. What's new?"

"What's new is sunshine, number one," answered Hayward. "What's new is two-year-olds. Talking about Rachel Alexandra, I don't mean to swear on the radio, but she's running in the Haskell."

This shot like an arrow over Wolfman's head. He furrowed his brow. Was that a bad joke? What's the Haskell? Gary Contessa, Belmont's leading trainer over the spring, sat next to Hayward, and in his robust persona and voice blurted, "I've heard Charlie Hayward will be in a dunk tank by the jocks' room for all the people who are upset with NYRA."

"Myself, Steve Duncker, Hal Handel," Hayward said.

"No matter how much people like you . . ." Contessa said.

"Twenty thousand people to dunk Charlie Hayward. Putting a Speedo on or suit and tie?" asked Wolfman.

"I don't think anybody wants to see me in a Speedo. Suit and tie," answered Hayward.

At last it was time for his morning break. He would have his fourteenth interview before he summoned his executive team together for the "Huddle," usually scheduled for 10:00 a.m., outside the administration building. Until then, it was another cup of coffee. And letting the sounds of the morning ring in his mind, such as a man singing to a flock of women, he crooned, "I don't know why I love you, *IIIIIIIIIII* just do."

$$\sim$$

From atop the grandstand, looking down upon the grounds, vendors and workers were ferrying goods on dollies, all sorts of beverages, from beer to soft drinks. They looked like ants carrying grains of sugar to their hill, their tunnels.

∽

The circle started to form with the members of NYRA's executive board, some fifteen members in power suits, all hooked to their BlackBerries. From up above they formed a ring on the asphalt, knights of the round table without the table. Ellen McLean, the newly hired CFO, filed out. Dan Silver was in the paddock for a quick interview, but Hal Handel was on time and saw Dave Smukler, senior vice president of human resources and labor relations, follow. "The man, the myth, the legend," Handel said. From scattered hovels around Saratoga Race Course, the other members came as if pulled by a magnet, until at last Charlie Hayward finished the group and closed off the circle. "Encouraging," Handel said, looking around at all the people.

They leaped from subject to subject, each with their own fiefdom. The topics of conversation zigged and zagged and lacked fluidity. There was no way to transition seamlessly with so much to cover. There was legal counsel, and there was finance. There was customer relations, and there was OTB relations. There was simulcast, and there was the racing secretary. And all of the information got funneled to the CEO.

"We'll be all right," Hayward said. "Let's get started. Welcome to Saratoga everybody. I'm glad to have you here. I'd like to welcome our new CFO, Ellen McLean, who came up on Monday and she's worked really hard, but she is leaving, is taking two weeks' vacation." Having already planned her vacation prior to her interview, this Brown and Harvard graduate took some flak.

"A little bit of news," Hayward continued. "We are announcing momentarily that we are turning the signal on at the Nassau OTBs. It was decided when Nick Kling made a comment. He said, 'The bottom line is that everyone knows you're right and everyone knows Nassau OTB's an idiot, but they're going to blame you and that's what they're doing.' They made another pass with the New York State Racing and Wagering Board. We're going to put out an announcement that we are going to countersue and hopefully get the suit together early next week. The good news is that the customers have been taken care of."

"I want to give a tip of the cap to Kevin and tip to Kimberly for why everything looks so good," Handel said to Kimberly Justus, director of guest services, and Kevin Gremillion, who works with the grounds crew.

Don Lehr, next in the huddle this day, Hayward's PR man and numbers guru, announced the figures of the attendance and the on-track and off-track handle in millions during every huddle. "I reviewed last year so now we know where we are this year. Last year, Opening Day, 18,127, 2.8, 11.4."

"We'll kill that this year," Hayward said.

"Sixty-nine betting interests," continued Lehr. "In 2007, 30,052, 3.4, 15.2. In '07, ninety-eight betting interests. Ten races both years."

"We've gotta have 110 betting interests," Hayward said. "How are the scratches?"

"Pretty good," said racing secretary P. J. Campo.

"Also, we're putting the West Virginia Derby in the program and Monmouth for the Haskell," said Liz Bracken, vice president and director of Simulcast Services, eager to show the Kentucky Derby winner, Mine That Bird, and Rachel Alexandra in their races for the weekend.

"I think we should do it," Hayward said. "How much does that cost?"

"Six hundred thousand programs, thirty to thirty-five cents a program," replied Jerry Davis, director of admissions and parking.

"That's expensive," Hayward said.

"That's with upgraded paper, twenty-four to thirty-six pages," added Davis.

"I think we ought to do it. That's gonna drive some handle, presumably," replied Hayward.

"Absolutely," Campo added.

"We have a lot of clerks, more than last year," related Patrick Mahony, senior vice president of Pari-Mutuel Operations. "The grandstand, we're still waiting on that."

"It will be done by first post?" Hayward asked.

"Yes," answered Mahony.

"Though you've probably seen Kim, this is Kim's first year at Saratoga, so be good to her," Hayward said, and then he turned to Patrick Kehoe, senior vice president and general counsel.

"Just VLTs and OTBs, a little action on Hard Rock," Kehoe said, standing erect behind a slick pair of sunglasses.

"So our moderate enthusiasm might be warranted?" asked Hayward.

"Yeah. Moderate," answered Kehoe.

"Vandenburgh killed Delaware North on the radio," Hayward said. "Did you hear it? I tried to get him to ease up, but he wasn't having any of it."

Hayward then moved onto race replays and photo finishes. "What we decided to do was after an official race, you can stream the replay," he continued. "So if a race goes off at 1:27, you can watch it, in effect, at 1:30. It's the equivalent to watching it live. I think it could be huge. Credit that to Mr. Lehr, he stole it from football."

"Good work, Don," Handel said, tongue in cheek.

"The whole slate of interviews that Ed Lewi coordinated," said Dan Silver, director of communications, "I hear it is the largest we've had. So that's a positive indicator. MASN [Mid-Atlantic Sports Network] is piggy-backing on MSG+. They're taking MSG+ feeds. Just have more coverage for us."

"Now the media rock star," Hayward said, motioning to Campo. "He does TV, he does radio . . ."

"Thanks to Kevin and that huge project," Campo said. "That day we had nine canceled races. That's put to bed. We don't have to worry about that."

One day in 2008 it rained with such ferocity that the top of the homestretch failed to drain, and it washed out. Some of the jockeys went out for that race and reported that there was a gaping hole in the track and insisted that the race day be cancelled.

"This is what it's about," Campo said. "We all work hard for this thirty-six days, so we all should enjoy a part of it and see the animals run on that oval, just enjoy these six weeks."

"I heard Darley has sixty-two two-year-olds," Hayward said. "Eoin Harty said he has a freak. I spoke to Contessa this morning when we were on PYX and he said, 'I've got a bigger freak, so we're going to see which freak wins.' How's the field for this week's stakes races?"

"We have eight in the Jim Dandy and ten in the Diana," Campo said. "The first week is pretty smooth. We're starting on the right track. This is the only place in the country that is racing six days a week and has not cut any days. That's something for us to be proud of."

With nods and acknowledging faces, the group shifted into place before Hayward said one last thing: "I'm having a party, informal, at my house this Monday. The invitations will be in the mail."

The huddle broke, and Hayward went to speak with his friend, Steven Crist, from *Daily Racing Form*.

∽

Steven Crist and Charlie Hayward had met in the 1980s in New York while Crist was a cub reporter covering horse racing for the *New York Times* and Hayward was in the publishing business.

In the mid-1990s, Crist was a vice president with NYRA in charge of simulcasting, marketing, and corporate development when Hayward was named a trustee. Crist remembers Hayward as a "very sympathetic voice and ear with what I was trying to do with NYRA, which wasn't necessarily the case with the rest of the board of trustees, so he and I got friendly then."

Hayward resigned in 1996 from his post as president of Little, Brown, and Crist left NYRA at this time, so the two found themselves jobless and motivated. They sat down together over lunch and tossed around ideas. Hayward was in publishing, Crist was a writer, so they thought, *let's start a racing magazine.*

Crist had experience. He was approached in 1990 by representatives of British media mogul Robert Maxwell to edit a new periodical called *The*

Racing Times. Its purpose was to compete against Rupert Murdoch's *Daily Racing Form* which, largely, had a monopoly over racing's coverage.

Crist went to work. He hired the best writers and quickly sponged 30 percent of the market. Then, in 1991, Robert Maxwell fell overboard from his yacht and drowned. Crist called it "weird, suspicious circumstances that have never been resolved." Maxwell's estate sold *The Racing Times* to Murdoch. He promptly folded the upstart and the market was again his.

One morning both Crist and Hayward read *Daily Racing Form* and on page 4 the headline read: "Primedia to sell *Racing Form.*" Crist said, oh, man, I had this lifelong mission with the *Racing Form* after my experience with *The Racing Times.* He said that he wished he had $50 million sitting around to act on the bitterness he harbored from his short time running *The Racing Times.*

"Well, you know we can go out and borrow money," said Hayward.

"I don't know anything about this," said Crist.

After a misstep, Hayward and Crist corralled enough investors to buy *Daily Racing Form* in August 1998. Hayward remained an outside consultant, electing to be excluded from day-to-day operations. After the first year he was in full time. At first Crist was the CEO and Hayward was the president, but three years later Hayward took over as CEO. Crist then became chairman and publisher, his current posts.

Over the six years they spent working at *Daily Racing Form*, they forged a great relationship, one built on respect for the task, racing, and each other, so much so that when the NYRA CEO position became vacant, it was Hayward who confided in Crist. They both realized they were a quality one-two punch, with Hayward the sociable head of state and Crist, in his own words, the "antisocial, swirly, hothead."

The *Daily Racing Form*, by 2004, was sold for a third time in six years, and Hayward was not fond of the new ownership group. Around this time the CEO position opened up at NYRA. The board of trustees offered the job to Hayward, but Hayward needed to consult with Crist. Hayward said, "Let's get dinner and let me pick your brain about the NYRA job. You think I should do this?"

"Absolutely not," Crist said. "You have no idea how filthy and awful the whole politics part of it is. Why do you want to put yourself through this? You're not going to have any fun. It's going to make you hate racing."

The more Crist spat out the broken parts, the more Hayward's fix-it gene expressed. Crist could already see in his eyes that he wanted to do it; he saw the glint. Hayward went ahead and took the job.

Crist knew that Hayward wouldn't create a clever, earth-shaking plan, but he did know that Hayward possessed a good analytical mind when assessing a situation and that he had the people skills to get things done. "He's the boss where his employees think he's getting a fair shake from, he takes time to talk to people. He goes out for a beer, makes you feel important. He's not a guy who's going to stay up all night studying figures and doing math. But he'll accomplish more face-to-face with someone in a half hour than most of us can."

Crist also knew that unlike other racetrack operators, Hayward actually liked horse racing, that on his day off he would like to go to the grandstand in his shorts with a beer and cigar and play the races.

When a horseplayer, or an executive, or both, comes to New York the question often mulled over is, "Boy, if somebody else was running this place . . . ?" Or, "If only they would let me have my way . . . ?" Hayward stepped in front of this bullet.

It came as no surprise to Crist when Hayward landed the NYRA franchise. Part of that was Hayward's savvy, but, as Crist noted, the status quo in politics is always the favorite, and NYRA always had the land.

It all started with a glint that Crist had tried to extinguish.

～

Earlier in 2009 *The Blood-Horse* magazine published an extended feature on Charlie Hayward titled "Good Job, Charlie." In the story it was exposed that while working in publishing and selling books in Chicago, Hayward and his friend, William Shinker, would slump into Hayward's rust-colored Pontiac convertible and peel down the streets. In the article Shinker said, "Charlie definitely liked the ladies, and the ladies like him." It was the kind of quote that would not ruin him but just cause him momentary embarrassment.

～

Hayward and Handel made small talk about Opening Day in Handel's office, Handel sitting with one leg crossed over the other, his shoe-shine box resting on the floor. Steve Duncker, the chairman of NYRA, walked in and shadowboxed with Hayward like they were fraternity brothers. They spoke of the weather and the optimism that comes with so much ahead and so little behind.

"This guy's a chick magnet!" Duncker said, while Hayward arched his neck back. "The ladies love Charlie, and Charlie loves the ladies!"

Smiles and laughs filled the room, and Hayward was eager to see the first race go off. After some six hours of interviews—and more to come—it would be nice to see a race, and get this meet rolling for P. J. Campo, the racing secretary.

"Win one for the Peej!" Hayward said.

"Win one for the Chick Magnet!" Duncker said.

"C'mon, help me out," Hayward said.

∽

Calvin Borel was given a leg up by Kentucky-based trainer Ian Wilkes for the first race of the 2009 meet. His horse was 24 to 1, by no means a contender on the board. There were twelve horses in the field of grass runners and an apron full of horse-racing fans eager for the meet to start. Once a year race caller Tom Durkin implores the crowd to join him when the gates blast open. He asks them to say, "And they're off! At Saratoga!"

With all of them in line, the fans did just that: "AND THEY'RE OFF! AT SARATOGA!"

Borel's horse loped out of the gate and after a quarter of a mile found himself in last place. And that was where he stayed. The entire way around the oval. Dead last.

∽

By mid-afternoon the winds had picked up and a Häagen Dazs umbrella was turned inside out. By 3:11, raindrops fell at a leisurely pace. A TV cameraman, looking at the radar on his iPhone, said, "We're gonna get clobbered."

Charlie Hayward bumped into Mike Francesa, formerly of *Mike and the Mad Dog* show. Francesa had booked Dino Amoroso of the Nassau OTB Network to come on his show. At the last moment, Amoroso put his PR guy, Robert Zimmerman, in his slot and dodged the show.

"Did you get the feed running?" Francesa said to Hayward.

"Well, here's what happened. A journalist friend of mine said, 'Listen, everyone knows you're right, and everyone knows they're wrong. But everyone knows they're a bunch of jerks and they're going to blame you.' And that's what happened. So I went to Chairman Sabini of the New York State Racing and Wagering Board and asked him to ask me to turn the feed back on."

"Did he?"

"Yes, and then we said we're countersuing them for damages, which we weren't going to do before."

"And the feed was switched today?"

"Yes, well, come with me and we'll find out for sure."

In the administration building Hayward learned that the switch had been made but that the feed was not running that day, however, it would be for the remainder of the meet.

∽

Prior to the feature race, the rains came as if to remind all parties involved that late summer in Upstate New York is a force to be reckoned with. With his phone to his ear, Hayward said, "$1.4 million? Should be a 40 percent increase. How much did that late scratch cost us? The scratch cost us $300,000. If it weren't for that, all-source would be up 10 percent."

Earlier in the card a horse was a gate scratch, meaning that at the gate the on-track vet saw something suspicious and withdrew the horse from the race. But all wagers on that horse were refunded and bettors were provided with a consolation that cost NYRA $300,000. Hayward dialed up Campo about taking the tenth race—a grass race—off the turf because of the rain.

"Say no more, it's your call. We'll live to fight another day," Hayward said.

Don Lehr entered his office, and Hayward excused himself. After an absence of ten minutes, Hayward came back to his office, flustered, running his hands through his hair. He was admittedly peeved, throwing a folded piece of paper onto his desk. There were just a few more interviews to do, but the mood had changed, and the rain continued to pour with no indication of slowing down.

8

The Problem with Pairs

The third day of the meet brought with it weepy clouds, the type that, should they be so inclined, would last all day. The radar was an amorphous emerald amoeba drooling over Saratoga Race Course and the Oklahoma Training Track.

Despite the rain and its zags across the sky, not a single umbrella was utilized on the Oklahoma backstretch. Trainers wore windbreakers, raincoats, and ball caps. Well, one red-and-white umbrella did bob its way into the hands of one spectator. Confused that no one else had an umbrella, this person was, at once, self-conscious as to the lack of umbrellas. That was when Hall of Fame trainer Bill Mott, aboard his pony, galloping a horse, yelled as if berating a child for having his hand in the cookie jar. The horse he galloped became spooked by the umbrella and failed to focus, was erratic, and Mott let this person have it. The umbrella collapsed and, for an instant, was considered for disposal.

Nick Zito's barn was particularly somber, one where the snorts of the horses were the greatest chatter. In the mud to the southern edge of Zito's barn, by the dormitories, were discarded chicken bones, bottle caps—both metal and plastic—mesh netting like one would find wrapping clams or mussels, plastic knives, forks, six-pack rings, and Q-tips.

Zito sat in his Mercedes GL450 SUV with the engine running. Raindrops freckled his windshield while the wipers erased the blemishes. His ball cap was cocked and twisted, tilted up high on his forehead. His face revealed a look of deep frustration, of needy clients always being at his ear. Zito had just one horse entered today. The rain kept falling, and his wipers kept wiping.

༄

Calvin Borel booked one mount this day, one horse that went off at 15 to 1. She was a nonthreatening fourth but earned Borel $1,860 in purse money. After he hopped off the horse and weighed in, he was met with swarms of fans that recognized his crinkled face. On the move, walking as fast as one could walk without breaking out into a jog, he signed photographs—him atop both Mine That Bird and Rachel Alexandra.

Borel's fiancée, Lisa Funk, remembered that just a few years ago, when the two came to Saratoga in 2004, 2005, and 2006, that they had walked around the grounds cloaked in anonymity. His physical stature might have been the only indicator that perhaps this man was a jockey. Ah, but many jockeys come in and out of Saratoga, riding one horse for one trainer who has one shot to say that he competed at Saratoga for one day before receding to the margins.

Funk had attended college at the University of Kentucky in Lexington in 2001 as an English lit major, perfect for anyone who grew up loving either college basketball or horses. Funk loved horses. She first sat in a saddle at age four, riding hunter-jumpers mainly. She had dreams of international show-jumping stardom; the racetrack seemed as real as a unicorn. When she became a Wildcat (Kentucky's mascot), she rode for the equestrian team. It wasn't long before she discovered Keeneland, a track whose elegance rivals or possibly surpasses Saratoga's, depending on whom you talk to. Funk figured that she could do well as a cocktail waitress in this environment, where owners and trainers watched the races. And rightly so—this job helped put her through school.

While working, a girlfriend of Funk's told her that she might want to try galloping racehorses in the mornings. The woman's husband, Ron Moquett, was a trainer, and he needed extra help. Funk's girlfriend said that they would teach her everything she needed to know about galloping and jogging horses. It shocked her at first. Imagine raising show dogs and then being asked to raise greyhounds—that was Funk's comparison.

At the time, Calvin Borel labored through a nasty divorce. He rode horses for Moquett, though Moquett was closer to Borel's brother Cecil. Cecil and Moquett thought that Funk would be the right match for Borel, the right blend of charm and heart. Cecil even asked Funk, "Why don't you date Calvin? He's such a nice guy. You'd really like him."

Funk hesitated. It was the end of the summer and school would start in just a couple of weeks. She had heard horror stories of womanizing jockeys and thought that this was a pool better left unwaded. But Cecil kept at her, and Funk succumbed, telling him, "We'll all go out together and scope him out and see if I like him." They went on several dates, and Funk and Borel were drawn to each other like iron to a magnet. Funk thought, as corny as it sounds, that it was a "meeting of two souls. We both are so committed to horses and love horses so much that I understood who he is and what makes him tick because it's what makes me tick as a person."

After a two-week courtship, Funk moved in with Borel and scrapped school. For her it was a shock and a leap of faith, but she also thought that this could go really well, or really, really badly. She would eventually go on to finish her English lit degree at the University of Louisville in 2006, and things with Borel shot to the moon.

Given Borel's ongoing divorce, he needed Funk to be the mast he latched his sail onto because, as Funk recalled, Borel experienced a great deal of vulnerability, especially since racetrack divorces ripple through the backside. "People will make up all kinds of things if you don't tell them what's going on," Funk said. Borel feared his business would suffer. He was a rider just scrapping by working herds of no-name horses, Kentucky Derbys being a pinpoint in the sky.

Borel's finances were scattered, and it was Funk who corralled them and ensured that his taxes were in order, that he was incorporated, things that, once settled, allowed Borel to be Bo-Rail—the fearless, rail-skimming rider. Five Kentucky Derbys passed before Funk finished school, and there were some dry years before 2007, before Street Sense put the spotlight on Borel.

In those arid years the owners for whom Borel rode were transitioning out of the game, and John Franks, one of Borel's most consistent owners, passed away, dispersing all of his horses. Hall of Fame jockey Pat Day still commanded the top mounts in Kentucky, so Borel had to coax the most ability out of his junior varsity talent. "It wasn't always rainbows and sunshine," recalled Funk.

Funk watched Borel in action, deciphered his moods and decrypted his body language. She knew that when one loved something as much as he did that one never gives up. Funk never saw Borel hang his head or lose his vision. Borel still woke up every morning. If a trainer stripped a horse from him, he'd find another horse and try to beat that horse, that trainer, and that jockey. Several times he did.

Despite the resilience Funk witnessed in Borel, she still saw that it crushed him to be taken off good horses, horses such as Dollar Bill, the Dallas Stewart horse that would finish fifteenth in the 2001 Kentucky Derby. She saw the disappointment because she understood that "he loved what he did so much. He loved the game no matter how rude the game was to him, how demeaning it was to him. The game's the game. He understood that one day if he just kept at it, opportunity would find him a good horse and he'd be able to show what he was made of."

She never saw him too depressed; rather, he was emboldened by rejection. "That's just his outlook on life." said Funk. "When you love what you do, there's nobody that can tell you that you can't accomplish something, and he's going to die trying."

Funk had restructured Borel's path in many ways and watched him, like other jockeys that wallow in obscurity, make a decent wage but never strike that upper echelon. She couldn't forecast the covers of the New York Times or the meetings with the Queen of England. It chiseled at Funk to watch Borel suspended in this jockey purgatory. When Borel woke before the sun, Funk knew all he needed was for someone to believe in him, *really* believe, to give him a horse and not take it away. But as the years passed she also began to resign herself to the fact that he was past his prime, already thirty-four, then thirty-five, and by then jockeys are who they are. It was thought that when John Franks passed away that Borel's chances had been grounded.

Funk pushed Borel. She got under his skin, because she knew he had it. But she started to see the flame flicker at wick's end. "You're such a good jockey," she said, "C'mon! What's the deal?"

"Well, you don't understand. This is a waiting game," Borel replied. "I have to wait for my business to come back around."

Funk learned that the horse business comes in tides but lacks the predictability of the moon's phases. But she watched Borel head out every morning, and just like Borel had said, it was just a matter of time.

Funk reflected that you try these different keys in different doors and none of them open. But you keep trying. And finally, you slide one in, turn it, and it opens.

The key, in 2007, was Street Sense.

∾

During the 2009 meet, Borel found that the weight of the year slowed him down, tiring his already fatigued body. So he and Funk spent much of their free time outdoors, away from the track, hiking the mountains and paddling the rivers. With food packed for a day, the two set out on a canoeing trip on the Battenkill River in Vermont. They shared a canoe, Funk in the front with the camera, Borel in the back manning the rudder and steering the canoe in the benign current. Along the way were pit stops where they rested to share a meal.

They encountered at one stop a minivan filled with a vacationing family from Pennsylvania who stopped to have lunch by the side of the Battenkill. The father saw, out of the corner of his eye, a recognizable face. Borel, used to the weight of eyes, caught the father's eyes as well but kept to himself. *Here?*

Borel and the man exchanged indirect glances. The man worked up his courage to approach Borel, while the man's daughter hid in embarrassment, imploring him to stay by the minivan.

"Are you Calvin Borel?" he asked. Borel nodded.

"No, Daddy," the girl said, as her father retreated to their camp to find anything for Borel to scribble on, before, at last, finding a T-shirt. Anything would do.

"We are going to the races this weekend," the father said.

So Funk and Borel gave them horses to bet on, this random family from Pennsylvania, by the side of the Battenkill River.

The family returned to their van and drove off. The day was postcard beautiful as Funk and Borel continued down the Battenkill, with Borel's back turned to his fame, no autographs, no interviews.

～

Two hours had passed, and now Funk and Borel were roasting in the sun. They neared what was to be their final destination, another riverside stop where the canoe company would ship them home.

Funk faced Borel in the back of the canoe, turning her own spine to the bow. She unsheathed her camera and snapped pictures of the landscape as Borel wielded the paddle as if stirring cake batter of the largest kind. "Are you going to steer?" he said.

Funk pivoted forward and was eye level with a tree branch just five feet ahead. Funk, in seconds, wrestled with the option of steering or abandoning ship. If she were the captain, she would opt to break code and plunge into the Battenkill. The ship, should it go down, would go down without her. The weight of her flight capsized their canoe, and she, Borel, and their belongings spilled out. They thrashed for their stuff and their canoe. While immersed in this chaos, they failed to notice that onlookers—other paddlers—at the riverside stop were keeled over in laughter. Borel was steamed and vowed never to share the same vessel with Funk again. They next time they ventured into the river they would rent separate vessels.

～

Nick Zito, in a ball cap and raincoat, walked to his box, his umbrella like a cane, and sat by himself. His phone was pressed to his ear. His horse, Dancing Digits, crept into the gate. Zito clamped his phone shut, fixed his eyes on the television in his box, and then turned his attention to the track. His horse, with Johnny Velazquez up, shot to the lead and cleared the field, heading to the wire. With Dancing Digits fifty yards away from apparent victory, Zito stood and descended to the winner's circle. The ease with which he did so signified a man who had been there before. Photographers snapped shots of Zito. He kissed a woman who stepped into the winner's circle. "Here's my lucky charm. Johnny said, 'Let 'im run.'" Zito then turned his attention to Dancing Digits and his groom who were entering the winner's circle. "Circle him around. Here we go!"

The photographer snapped several pictures, the flash flickering with every snap. Zito notched his first win of the meet.

❧

Charlie Hayward hustled to the Parting Glass, his urgency implying that he had other places to be. This was payback for the meeting he had missed earlier in the year when his Volvo was wrecked by an errant projectile. Tom Gallo, the gregarious racing manager for Parting Glass Racing, expressed his joy over having Hayward present. "I'm the ringleader of this circus. The past couple of days, if you didn't get the seats you had last year, if you had B and now you're D, or you didn't get the parking space, or table at the Turf Terrace, or not getting the race for your horse, at 6:30 at the racetrack tomorrow, you can get even. Or if you're sick of Andy Serling giving you the wrong horse, and if you hit the target, they will be dunked in." Turning to Hayward, he added, "Picture him in the Speedo he'll be wearing tomorrow. Take a shot and get even with NYRA."

"One thing about the dunk contest," Hayward said, "the others will be throwing from twenty feet away; for me it will be 150 feet for the same price. We've got breaking news today: opening week was brutal as far as weather was concerned last year. Hal Handel said the only good thing is that it makes us look smarter this year. We're off to a great start. The entry box is full. P. J. said, 'I could make seven days of racing.' I tried that and got killed."

Hayward proudly recounted how attendance was up and that the betting handle was also on the increase. But, still, the matter of VLTs surfaced, and Hayward was quick to say that he had guessed twelve times and had been wrong twelve times. "I think a really good Saratoga meet can make a change in the industry to move forward."

"That's Charlie's way of asking you to double your bets," Gallo interjected. "If you're a $2 bettor, bet $5. If you bet more, you win more, right?"

"Jess Jackson was quoted as saying he'd love to see the horse race in Saratoga," Hayward said, of course referring to Rachel Alexandra. "It would be great if we could see the filly against those boys in the Travers."

And with that Charlie Hayward departed with quick steps, shaking a few hands on his way out, his suit jacket billowing out like a cape. Unfortunately for him, something would happen that would cloud the Travers picture for Rachel Alexandra.

❧

Friday came and went and Charlie Hayward conveniently missed the dunk tank; so too did everybody else. "Yesterday was not so good all the way around," Hayward said during Saturday's huddle. "I've got to do the OTB show and there's a lot of bullshit going on. Have we fixed the fiber? Do we know what that was? How much did that cost us?"

"The first race all-source handle was down by half," Pat Mahony said. "I wouldn't attribute that all to the signal.

"We did $900,000 last year and $412,000 this year," he continued. "The Tote went out with about three minutes to post. The second race, what happened was the software failed and the Tote had to restart. I asked the stewards to give me some time, but it came up after the field broke. There were people stuck at the machines during the second race."

"So, we were down $140,000, it cost us a hundred and change," Hayward said of the second race. "Okay, so go around. Kevin, the bulbs."

"We're working with Tote," said Gremillion. "It's not like going to Home Depot to replace it. We have two lifts working simultaneously so they can constantly work."

"Yeah, we're getting killed," Hayward said, shaking his head, thinking how is it that the press, the crotchety press, is more concerned with bad lightbulbs on the infield?

"Where we run into complications is when the socket is not there and we won't know until we change the bulb," said Gremillion.

"Communicating," Hal Handel chimed in, "there were major screwups yesterday. Let us know when there is a malfunction. Maria Diaz will be the repository of bad news. Do a better job in crisis mode."

"I called Dan at one minute to post on the uplink issue," Hayward said. "You know how shit gets around the press box. It spread the rest of the day and we have to run down this bullshit. That was great the Tote recovered from the fuckup. Well, Steven Crist took on OTB and dinged us a bit. You'll read that tomorrow in the *Form*."

"We're up against some tough numbers," Don Lehr said. "We had the Vanderbilt, the Diana, the Go For Wand, and the Whitney last year. We had 27,000 people here and $5.1 million on-track."

"$10 bet, over-under $5.1 million?" Handel prodded.

"Uhhhh, I feel good one way then . . ." said Lehr.

"Oh, come on!" said Handel.

"I feel a lot of positive energy here," Lehr said.

"If we can get anywhere near those numbers then with this Fasig-Tipton Festival, we'll destroy those numbers from last year," Hayward said.

"If all goes well," P. J. Campo said, "we'll have the Derby winner, the Preakness winner, and the Belmont winner here next week. Right now we're all set and we know where they're going. Hopefully a hell of a race unfolds."

Hayward turned to Handel with a smile and a nod, "There was a band playing Jimi Hendrix. Purple Haze."

"Bring back good memories?" Handel asked.

"We're all set with the Mine That Bird telecast?" Hayward asked his marketing director, Neema Ghazi.

"I think so, I'll follow up on it," he answered.

"The point is we want to alert people on it," Hayward said, turning to his OTB officer, Bob Polombo: "We do have a $126,000 carryover. Mr. Polombo will, of course, contribute but not hit it. If you go in with him, the funny thing is, you think he takes your money and places the bet."

Polombo, tapping an unlit cigarette to his palm, shook his head as the meeting disbanded.

∽

Hayward turned the key to his golf cart and whipped the cart around to drive to the backside to do a television spot for the Capital OTB network. The fiasco with the uplink feed still burned him. NYRA relies on the satellite feed because 82 to 85 percent of its revenue comes from off-track sources. NYRA owns a satellite truck on the property that transmits through a fiber wire to uplink the truck to a satellite. The signal goes up encoded so no one can steal it. A decoder at the other end translates the signal and shoots it down to providers. There was a miscommunication in the NYRA elite with regard to the defection in the fiber, and bets were not placed on the second race. Hayward and Mahony knew the system failed to operate, yet they could not pinpoint exactly what went wrong. The worry was that it could happen again. "There's a lot of shit going on all the time," Hayward said.

The golf cart hummed as Hayward waved to some fans who recognized the man in the suit with the wavy silver hair. He took time to reflect on Opening Day. Thanks in part to a cooperative Mother Nature, it was a success. For Hayward, in his thirty interviews, it was about managing expectations, blaming the weather, and alerting people that while the economy was slow, it was turning around.

Reporters, all reporters, hark on attendance. For Hayward's money, he'd rather talk about something else, but people want to talk about attendance as the one indicator that the skies are blue. "I was just saying to Hal, he used to run Monmouth Park," Hayward said. "Yesterday they had 5,500 people and a $385,000 handle. That's $70 per cap. We had 15,000, $2.4 million, $150 per cap. There are a lot of casual fans, that's what I care about, but people want to talk about attendance, so we tout attendance."

Hayward steered the golf cart up to the Capital OTB television set and clicked the brake into place. Bob Polombo, Hayward's OTB relations officer, stood waiting. With a slap on the shoulder, Hayward said, "It's gonna be a great day."

∾

After his interview Hayward took off his microphone and slipped back into his golf cart, the cart swaying with the added weight. Again, he thought that the uplink story was huge, but that 80 percent of turf writers are myopic over the races and not the big picture. He thought that even if they knew, they wouldn't write about it. Hayward was worried that there could be a labor slowdown because the pace of the bulb installation on the Tote board proceeded like a lame horse. "No place you hear more rumors than at a racetrack," Hayward said.

A metal gate opened and Hayward guided the golf cart through it and kept it on the heels of patrons. "We're taking life in our own hands," he said. " 'NYRA president runs over a patron.' That's not a good story."

Back at his office, two unfinished cups of coffee sat on his desk. Hayward reclined in his chair and dialed his wife, Betsy Senior. With her on the phone, he coughed. "Gosh, I'm sorry. . . . We talked about the screwups."

∾

Calvin Borel stood on the scale just outside the jocks' room and handed his tack to his valet. With his helmet fixed and ready, he walked into the squinting light and was swarmed by fans looking for an autograph. "C'mon, Calvin, let's go, baby!"

Borel had Warrior's Reward to ride in the Grade 2 $500,000 Jim Dandy Stakes. He opted to ride him in this race rather than travel to West Virginia to ride his Kentucky Derby winner Mine That Bird in the West Virginia Derby. Jockey agents questioned this move. Certainly you take off Mine That Bird to ride Rachel Alexandra, but to take off the Derby winner for an unproven—though talented—colt? That reeked of smoke from burned bridges.

The Jim Dandy had particular interest because of a horse named Kensei, Rachel Alexandra's stablemate. Both share the same owner, Jess Jackson.

This race is the traditional Travers prep, trainers looking to get a race over the surface four weeks prior to the Travers. Kensei's presence raised questions about the strategy around Rachel Alexandra. What if Kensei wins? Jackson couldn't run his two horses against one another, could he?

Kensei won. Kensei, ridden perfectly by Edgar Prado, won the Jim Dandy, and it would seem that he would be pointed to the Travers. But would Jess Jackson run Rachel Alexandra against Kensei? No way, no how. Kensei's win muddied the picture for those who hoped to see Rachel Alexandra challenge the Derby winner and the Belmont winner. Still, the Travers was four weeks away, and anything could happen to a thoroughbred racehorse. In the winner's circle, Joe Calderone, a television reporter for Capital News

9, said, "Jess Jackson has the top three-year-old in the country with super filly Rachel Alexandra. Now he has the Jim Dandy winner."

Calvin Borel finished second aboard Warrior's Reward. With choppy steps he signed autographs while on the move. He went into the jocks' room and showered. He came out with his luggage in tow. Tomorrow he would be aboard Rachel Alexandra in the $1 million Haskell Invitational. The wheels to Borel's suitcase grumbled on the ground, and a fan called out to him, "Go get 'em tomorrow, kid!"

Borel nodded in recognition, smiling so that his skin folded over his eyes.

∽

The air whistled over her ears. Rachel Alexandra splashed in the mud with Calvin Borel aboard, the two thrusting to the front of the herd. She was flanked by two colts, Munnings and Belmont Stakes winner Summer Bird, the pair of them heaving to keep pace. Borel was a static ornament welded to the back of this airborne horse. Borel often thought that it was as if Rachel Alexandra flew over the ground, hovering like a water bug barely breaking the surface tension of a puddle. It was a fool's errand for Munnings and Summer Bird to be in her orbit, for Rachel Alexandra and Borel toyed with them. Her ears flopped the way a champion sprinter's cheeks jiggle when relaxed under duress.

And like the way wine combusts over a stove top, Rachel Alexandra exploded. In three strides she cleared Munnings and Summer Bird. Borel showed her the whip like she was held up at gunpoint. Her legs curled under her belly. They launched her body some thirty feet per stride to the wire. The camera was anchored at the wire, and you could have taken a yoga breath before you saw Summer Bird and Munnings finish, in that order.

Borel stood tall in the irons and pointed to the shooting star below.

∽

Nick Zito watched the race from afar. Needless to say, he was impressed. It just made his job that much tougher if he were to try and take her down.

∽

Kensei won the Jim Dandy, and the following day Rachel Alexandra won the Haskell. Questions began in earnest as to where each would race next. And with the first week barely finished at Saratoga, no question would be asked more, and no question would get squashed as much. For Jess Jackson, it was a good problem to have: two elite horses that could run wherever their talent dictated. But for Charlie Hayward and NYRA, the complication of their next races would prove to be a source of frustration.

And Week 1 had barely expired.

∾

Hal Handel looked up to the sky on the final day of Week 1. The previous day had been wet up and down the East Coast, so when Rachel Alexandra ran in the mud in New Jersey, so too did the horses at Saratoga. "Little sunnier today," he said.

"We had a great day, despite the weather," Charlie Hayward said. "I felt sorry for the folks at Monmouth. The weather killed them. That's usually their biggest day of the year. They said they had 37,000. Their on-track was 2.5. We did 2.9. They got killed with the weather. Rachel Alexandra, as you all know, ran incredibly impressive. P. J. will let us know what that means for our future." To this Campo nodded and smiled. "They got torrential rain," Hayward added.

"It was interesting yesterday, I was disappointed with how much was bet on the Haskell," Handel said. "The off-track on-track being waged was down. The stakes races are more competitive. It's an indicator of how the world has changed. The big days of the summer are here. We're the centerpiece. The competition has slid backwards. We should have a great month."

"We're out-handling and out-attendancing them," Hayward said.

"Del Mar is living on reputation. It's beautiful, but we're the show," said Handel.

"It's the end of the first week and we have no payment from Nassau OTB. I'm taking their box away," Hayward stated.

"Nice," Handel said, nodding and smiling.

"I gave them a week. That's the end of that." And with that remark Hayward buried his relationship with Nassau OTB, and as far as he was concerned, they no longer existed. "In addition, we need to get people in here and find ways to educate them," he said.

Kim Justus said, "There's a guy who stays in the luxury suites; he teaches fans in the luxury suites to read *Daily Racing Form*. If it's not full, he goes to the Curlin Café and the tents. He doesn't give them picks."

"Educating them on how to read the *Form*? That's great . . . Mr. Lehr?" asked Hayward.

"Yesterday, despite the rain early on, we had 35,862, down 7 percent. We were down 16 percent from 2.9, all-source down 8.9 percent. When Monmouth fell apart, our betting picked up," Lehr said. "Through Sunday our numbers are up 10 percent. In attendance, we're up 2 percent. On-track wagering is down, but all that said, .6 percent, call it even. We should do great today. We had 10,000 last year, 1.8 on-track, 9.7 all-source. We have a shot at 9.7-plus to make this. Let's call it even. Last year, I think we had ten races with eighty-five betting interests. It was cloudy and muggy. Last year was not a killer day. Typical numbers. We have a shot."

"I think we can get better today," Hayward said.

"This year has been bad, good, bad, good, bad, good. Last year it was two horrendous days, two good, and two iffy days. I have the exact percentages upstairs," said Lehr.

"Things to consider," Campo said, "last year was the Whitney. Those are huge numbers to go against."

"That's a good point," Hayward said. "The Whitney is far and away our best."

"We beat Saturday last year," Lehr said. "The weather looked okay this week, whereas last year it was disastrous. Big-time upswing here."

"We're going to have the Top 5 sprinters in the country here," Campo said, then paused, thinking of Rachel Alexandra. "Now we play the guessing game."

"There's a lot of speculation about Rachel Alexandra," Hayward said. "Given Jess Jackson's PPs [past performances], we won't know for a week before the race. She could run against the girls in the Alabama, but she has nothing to prove against them."

"She has nothing to prove in the Travers," Campo said.

"She's got to run against the boys," Hayward said.

∾

By noon, Mine That Bird, following a disappointing third-place finish in the West Virginia Derby, was two hundred miles away from Saratoga Springs. His trainer, Bennie "Chip" Woolley, was optimistic about running his horse in the Travers Stakes. That was cause to smile, but Charlie Hayward seemed peeved while in the paddock. People passed by its boundaries in Hawaiian shirts and three-piece suits. Girls, smaller than jockeys, stood by with pen and program hoping for an autograph, their pigtails bobbing on their shoulders.

Steve Duncker, chairman of NYRA, sidestepped Hayward, taking jabbing punches at him as if he were working a speed bag.

Prior to the main stakes race, Hayward, Duncker, and Handel walked from the paddock to their box in the grandstand. Their ties swung like pendulums while fence-hugging onlookers gawked at the dapper elite just feet away.

Ten yards in front of the trio were two young women, one blonde, one brunette, with pink-and-white dresses that hugged their figures. Duncker took his right hand and glued it to Hayward's head, aiming him like a hockey puck. "You're eyes are better than mine," Hayward said. Someone called out Hayward's name, and he jettisoned. "It's like walking with the mayor," Handel said.

∾

Hayward ducked into the Saratoga Room, a private dining room, carpeted from wall to wall, where champagne toasts take place after stakes races of $80,000 or higher for the winning connections. With the hum and hustle just outside, and where the humidity is Bayou-like, the Saratoga Room is a vacuum of calm and cool. One could imagine a three-piece orchestra playing in the corner. Instead there are tables and two automated betting machines. Hayward bellied up to one machine and did an exacta box with the 6 and the 1—meaning they could finish in any order as long as they placed one and two. He then wanted to do a straight exacta, 6–2, but, unknowingly, hit 6–1.

Hayward's strength as an executive is that he's a player. In 2001, while still president of *Daily Racing Form* and just after the terrorist attacks on New York City and the Pentagon, Hayward flipped through past performances at Santa Anita while on a visit to the California track. He had meetings with the executives of the track and wanted to play the $1 million guaranteed Pick 6—a bet where the player must pick six consecutive winners. He looked at his watch. *Will I have enough time to place this if the meeting goes long? Better place it now.* He crafted a $64 ticket, not how his friend Steve Crist would approach it, but it was a live ticket, and any live ticket has a shot.

He walked out onto the apron of the track and saw that of the two horses he had in the first leg—a 17–1 and a 4–5 horse—the 17–1 came in. Five races to go. Hayward dove into another meeting. In the back of his mind he knew he had one race singled and was two deep in the next three. He hit the single. Hit the next three. That's five out of six with one leg to go.

Hayward sat with *Racing Form* columnist Jay Hovdey. Hovdey brimmed with excitement. Hayward now had a 9–2 and a 7–2. It was a big field, nine or ten horses, a sprint; the favorite was a big horse for the course. The 7–2 was a closer. The gate opened. The 9–2 dropped to its knees. Hayward thought he was out, that was until he saw the 7–2 tracking in fourth. The 9–2 recovered, and as they both neared the wire, Hayward urged them home. The pair finished first and second. He hit the Pick 6 for $50,000. He also hit the Pick 5 for $12,000.

Hayward filled out his tax forms and asked for a check. The clerk told him they couldn't write him a check because "it will take too long." Hayward had a flight to catch back to New York in the morning. The sun had set into the Pacific Ocean. He looked at his watch again and then asked for cash.

The clerk peeled off $50,000 worth of $100 bills, and Hayward stuffed them into his pockets.

The following day he put the money in folders and crammed it inside a briefcase. Hayward worried that with the heightened security that he would be searched, that all the cash would be found, and that it would raise some red flags.

They never saw it. He flew across the great expanse of the United States and touched down $50,000 heavy.

His wife, Betsy Senior, was there to greet him. He peeled off $10,000 and let her in on the score. "It was the wisest investment I've ever done," said Hayward.

∾

A stroll with Hayward to his box proved that he was not just a figurehead but a personality, even with his inaccurately numbered betting slips. What you see is what you get, he thought. And when the race he bet on wrapped up, he was surprised to see that he had mistakenly hit 6–1. It was of no negative consequence, for the six finished first and the one finished second, so he hit the exacta twice for $900. Happy, he went back to the Saratoga Room where he waited for Duncker. Handel, on most occasions, spent his time watching races from the televisions of the Saratoga Room. The door swung open.

"You guys ditched me!" Duncker said.

"What?" Hayward said.

"You said you'd sit with me, then I look back and you're gone," said Duncker.

"I didn't say I'd sit with you," Hayward replied.

"I did," Handel said.

"Your beef is with Hal then," Hayward said.

Week 1 was officially over. Hayward, Duncker, and Handel noted that today was good, and that they should kill the numbers from last year. Attendance was even up 10 percent, so naturally the mood was light.

Hayward snatched a handful of popcorn from the hors d'oeuvres table and put his fist to his mouth as if singing into a microphone. The table had various cheeses, along with strawberries and raspberries. Hanging on the walls were paintings that predated television, images of prestige and promise. "We're now in the black," Handel said. "Now we've gotta stay there."

Week Two

9

A Shot at No. 3

On the Oklahoma backside, owners' cars, with license plates from California, Kentucky, Florida, and New Mexico, crawl by. The owners are visiting the barn to see their horses, and Nick Zito's barn is no different. Zito's stable is often lined with the cars of clients and racing managers. Tracy and Carol Farmer, owners of the eight-year-old Commentator, sit at Zito's patio table. The Farmers are soft-spoken, slow-moving people, quick to smile.

"Carol and Tracy Farmer," Zito said, and leaned down to shake hands and hug.

"Do you stop?" Carol said with a laugh.

"I've got a politician's job," Zito said. "I'm a mayor."

"I'd say you'd make a good senator," Carol replied.

Zito kissed Carol on the head and then got into his golf cart to head to the track to watch Our Edge, his Travers hopeful, breeze over the Oklahoma Training Track.

∾

Maxine Correa, a mother of one, with strawberry-blonde hair hidden underneath a jockey helmet, climbed aboard Our Edge and trotted to the track. Zito gave her instructions regarding what he wanted his horse to do. Our Edge was on a three-race winning streak. "He's doing well," Zito told a man as he leaned against the rail. "This is a big step for him. He ran a great race in the Barbaro. It's a big, big step. Long shots have won before, am I right or wrong? He's on a roll."

Zito won three races in the first week of the meet, which put him in a tie for second place. No doubt with this in mind, a person came up to Zito and said, "Congrats, the barn's going good."

"Thank you," Zito said, before turning his attention back to the track where Our Edge broke from the half-mile pole. Saratoga is hard. There's a lot of pressure. Zito knows this but would rather the pressure come from within, otherwise he may find it from the people who pay the bills. "If you put too much pressure on yourself like I do, you try to do well," he said. "You put extra pressure when you don't need to. It's silly. Saratoga is special to us. If we don't put extra pressure on ourselves, our clients will put the pressure on us."

Correa, statuesque and calm, kept Our Edge on pace. Zito motioned his chin to indicate that Our Edge had just passed. His stopwatch beeped. "Fifty, nice and easy," he said. "How about that? I told her fifty. That was perfect."

∼

Irish tap dancers drill on the apron of Saratoga Race Course. Teenage girls in skirts, high socks, and tap shoes dance in percussive punctuation with straight arms and bobbing curls. The air swells with a cacophony of drumming feet in cosmic unison. The legs dart, the heels flex, and the feet rattle like Gatling guns. Then, all at once, they ease off the trigger to silence, a cease-fire, to the applause of onlookers.

The smell of breakfast wafts through the air. The trackside restaurant is an open-air one and exposed to the main track, where people can eat breakfast while watching the horses train. It is an intensely kinetic backdrop, with the fragrant odor of eggs and croissants mixing with the buzz of conversation and the high pitch of silver clanging against plates.

Charlie Hayward begins every week here with radio host Paul Vandenburgh, the official kickoff to a new week of racing where he can reflect but also forecast. Hayward hustles in from his office in a shirt and tie, balancing his lidless Styrofoam coffee cup.

"He doesn't realize how popular he is," Vandenburgh said into his mike.

"It was a great first week," Hayward said. "We've had a lot of freaky weather. We're up in attendance 13.5 percent, and the on-track handle is up 5 percent."

"Talk to me about Week 2. Do you put an importance on Week 2 numbers in your head?" asked Vandenburgh.

"Week 2 is important," Hayward replied. "Last year was not strong at all. I hate to do this, but the weather looks good and I think we should knock the ball out of the park."

∼

After only six days of racing, Calvin Borel had some action, but not what you would call a "busy go of things." Strangely, for reasons unknown, the few horses he had booked had been scratched. Sometimes they were part of a coupled entry, and other times they reached the gate and were scratched just minutes before post time. It was almost as if he were being conspired against, as if there were a jealousy permeating the ranks of the elite New York jockeys. This might have been true on some level, but Borel is a Kentucky rider, and to crack into the New York colony would take time, if it happened at all. Imagine the shoe on the other foot: Would New York riders invading Kentucky take all of Borel's business?

For the time Borel hovered around the jocks' room in a blue bathrobe and shower sandals. He sat on a bench in the sun with his right leg crossed over his left, smoking a Marlboro Light. He angled his chin to the sun. His eyes were closed, and there was a muted grin stamped on his face.

⟳

Charlie Hayward received an e-mail from Ed Lewi's Mark Bardack on Tuesday, August 4, 2009, to alert him that a quote of his from an article in *The Saratogian* was used in a *New York Times* editorial.

Charlie,

Assume you saw this editorial. Does it get any better than this!!!! I hope Betsy is framing it for you. It is a keeper from now to eternity. Awesome, awesome stuff.

Mark

The Off-Track Betting Mess

As everyone who has ever bought a chip knows, there is only one sure way to make money gambling: own the house. So how is it that New York City's off-track gambling parlors are nearly bankrupt? These seedy, storefront operations take in almost $1 billion a year, yet the New York City Off-Track Betting Corporation is about $46 million in debt.

Attorney General Andrew Cuomo—or somebody with subpoena power—needs to investigate how operations that should be able to help keep the state afloat manage to lose so much money instead.

Investigating OTB operations in New York State will be like digging into a toxic swamp, but here's the place to start: politicians have used these betting parlors for years to house friends and family who needed jobs. They are patronage nests. And the extra layers particularly infuriate those in the horse racing business in

New York State because they siphon off profit that is supposed to go to the Saratoga, Belmont, and Aqueduct racetracks, which really need it.

During a recent interview with *The Saratogian* newspaper, Charlie Hayward, president of the New York Racing Association, described the problem succinctly. "Racing in New York could be profitable if we just solved the OTB problem," he said. "They really have become places where good local politicians are sent to max out their pensions."

Gambling is destructive enough in the way it cleans out the pockets of too many people who need every dollar. When these parlors don't make enough money to pay for themselves—much less help the state's horse racing industry—they are a drag on everybody. Mayor Michael Bloomberg wisely stopped New York City from subsidizing these dreary establishments. Governor Paterson must also make sure not a single taxpayer dollar is going to keep New York City's gambling dens alive.

Hayward chuckled as he headed out for the day's huddle.

∞

Hal Handel hammed it up with Bob Polombo, taking friendly jabs when Hayward stepped out of the administration building. "You'll have to excuse us," Handel said. "There should be an age when one retires," he said, looking at Polombo. "Unfortunately we're both there."

"We had a great first week," Hayward began, "I'm sure Mr. Lehr will regale us with these numbers."

"Today we've got step dancers, Guinness, green popcorn," Handel said, and then, ribbing Polombo again, "This man who looks like the Godfather next to me is half Irish, though he won't admit it. Why don't you come out today?" Polombo shuffled uncomfortably, flicking his cigarette, and mumbled under his breath while Handel laughed.

"There was a true statement made in *The Saratogian*," Hayward said. "They made it sound like it was all the OTBs. It was interesting. First it ran in *The Saratogian*, then the *Post* ran with it, then the *Times* ran an editorial. The nice thing about yesterday was NYC OTB's new president, Sandy Frucher, was there and he said that things have got to change and he plans to involve NYRA."

"Not to pile on," Don Lehr said, "but the *New York Times* editorial is nothing less than a watershed moment. The *Times* never reports racing without a negative, referring to OTBs as 'gambling dens' and 'dreary establishments.'

[That] it came back that Charlie's quote was 'succinct' is nothing short of revolutionary."

As he did every morning, Lehr turned his attention to the numbers for the upcoming day. "We're up, as you know, our numbers killed last year. The second week looks good."

"So the real indicator is the third week?" Hayward asked.

"Yeah, if the weather is good, we kill Week 3," replied Lehr.

Dan Silver, NYRA director of communications, stood cradling a sheet magnet the size of a pizza box with Tracy Farmer's colors for Commentator. "They sent us all the magnets except Commentator. They had to overnight it."

"Down at 11 o'clock in the paddock for the post draw for the Whitney," P. J. Campo said. "Summer Bird is here. He shipped well."

"How big is the Whitney?" asked Hayward.

"Seven," replied Campo.

"Okay, let's go get 'em," said Hayward.

"Week 2!" Handel punctuated.

∾

Reporters, with notebooks and voice recorders in hand, huddled within the paddock's fences. A metallic board labeled for the post positions provided the backdrop for the "stage." A podium stood before it. There would be six horses running in Saturday's Whitney Handicap instead of the forecasted seven after Asiatic Boy was scratched.

Bagpipes chimed in the background and Saratoga's race caller, Tom Durkin, shook his head and picked at his ears. The trainers who had horses in the race filed into the paddock. Dallas Stewart, trainer of Macho Again, was holding hands with his wife. Barclay Tagg, trainer of 2003 Kentucky Derby winner Funny Cide, was standing with his assistant trainer, Robin Smullen. Amidst the crowd stood Kiaran McLaughlin, and finally, to the side, on his phone, was Nick Zito.

Durkin, in a tan fedora and matching blazer, had the look of someone who would rather be, well, anywhere else than in this paddock hosting a post draw. "I'll ask that you all turn off your cell phones. Someone here has the rather annoying ring tone of bagpipes," he commenced. "If any of you have questions for Nick Zito . . . if he stops talking." A stone-faced, unamused Zito barely looked up.

Zito played with a black marker while a photographer took pictures of him. Zito, at first, tried to get out of the way, thinking he was in the way, but the photographer let him know that, yes, the photo was meant for Zito. Zito folded a piece of paper and slid it into his breast pocket. He crossed his arms and let out a prolonged exhalation.

"We've got six in the box," Durkin said, as he pulled out the pills that corresponded to post positions. It finally came down to Commentator. "What post do you want?" Durkin asked.

"It's doesn't matter," Zito said. "No, sir." Commentator was assigned the far outside post, Post 7 in this case. Zito wrote it down on his sheet of paper.

"Nick Zito, please?" Durkin asked, and Zito walked up to the podium.

"Good to see you," Zito said.

"I will spare you my Commentator joke today," Durkin said, addressing the crowd.

"It was good," Zito said, and then, turning to the crowd, "You ought to hear it."

"Okay," Durkin said. "Two potatoes get married: a Long Island potato and the other was an Idaho potato. She was a regally bred potato. Soon they had kids, little sweet potatoes. The baby was the princess of potatoes. She grew up and fell in love, but her father, when she went to get married, said, 'You'd better marry in the same regal line. You're a regally bred potato.'

'His name is Walter Cronkite,' she said.

'You can't do that,' her father protested.

'Why! Why can't I marry him?'

'Because he is a common . . . tater.'

Zito smiled and said, "That's not bad," though the audience groaned.

Zito's New York roots surface in the respect he has for the great New York races, the Whitney Handicap being no different. For him it is the most meaningful race of all. Zito won his first Whitney in 2005 with Commentator, ridden by Hall of Fame jockey Gary Stevens, when he held off eventual Horse of the Year, Saint Liam. Commentator won the Whitney again in 2008. Commentator went to the front and never trailed, his signature running style. Zito said, "He showed pure desire, pure heart." Zito remembered that 2005 race, that it was Commentator's first race "going long" (that is over a mile in horse-racing speak). He had only one prep race, at seven-eighths of a mile in January, and then came to Saratoga off a layoff for the win. "To win a Grade 1 the way he did, he's a great horse. They ran 46 and 2 for a half-mile. I told Gary make a sprint out of it. Go as fast as you can. We're better off letting him run."

"It sounds like Homer Simpson who had a horse that he had to train and he said to the jockey, 'When the gates open, run real fast!' " Durkin said.

Zito nodded again, not amused. "If he does what he did it will be tremendous. Saturday will be great. You say to yourself, 'How lucky and blessed that he is this old and doing what he does. He's a great athlete.' "

"You said you'd be happy if he never ran again if he won?" asked Durkin.

"We all misspeak," Zito said.

A few days earlier, Zito was asked that if Commentator won, would he retire him? He responded that yes, if he won, then that was it for him. A trainer can advise but seldom has the final say. Had he not had sympathetic owners, it could threaten the relationship so much that they could take their horses to another trainer. Here he corrected himself. "That's up to Mr. Farmer whether he runs again, but if he pulls this off, what better way to go than to go out a winner? We all misspeak sometimes. Even you."

After a long pause, Durkin said, "*Fine.*"

Zito left the podium hoping that his horse would get a good trip and, above all, that his horse would come back safe and sound in three days.

∾

"Okaaaaay," Charlie Hayward said, summoning the huddle, "just did a radio show with Rodger Wyland and heard that Rachel Alexandra is nominated for all the races, even the Pennsylvania Derby. She can't run in the Pennsylvania Derby, can she?"

"Sure," racing secretary P. J. Campo said, with a toothy smile.

"They also nominated her to a 4½ furlong race in West Virginia," Dan Silver said.

"That makes me feel better," Hayward said, leaning back on his heels. "It keeps up the tension."

"We're doing good," Hal Handel said. "Business could be better, but the meet is off to an extraordinary start. To have two horses like Mine That Bird and Summer Bird, to have two horses like that, thrilled to be here, go ahead over there. It's nice to see them train."

"We're up 48.4 percent on attendance, 29.6 percent on-track, we're beating '07 which was a huge year," Don Lehr said. "These numbers are really quite good. Today last year was sunny, warm, and beautiful, 19,345. Coming in from the lot it was three-quarters full and the picnic tables are full. We did 3.1 million on-track last year. We can hit that, 14.7 all-source."

"That's a far stretch from Aqueduct in February, let me tell you," Campo said.

Then Handel, always prodding Lehr, said, "Interested in a $10 over-under?" Lehr nodded.

Campo interrupted, urging Lehr to renege. "No, no, you're on a roll."

"He already said yes, he jinxed it," Silver said. "Now we'll get 2.6."

"He's a chalk player anyway," Hayward said, smirking.

"I'd like to thank Mr. Handel for the opportunity," Lehr said dryly.

∾

The clerk of scales yelled at the jockeys, "Gotta move guys!"

Calvin Borel put out his cigarette and followed his assigned security officer out of the jocks' room and onto the jockeys' path. "Let him walk, please!" said a security officer.

"Calvin! Give Rachel a kiss for me!" yelled a fan.

"Good luck, Calvin!" shouted another fan. To this Borel gave a nod, accompanied by a thumbs-up. The fan responded, "Go Calvin!"

Borel scooted into the paddock and gave another jockey a pat on the back and then went to high-five with Gene Stevens, the delightfully tacky and narcissistic publisher of *Post Parade*. "Like this, like this," Stevens said, putting out his fist for a fist bump. Borel fumbled his fingers before balling up his hand for the bump.

Borel galloped by on his horse Maria's Moon, while in the winner's circle Sam the Bugler entertained three women, taking pictures with them and playing some songs. "You wore that pink dress just for me? You girls having fun?" he said. "You're next. Yellow's my favorite color."

A man approached Sam the way a fraternity brother might. "All these women are single," he said. "I'm not single," Sam said. "That doesn't matter," said the man. "It matters to me," Sam replied.

Out on the oval, Calvin Borel shot Maria's Moon to the lead. Borel had yet to win a race this meet, but this, at least, seemed promising. "Calvin Borel and Maria's Moon still lead the way," Durkin announced. Soon enough, Borel was swallowed by the field and cantered home seventh. Borel hopped off the horse and weighed in before handing his tack to his valet. He took off his goggles and handed a pair to a child along the walkway. "Step aside, jockey's coming through!" Borel's escort said. Borel then autographed six pictures of him aboard Mine That Bird, aboard Street Sense, and aboard Rachel Alexandra. "Gotta have you in the eighth!" a fan yelled. Borel would finish sixth in that race.

Borel signed his last autograph and ducked into the jocks' room, leaving a few people without Borel's ink on their programs or photographs. "He blew us off," one man said.

∽

Charlie Hayward swung open the door to the Saratoga Room and was surprised that Janine, the head server, had set it up for a champagne toast. Hayward thought that today's stake's purse fell below the "champagne line."

"Champagne for this?" he said.

"Yeah, $80,000 and up," said Janine.

"What's it today?" asked Hayward.

"$96,000—wanna start drinking early?" asked Janine.

"No!" Then Hayward directed his attention to the betting machine. "Let me make a wager and go back and see the boss."

The boss, of course, was his wife, Betsy Senior, who managed an art gallery in Manhattan. Senior bears an uncanny resemblance to actress Tina Fey, her eyes, her smile, everything. She forges strong relationships with artists, asking them to do various projects. One such exhibition was "The Book as Image and Object," where Senior had sculptures and images of books. Senior grew up in suburban Connecticut and eventually went to Stanford University, where she studied art history.

Senior met Hayward in the summer of 1996 through a mutual friend. Senior, recently divorced, asked her friend if he knew any single men. He immediately said that Charlie was a great guy, but that currently he didn't have a job. This was around the time that Hayward resurrected an unprofitable division at Little, Brown and turned a profit of several million dollars. After this performance, Hayward was told to cut the staff in half, the same staff that made their gains possible. He would have nothing to do with that and resigned, saying it was a breach of trust.

Senior's friend set up a dinner party and the two sat next to one another and found the evening pleasant enough. Both talked about the horses, which Hayward loved and with which Senior was familiar, having watched the big races growing up. Senior fell for him because even though they had different life experiences, they had similar outlooks, the same moral outlook, and, as she said, they were "very much in tune in terms of a view towards people and how you treat people and how you move through life." She added, "I think he has great generosity of spirit, and people appreciate that."

The pair had taken up golf four years earlier. On one occasion, when Senior was sitting on her porch, Hayward asked how her round went with her girlfriend. "I shot a 113," she said, half embarrassed.

"That's not bad," he replied.

In the background, Senior heard a muffled, babyish voice. "That's his kitty voice," she said, then impersonating him, "*Mistah Nomah!*"

She said it with a smile, the same smile she flashed as Hayward entered the paddock to meet both her and Don Lehr—after he had placed his bets, of course. Senior pulled a *Daily Racing Form* out of her purse which, it must be said, was uniquely wonderful.

Hayward faced Lehr, prompting him on his friendly wager with Hal Handel, "Mr. Handel says you're building a strong lead," said Hayward.

"Yes, unless Mr. Mahony lets the mutuel clerks go home," Lehr replied.

John's Call, a seventeen-year-old horse, a Saratoga legend, came into the paddock to lead the parade for the stakes race named in his honor. Hal Handel arrived, "John's Call, seventeen years old. An inspiration to us old guys."

Hayward, having not heard Handel, turned to Betsy, "He must be nine."

"Seventeen years old," she said.

"Seventeen! I remember well," he said, and then he turned to Handel. "Lehr was looking for his ten bucks."

"I told him there must be a Tote malfunction," Handel said and smiled.

∽

On tap for the following week was the Fasig-Tipton Festival to kick off the Saratoga Yearling Sale. The ruler of Dubai was expected to be in attendance for this event. With the economy acting like a three-toed sloth, this sale would be a litmus test for the horse business. Were current owners willing to pay top dollar for new horseflesh? And, more importantly, were new owners willing to take a chance? Either way there was a cocktail reception to be had at the sale's grounds on East Ave, three hundred yards from the Saratoga Race Course.

Hayward slipped into his Volvo. His parking tag read 0001. He pointed to the spot on his hood where the projectile had hit, derailing his trip to Saratoga in late May. He parked the car and he and Senior crossed the street. "Go around to the left side?" he said. "Let's go through here."

The night air was feather-light and the evening sky a deepening shade of baby blue. The trees were lush and whispering. Champagne, garnished with sliced strawberries, bubbled on a table waiting to sizzle down throats. People were dressed in tuxedos and gowns. Servers walked about with hors d'oeuvres: shrimp cocktail and scallops with corn salsa. Hayward ordered himself a Dewar's on the rocks and a glass of wine for Senior.

A gentle murmur of conversation escalated with each glass of champagne, the open bar the volume dial. Hayward and Senior, after finishing one cocktail apiece, departed for another function, this one hosted by Saratoga Springs socialite Marylou Whitney.

The heels of their shoes clicked on the pavers as they exited the grounds. Left behind was a crowd of increasing size and flutes of champagne bubbling in the summer air.

10

Where He Still Races

If races could be ranked, then it might be true that the Whitney Handicap was Nick Zito's No. 1 race of the meet. It had everything to do with Commentator, a super-talented, overachieving, hard-knocking horse who defied the clock. Horses don't keep their edge this long. Commentator won the 2008 Whitney—three years after his first—by going to the lead and holding on to win by daylight to record the highest Beyer Speed Figure of the year: 120. Zito thought it was a brilliant effort in a tough spot, and he reveled in Commentator's athleticism. Zito has trained thousands of horses, yet none seem to hold as dear a place as Commentator. "If he can pull this off, what great thing can you do than to go out as a winner? More importantly, he's such a great horse."

Zito watched his horse work out in the mornings and basked in what he saw. How can a horse of that age run over a track as deep as the Oklahoma Training Track drill that well? He thought Commentator moved like silk. Coming into the 2009 Whitney, Commentator had just two races to prep for it the whole year, so Zito's concern was that he lacked the action between the fences to be competitive. Still, Zito shook his head. He said Commentator was a horse that thought he was a four-year-old colt, who would take a bite out of your arm. "It's unusual for a horse his age to run on a high level like that. He's a star."

∽

Always in the back of Zito's head was Wanderin Boy, another older horse he trained, who won four graded races, ran with heart and mettle, and broke down in what was to be his final race in the Cigar Mile at Aqueduct in 2008. While Zito aims for the Triple Crown races, something his peers have stamped him with, he holds special respect for the older horses and the clients who hold onto their cards, those who keep their horses in training. Wanderin Boy was one such horse. The difference with him was that he was still a *horse*, not a gelding. Most horses with a resume like Wanderin Boy, who also have their plumbing intact, are quickly ushered into the breeding shed. But he was the exception.

Zito called Wanderin Boy a treasure, a true professional. Then down the homestretch of the Cigar Mile Wanderin Boy's sesamoids—bones, in what you would call the ankle—shattered. He was then taken off the track for good. Nick Zito could not be found.

Naturally with Commentator's presumed last race just hours away, Zito, above all, hoped that he would come home with his life in tow.

~

The paddock swelled with onlookers who huddled around Stall No. 7 to watch Nick Zito saddle Commentator. Zito put on the saddle pad, the saddle, and the saddlecloth and tugged the girth until it was tight under Commentator's rib cage, the final wrap of tape around the wrists of a prizefighter.

Television cameras zoomed in on Commentator. He bounced on his hooves and walked in circles to warm up his eight-year-old legs. Soon John Velazquez, the jockey who won the Whitney on Commentator in 2008, entered the paddock and shook hands with Zito. He knew the drill: take him to the lead, and see if the hare can win this thing again. Slow and steady does not win the race. Zito gave Velazquez a leg up and watched Commentator canter out of the paddock and onto the racetrack.

~

Zito went up to his box where his wife Kim, sat waiting for him. She wore an ornate, crimson hat. Zito wore a navy blue suit, conservative yet formal. Bottles of Saratoga sparkling water stood in unordered ranks on their counter. Zito reached for a bottle out of an ice-filled bucket and twisted the cap. The seal crackled, and he tipped it back.

~

The fuse was lit, and the cannon that was the starting gate launched six horses. Commentator, as everyone suspected, zipped clear of the field, angled to the rail, and got the lead. Zito shaped his lips as if blowing air on kindling to start a fire. He watched the early part of the race unfold on his television. With his eyes still fixed on the screen, Zito reached down and tied his shoe. The fractions came up with a half-mile run in 46.36 seconds, a blistering pace for a horse half as old as Commentator. Zito shaped his lips again, this time as if blowing a fire out, and then resumed chewing his gum. Zito's eyes went from the television and back to the track, watching Commentator arc from the backstretch to the top of the lane at the eastern edge of the main track. "C'mon!" he yelled.

Zito yelled for his old horse, his buddy, but his yells could not stop the other five horses who wanted a piece of the old man. Bullsbay, who tracked the pack in fourth through much of the race, swallowed Commentator as they straightened out, clearing him by one and a half lengths. Commentator felt the fatigue, felt his age, but dug in, his head driving forward, his mane flopping in the Saratoga breeze. Macho Again, a classic stretch runner, came late and plodded by Commentator just yards before the wire. Commentator took third place, just four and a quarter lengths behind the winner.

Kim Zito patted her husband on the knee. Zito stood up and buttoned his blazer. He passed a seated Tracy Farmer and Farmer gave a politician's pressed-thumb, "Well done! It's phenomenal what you've done with him."

Zito's feet sunk into the track and he greeted Commentator. He looked him up and down and felt the heat on his brown coat. Not a scratch.

∾

The story was not Bullsbay winning, the story was wherever Commentator finished. The proof was when the reporters swarmed Zito as if Zito had punctured a beehive. Zito was ready and he leapt into the questions: "We were playing catch-up. He was tough today. He tried as hard as he could." Zito did not blame the track, nor did he blame the long layoff—he did not blame a soul. "We had a shot coming home. I think Father Time catches up to everybody."

Tracy and Carol Farmer had told a reporter that the decision to retire Commentator was up to Zito. To this Zito said that the Farmers were wonderful to do that, since, in the end, Commentator was their horse.

Zito left the winner's circle alone, probably thinking that sure, while winning this race would have been ideal, it was still a hell of a race to go out on.

So he followed the jockey path through the clubhouse with his hands in his pockets. "Keep your head up, Nicky," a fan said. Zito toed a serpentine line, and people parted to create a seam through which Zito could walk. They looked back and whispered to one another: Was that actually Nick Zito?

Zito's chin dropped to his chest while he walked under the roof of the grandstand, weaved his way through tables, and glued his feet to the floor in front of a television. On the television streamed the replay of the Whitney. Zito stood like a sentinel, his arms folded, neck craned up at an angle. He made no sound. In this replay Commentator still ran, still fought. There was the head-on shot, the pan shot, illustrating the many views of defeat. It was on this screen that Commentator still raced. At last Zito tore his eyes away from that screen with his head low, scuffing his feet across a worn path back to his barn.

⌇

Charlie Hayward pulled for Commentator, always a fan of a good underdog story. This was evident since, above all, Hayward rooted for the Boston Red Sox, for anyone who has rooted for the Red Sox up until 2004 was to be uniquely, and Calvinisticly, New England.

Earlier in the day, prior to Commentator's third-place performance, Hayward approached Don Lehr in the huddle to get the numbers and to find out if he had won his side bet with Hal Handel. "Despite Pat letting 50 percent of the mutuel clerks go, we crushed last year's numbers," he said with that slowly curling smile. "We were down a little bit all-source. That was nice. Last year, Saturday was the beginning of a spate of bad weather. We had rain at 11:00 [a.m.]."

"Yaddo!" Hayward said, in reference to racing secretary P. J. Campo's scheduling of a state-bred stakes race as the main feature for a Saturday card in the middle of the 2008 meet. The meet starts and ends with a flurry, so the middle often suffers. Yaddo Day was no different, perhaps even the embodiment of how bad the middle can get. Campo took a beating in the press and got ribbed to no end by those in the NYRA inner circle. "Yaddo!" repeated Hayward.

"No, it was the Test," Lehr interjected, "we had 20,000. We should crush that. If you gave me the over-under at 5.1 I will not take it again. We should come close to '07. I'm hesitant to do comparisons to '07 because I don't want to jinx it. Maybe a little hazy sunshine, but we look good."

Hayward thought of the crying and whining yearlings on Madison Avenue, just off East Avenue. He could hear them from his house on Fifth Avenue. With a nod as if to gesture that it was time for horse sales, Hayward said, "The Sheik is here."

"He is?" asked Lehr.

"Today," replied Hayward.

⌇

It came to Hayward's attention that they drew over 40,000 patrons on Whitney Day, completely smashing last year's numbers but also giving them some hope that as long as the weather was good, there was no limit as to what Saratoga could do.

It was worth a flute of champagne, so after the Whitney, after Nick Zito walked back to his barn like a broken prizefighter, Hayward and Handel entertained the winning connections of the Whitney in the Saratoga Room.

A day like today made them feel confident that they were doing something right, although Hayward exited the glow of today's success by saying, "The smart guys that bring you Saratoga are the same idiots that bring you Aqueduct in the winter."

Charlie Hayward walked across the parking lots to the Reading Room, off the grounds southbound on Union. He wanted to shake some hands, have a drink, and see Boyd Browning, president and CEO of Fasig-Tipton. While on the way, some wayward race fans yelled out to Hayward, "There's Mr. Right! Yeah, Pick 6!" They stuck out their hands and high-fived Hayward. He smiled.

A friend rolled down his tinted car window and yelled to Hayward, "Big Day, sir!"

"Big day . . . huge day!" Hayward said, smiling.

There was never a partnership between NYRA and Fasig-Tipton. Because the horses purchased at Fasig-Tipton sales often ran at NYRA tracks, it seemed like a simple pairing, like wine and cheese. Why not? You sell them. We race them.

Hayward had his usual Dewar's on the rocks and mingled with the crowd, occasionally sampling the hors d'oeuvres like a hummingbird extracting nectar from a flower. He met Boyd Browning, and the two shook hands. They expressed their fondness for their new partnership, though the conversation looked a bit uncomfortable. Perhaps it was Browning's superfluously pink cheeks. The two, again, brought up how foolish it was never to be paired like they were. "You hit them from your side, and we hit them from our side," Hayward said.

"And take all their money!" Browning said, putting his fist out for a fist bump. An ice cube could have melted in the time his fist hung in suspension, waiting for some sort of contact, some sort of reciprocation. "And take all their money!"Browning repeated. And like the moment's hesitation before kissing an aunt with too much makeup, Hayward bumped fists with Browning.

After the Whitney, when the dust had settled, Nick Zito met with Tracy and Carol Farmer just outside his barn. In the company of their favorite horse, they had a decision to make. The discussion lasted only a few minutes.

∽

Nick Zito's barn was the compass's center the day after the Whitney. During the break, when John Deere tractors harrow the training track, is when most trainers talk to reporters. The press wanted to know the fate of Commentator. Zito walked up to the cohort of people aiming recorders at him like an épée.

"Commentator is officially retired," Zito said. "I did that with Mr. Farmer. Physically, there is nothing wrong with him except his age. He'd have to run back in Grade Ones. This is the best thing to do. He'll go to Tracy Farmer's farm and let him down."

There are two public sides to Nick Zito. One is reserved, almost anti-social, one that grimaces at the attendance of those unwanted. The other is showy, a performer when he grips an audience, like this morning. He pulled out of his shirt pocket Commentator's past performances, the way a proud father would pull out a photograph of his eight-year-old son's Little League baseball card. "I keep it with me," he said. "He raced twenty-four times, fourteen wins, made $2 million the hard way. I don't see no Breeders' Cup money. He's been a real treasure. When he was on he was as good as any horse in America. The Mass Cap proved that. The Whitney proved that."

Twenty yards away, in a stall in the middle of Zito's shed row, stood Commentator, who poked his head out and tugged at his hay bag. "Look at him! He's so happy, look at him!" admired Zito. "He probably knows that's it. Look! It's a good sign that he's not in the corner of his stall, *uhhhhhhh*. He still wants to race. I'm glad Tracy's not here!"

For those who thought it would be a sad day for Nick Zito, the Farmers, even Commentator, would be disappointed by the lack of tears or melancholy. Zito was celebrating his horse, how he had survived.

By the middle of October 2009, a little more than two months away, Commentator would be ready to be ushered into permanent retirement. It would be a day as warm as a mug of cocoa. The Sallee horse van would pull up to the southern edge of the barn and deploy its ramp, destination Sheltowee Farm. "You know he can run," Zito would say. "We did the right thing. We don't want him breaking down some day, right or wrong? Fuck *that* shit! I was just hoping he won the Whitney then I was retiring him THAT. FUCKIN'. DAY! That would've been epic."

At the ramp, Commentator would pause before slipping into the van, and Zito would note how good he looked, almost like he wanted to saddle him up for another go. "Commentator, you're gonna be good buddy."

Commentator had nine different jockeys on his back over his twenty-four races. When he broke his maiden at Saratoga on August 9, 2004, Javier Castelleno recalled, "As soon as they opened the gate, boom! I said, 'Man, what kind of horse is this?'"

Commentator even gave the apprentice jockey Channing Hill a chance at earning his stripes: "I remember walking in the paddock and Zito telling me to hold on and basically that's all I really did and he almost broke the track record. That was one of the biggest mounts of my career. That was the first real, real nice horse I had ever been on—that really showed me what a nice horse was."

Gary Stevens was aboard for that memorable 2005 Whitney Handicap when Commentator defeated the eventual Horse of the Year, Saint Liam. "That was one of the funnest [sic] races I ever rode. After the first quarter-mile, I was laughing to myself because he switched completely off. He was rolling right along, but he was so well within himself when he was doing it, he was like a two-minute lick. When I picked him up and asked him, he cut."

And it was that victory that belonged on the medal stand along with Zito's career of Triple Crown wins. "I'd have to say that ranks as high as anything. It was true racing. He beat the Horse of the Year. He proved he could go two turns. It was a great, great effort. He had a lot of resolve that day."

Commentator's hooves clanged on the ramp and settled into place, aside other horses headed to farms south and west of Saratoga. "Hey, buddy. Normally he goes by himself," Zito said, "and now he's seeing all these horses. He's saying, 'Who are these horses?'"

"He's going home!" the driver said, home to Sheltowee Farm.

"He's saying, 'Normally I go by myself. I've got a lot of people on this thing,'" said Zito.

The engine to the truck snored out of its slumber and Zito sang "Sheltoweeeeee on a Sallee Vaaaaan."

Zito walked back to his patio table where he had an Italian sub waiting for him. He picked at his gums, sore from a dentist appointment he had earlier that day. He then pulled out his phone and dialed his wife and left a voice mail: "Hey, hon. Just put Commentator on a van. I know you're probably at physical therapy, but I just wanted to tell you that. Okay. Talk to you later."

Week Three

11

Old Smoke

In the Saratoga Room, where the champagne toasts take place and an endless stream of race replays runs for the winning connections, hangs a picture of John Morrissey, the track's founder. He rests on the wall just by the door, a bust of him in his later years, showing his mosslike beard, his hair wavy like the ends of al dente strips of lasagna.

Hal Handel sat in the corner and sipped from a sweaty bottle of Heineken beer. He looked over at the portrait and said, "He was an interesting guy."

∽

Racetracks are notorious for their characters, and John Morrissey was no exception. He was born on February 12, 1831, in Tipperary, Ireland. While he was still a toddler his parents emigrated to the United States, seeking opportunities that would have escaped them back home. They settled in the Irish ghettos of West Troy (now Watervliet), New York. Morrissey was the big kid, the bully, and his reputation slowly took hold as being a rabble-rouser, a broad-nosed hooligan whose actions spoke louder than his Irish brogue. His fists knew one language: pain. Morrissey soon befriended John Heenan, a boy tall for his age, though two and half years younger. The two kicked up dust in the streets of West Troy. But in 1843 Tim Morrissey, Morrissey's father, moved his family across the Hudson to Troy. Morrissey's river crossing burned an invisible bridge between him and Heenan.

No thanks to a cockfight gone sour, the fathers of the two boys severed ties, and the sons carried the banner of the Morrissey–Heenan rivalry. Both young men grew in stature, their bodies roped in muscle, their egos ever swollen. This rivalry would not be settled for years, but it would be settled.

∽

Until then Morrissey lived up to his reputation by bludgeoning foes to the ground, Irish immigrants whose pride was so often a balled-up fist landed on someone else's jaw. He joined the Taffy Dumbleton gang, famous for "chewing and screwing," or some variety thereof, whose members ran up bar tabs, refused to pay, and then pummeled the proprietor. Naturally Morrissey found his way into prison.

Once released, he was dogmatic in finding ways to profit from his bullheaded need to fight. The Eastern Hotel on River Street, a bar and whorehouse, was owned by sports promoter Alexander Hamilton (not the politician on the $10 bill). Brawls routinely erupted, and bartenders armed with "bungstarters" and "slung shots" kept no order. Even the police steered clear and allowed the Eastern Hotel to figuratively grow unfettered like a neglected lawn. Hamilton needed a new recruit, someone he could rely on more than his inept bartenders, and certainly someone more reliable than the Troy police force. Hamilton heard of a six foot, 170-pound seventeen-year-old punk who might be perfect for the job. Hamilton sent for John Morrissey.

❧

A couple days later, fashionably late, Morrissey lumbered into Hamilton's office. Hamilton eyed the boy like he was a horse up for auction. Not to be toyed with in the matter of meat on a hoof, Morrissey reportedly said, "If you want me, you'll pay twenty dollars a week." It was not a negotiation. Hamilton stirred. He had never paid a bouncer more than twelve dollars a week, and here was this brazen youth pushing *him* around? "I might pay you that," he said, "if you are as good as they say you are."

Morrissey, like trying out for the major leagues, got his shot at The Show. Infamous eye-gouger and nose-biter from the Albany docks, Bibber M'Geehan, stood at the bar. Hamilton was never in possession of a bouncer who challenged M'Geehan. And like the cockfight that had split the Morrissey and Heenan families, Morrissey and M'Geehan were caged and primed.

Hamilton escorted Morrissey into the bar, into the ring as it was, the Emperor to Morrissey's Darth Vader. M'Geehan put his drink aside, curled his hands into bite-size boulders, and eyed Morrissey with nervous eyes. Morrissey drew his right arm back and cracked M'Geehan on his bearded jaw; his knees wobbled, no longer able to support his two hundred-pound frame. Morrissey cradled M'Geehan in his arms and dumped him onto the street.

"Twenty it'll be," Hamilton proclaimed.

❧

Hamilton took enormous pride in his new bouncer and in the raw ability he saw Morrissey exhibit. The sports promoter surfaced. While on a trip to New York City, Hamilton bragged to "Dutch Charley" Duane that in his Eastern

Hotel, up the Hudson River, in Troy, he had a bouncer that could grind him or his friend into meat. Duane's friend was Tom Hyer, the reigning heavyweight champion boxer. Duane did not take Hamilton's taunt lightly and beat him, leaving a thread of blood from New York City to Troy.

Morrissey followed the scent all the way down to the city and burst through the doors of Duane's Empire Club hangout. To Morrissey's surprise and chagrin, Duane was absent. But to travel such a distance to seek out Duane and come up empty with neither a cut nor a bruise was a waste, so Morrissey bellowed that he was Irish and would fight any challenger. He failed to specify the number that could challenge him at any given time, and at least a half-dozen men accepted his call and beat him worse than they had beaten Hamilton. Morrissey lay unconscious, his body still heaving from the blows from the mob. The club's leader, Isaiah Rynders, put an end to the bloodbath and saved Morrissey from further beatings.

Rynders admired Morrissey's courage, foolish as it was, and Morrissey let it be known his appreciation for the intercession.

Morrissey, back home in Troy, had courted Susie Smith, the daughter of a ship captain for whom he once worked. She would, eventually, be the woman he would marry, but until then he took up relations with the "voluptuous" Kate Ridgely while down in the city.

Rynders had employed Morrissey as a runner for an immigrant boardinghouse near the waterfront. Morrissey was the enforcer, to ensure that rival boardinghouses didn't steal from Rynders' patrons. Tom McCann, a man "who was as dirty as he was handsome," was peeved to find that not only had Morrissey invaded his turf, but he had taken his girl, Kate Ridgely, as well.

It was either at a shooting gallery at the St. James Hotel or a barroom at the St. Charles Hotel on Broadway and Leonard Streets, but wherever the setting, there sat Morrissey. The presence of McCann, who was fueled by jealousy and had been trespassed upon on more than one front, silenced the room. Morrissey, showing a pompous coolness, got to his feet and said, "Men, what do you think you'd do if a fellow started by taking away most of your business and ended by stealing your girl?" He took off his coat. "Here I am. What do you suppose McCann will do?"

❧

McCann threw off his coat, hedged toward Morrissey, and stood just two feet shy of his foe's face. The bar remained quiet, in an awful trance, when Morrissey thrust his right fist into McCann's face and drew first blood. The melee was on, as the two became enmeshed, a tangle of flesh and sweat. McCann had yet to unleash his unsportsmanlike prowess, so Morrissey buried his head in McCann's shoulder. But McCann, the stronger of the two, heaved

Morrissey onto a cannonball stove. It vomited its throbbing coals onto the ground. Onto the coals went Morrissey, the heat of the coals melting his skin. Morrissey, all grit and barely uttering a grunt, honed his rage. A Morrissey supporter cast a pitcher of water onto the coals, swelling the room in vapor. Morrissey threw his adrenaline, an unrelenting barrage, machine-gun fists into McCann. The fight was won.

Morrissey's charred shirt hung in rags, glued to his back by melted flesh. Morrissey rose from the coals, and thus a new name was born: Old Smoke.

❧

By the early 1850s the Gold Rush was on and John Morrissey was no less ambitious than the next guy looking to sift through river muck. Gold aside, Morrissey found a chance at riches in the boxing ring as a prizefighter. His barroom brawls were for pride and protection, but out West there was a new fever.

George Thompson, a Scot, was a prizefighter from the British Isles who claimed to be the Best of the West, and when word reached him that this upstart from New York was on his turf, he needed to settle who was the bull and who was the calf.

Two thousand dollars was the prize, and with the money deposited, all that was needed was to set a date: August 31, 1852. Morrissey's fighting style was to use his otherworldly stamina and to bludgeon. He was a brawler, not a trained or skilled fighter. That was Thompson's style.

Morrissey launched at Thompson, and Thompson, using his repertoire of jabs and sways, drew first blood. Morrissey, undaunted, cracked the Scot on the jaw and knocked him down. Mexicans and Americans alike unified their frenzy into Morrissey's corner. Morrissey, like a gladiator, won the crowd.

Thompson sensed a shift in the momentum and cowered like a cub. Thompson was knocked down yet again. Knockdowns ended rounds, and while in a clinch, fighters could throw each other down, this according to the London Prize Ring Fighting rules, rules that should have benefited Thompson.

In the eleventh round, Morrissey pressed on Thompson, and the Scot, desperate, latched onto Morrissey's drawers and slung Old Smoke to the ground. This was illegal, so the fight and the two thousand dollars were awarded to Morrissey. Not only was he richer, but this Irish immigrant, this barbarian from the streets of West Troy, New York, was making a name for himself.

❧

California, notably San Francisco, where Morrissey took up residence, had a buffet of ways to steal money from gold prospectors, something Las Vegas caught onto a century later: gambling houses. San Francisco's casinos were ornate and pandered to whalers and gold seekers. They had games of chance: faro, monte, and roulette. These games favored the house and were quick to play; poker was thought to take too long with stakes far too low. Faro proved to be the most popular, in that hands were quick, and a gambler could get rich in a hurry. The converse of that was true as well. Morrissey liked what he saw. But what grabbed his attention most was horse racing.

Morrissey went to the track on the jagged course of Santa Barbara and won five thousand dollars on a black mare named Carencita over the bay horse Alameda in a ten-mile match race. It could be that part of Morrissey's inspiration for what would be Saratoga Race Course was inspired here.

No matter, with the five thousand dollars in his pocket, he was ready to head back to New York. This gold rush, in his mind, was played out. Waiting for him in New York were still more challenges, challenges he could not have predicted.

∽

Morrissey's return was indeed a king's welcome. He was a celebrity, the man who toppled the Scot, George Thompson. Morrissey also ran into Susie Smith, his longtime girlfriend, who had moved to New York City with her father. Morrissey dabbled in politics, going so far as to organize a gang for Fernando Wood, a Catholic mayoral candidate. Wood lost, but in so doing, Morrissey gained a political ally.

In other circles Morrissey's return from California was met by pursed mouths; he was not a hero to everyone; rather, he was a threat. Just as he was greeted out West by Thompson, back East it was Yankee Sullivan who needed to protect his turf in the ring. Before they squared off, Tom Hyer, the idle heavyweight champ, derided Morrissey's win against Thompson, calling him, in not so many words, an un-credible champion. Old Smoke challenged Hyer, but Hyer had gone soft, and the only remaining muscle that put up any fight was his mouth. Morrissey looked for other opponents and found one in Yankee Sullivan.

Since boxing was illegal, the disclosure of the ring's location was kept secret. They were to meet and set up their own ring with four posts hammered into the ground. Morrissey's men hung a scarf bearing the Stars and Stripes. In the opposite corner Sullivan hung a black scarf, which meant "victory or death." Despite the secret, thousands showed up to a little city named Boston Corners on the New York–Massachusetts border.

Sullivan was twice as old as Morrissey, Old Smoke being twenty-two at the time. But what Sullivan lacked in youth he more than made up for in cunning, smart fighting. Sullivan was twenty pounds lighter and thus increasingly nimble, able to skirt the sledgehammer swings of Morrissey. Descriptions of the fight elicit images of Muhammad Ali bouncing on his toes jabbing and backing off. By the end of four rounds, Morrissey's face was bloodied and swollen, and "a puffed eye had to be lanced before the fifth round could begin.".

It was in that fifth round that Morrissey knocked Sullivan to the turf for the first time. Both men were emboldened, hardened by the black scarf in Sullivan's corner. On went the rounds—fifteen, twenty, twenty-five, thirty, thirty-five. They were fleshless and pulped, zombies dripping blood. In the thirty-seventh round, Old Smoke took it to Sullivan and trapped him in a corner. Sullivan contorted and was on the edge of defeat. Morrissey felt the precipice of victory and rained a dozen blows when a brawl broke between the seconds and spectators. Sullivan was woozy, and Morrissey somehow squirmed out of the mess and stood back, disengaged, with heaving chest.

The referee called time for the thirty-eighth round while Morrissey stood at the scratch line, ready to fight, but Sullivan heard nothing, still engaged with the brawl. The referee called again, and again, but still Sullivan did not reply to the summoning. Sullivan had his chances, longer than the referee should have allowed, and the fight was awarded to Old Smoke, the new heavyweight champion of America at twenty-two years of age. Unbeknownst to Morrissey, he was nearly halfway through his life.

∾

John Morrissey swore to marry Susie Smith after the fight and said that he would no longer be involved in such behavior. Smith wanted to believe it and, one would imagine, so did Morrissey. But his win out West against the Scot was from a low blow and his win against Sullivan was amidst a sideline melee that Sullivan failed to pull away from. So Morrissey never defeated these fighters in the traditional sense. This was why his childhood friend, John Heenan, resurfaced, their rivalry every bit inflamed as it was when the Morrisseys crossed the Hudson River from West Troy to Troy, the cockfight of their fathers still unresolved and bitter. In due time, the score would be settled once and for all.

∾

While waiting for a suitable opponent, John Morrissey began building gambling houses in New York City like the ones he saw and frequented in California. But the image of him with the Stars and Stripes scarf tied around his waste like a belt precluded him. His fists, like anvils, were poised. He was shirtless, his gaze vacant on a broad horse face topped with close-cropped curly hair. While Morrissey networked in Downstate New York, John Heenan slugged it out as a mechanic for the Pacific Steamship Company in Benicia, California, where he too had traveled to seek the riches in golden treasure. It seemed he never left his rival's shadow. Much like Morrissey, Heenan was hotheaded and quick to brawl, but he also possessed a raw talent for fisticuffs. Morrissey had found a challenger.

Old Smoke promised his wife, Susie Smith, that this would be his last boxing match, and that he could commit to a legitimate life. "I shall have to fight to vindicate my character for honor and manhood, and to relieve myself from the persecution and assaults of my foes," Morrissey said. So he immersed himself in his training like he had never done before. If this was his swan song, then he left nothing to chance. His training regimen reminded one of the *Rocky* movies, archaic trials of strength and stress. Edward Hotaling, in his book, *They're Off! Horse Racing at Saratoga*, recounts Morrissey's commitment: "He got up at five, had sherry with beaten eggs in it, and headed out for a five or six-mile walk."

He continued:

Then it was back to the Abbey Hotel and his makeshift gym, which, in contrast to the grimy histories of the antebellum North, seems like some orderly, futuristic setting. He boxed a sandbag hanging from the ceiling and used three or four sets of dumbbells and pulleys. After a rubdown, he breakfasted on broiled chicken or mutton with no seasoning, a cup of tea, and a slice of toast. Then he took a rest, usually just a chat with his English trainer, two assistants, and friends. At eight-thirty, he went out again for an eight- to ten-mile walk, followed by a half-hour with rope, bells, weights, and bag and another rubdown. Lunch could be beefsteak and currant bread, followed by a glass of sherry. Then he did six or eight more miles, sparred with an assistant, hit the bells, pulleys, rope, and bag, and got a third rubdown. Supper was broiled chicken, a cup of tea without sugar, and a slice of toast, which he soaked in the tea. There could be no spices or seasoning, and little or no water—the reverse of today's regimens—on the belief he would have to work it off. After supper, he rowed or walked four miles and wound it up with a hundred-yard sprint at his top seed, which professional footracers called astonishing. He had a fourth rubdown. Then it was off "to his virtuous pillow, to sleep like a top." Here lay not the shadowy, gambling, fighting political hack of Saratoga legend but perhaps our first modern athlete.

As the date of the fight lurched closer, the event was quickly becoming a spectacle. The types of newspapers that planned on chronicling the fight were the *New York Clipper*, the Philadelphia-based *Spirit of the Times*, and, all the way from Canada, the illustrated *Leslies Weekly*. They would all fall upon Long Island Point, "beyond the reach of New York sheriffs."

They traveled west toward Buffalo and would, as they saw fit, duck across the Pennsylvania border to avoid the New York police. Leading up to the fight Morrissey repeated that he "felt like a racehorse." He was a svelte 173 pounds, twenty pounds lighter and two inches shorter than his rival. Heenan, then dubbed "The Benicia Boy," was in poor condition having suffered from a bad wound on his ankle.

Eight stakes were hammered into the earth, a twenty-four-foot square tethered by four ropes. The "scratch" mark was etched into the center, and since they fought on grass, both fighters were fitted with spikes, or cleats.

As 3:30 p.m. approached, the two fighters entered the ring to "settle a hate as old as their fathers."

Morrissey attacked. He charged with unscientific thrashing and Heenan, much quicker despite his larger frame, ducked and cut Morrissey on the left eye. Heenan's supporters shrieked, "First blood!"

Morrissey then tried to lock up Heenan, getting in close in an attempt to throw Heenan to the ground. Undaunted, Heenan broke the hold and tossed Old Smoke to the turf. Morrissey had never lost an "official" bout, and this, no doubt, was a troubling moment. In the third round, Morrissey finally knocked Heenan to the ground.

Heenan kept landing successful punches, punches that had little effect on Morrissey, his stamina and perseverance freakish. They rumbled for five more rounds, with Morrissey showering Heenan with punches. Heenan began to show signs of weakness, his legs unsteady underneath. That didn't stop him from backing Morrissey onto the hemp ropes, their abrasive skin like a switch on his bare back. It was then that Morrissey saw the "death blow," Heenan's right fist pulled back like the grim reaper's sickle. Morrissey ducked and heard Heenan's knuckles shatter on one of the eight ring posts. Heenan writhed, yet still managed to protect his face. Heenan missed his opportunity to win, and with his right hand rendered useless, all Morrissey had to do was land the final slam.

Morrissey threw Heenan to the ground five rounds in a row, yet Heenan still straightened his body from his second's knee by the time the ref called "time" every time. Round 11 would be the final round.

Morrissey bounded to the scratch and smashed Heenan in the forehead. The Benicia Boy wobbled, swung a counter and missed, and put an ear to the ground. Exhausted, he could not stand from his second's knee.

Morrissey's smile was "a ghastly thing to see. His eyes were nearly closed, his mouth cut, his lips and tongue swollen, his nose literally battered flat to his face." He was a "tottering tower of blood but victorious."

Heenan needed nearly a half hour before he could stand on his own. In the meantime, Morrissey stood alone and retired as the undefeated heavyweight champion of America.

John Morrissey traveled to Saratoga Springs in 1861 and brought his boxing winnings and his gambling notions to the nation's premier luxury town. One of his first casinos in Saratoga Springs was on Matilda Avenue, now Woodlawn Avenue. He was limited by space on Matilda and therefore could not build a casino that rivaled the great gamblers' halls of America and Europe. So Morrissey bought property at the corner of Union and Putnam to construct a "gentlemen's club house." It is the building that now sits in the center of Congress Park.

It took two stages to build the Saratoga Club House in 1870 and 1871. It was a front for what was largely considered illegal activity within its walls. Still, an advertisement ran in the nationally circulated newspaper *Every Saturday* that said, "Beginning on our right, and following the green cloths in course, we come upon the 'faro table,' the 'dice board,' the 'roulette,' the 'rough-et-noir,' again the 'roulette,' and, finally, a queer little game with cards which somebody tells us is 'Boston.'"

The games of chance were played on the first floor, but other card games, skilled games, were reserved for high rollers and special clientele on the second floor. As a rule, Morrissey excluded women from gambling and even wrote a letter to *The Daily Saratogian* smothering a rumor that ladies had been allowed to play at the faro tables. In this letter he writes on June 18, 1871:

To the Editor of the DAILY SARATOGIAN—Sir: The report is going the rounds of the newspapers that my house is open to ladies to gamble in. I desire to contradict the story, flatly, through your columns. I have lived in Saratoga nine years, and no lady has ever gambled, nor will ever gamble, in my house. By request, ladies have been admitted to look at the house and furniture, but the comment it has occasioned both far and near prompts me to decline any further visits from them. Furthermore my house is intended for visitors, not residents, of Saratoga.

Very Respectfully,
JOHN MORRISSEY

To which *The Daily Saratogian* bowed, parenthetically writing below Morrissey's letter: "We have already taken occasion to deny the foolish stories about the establishment of a ladies gambling house here in Saratoga, which originated, we believe, in the New York *SUN*. Mr. Morrissey's personal refutation of the story leaves no excuse for imaginative correspondents to perpetuate the yarn during the present season."

Apparently Morrissey's frequent donations to local churches, charities, politicians, and law enforcement kept any meddlers at arm's length.

Prior to the founding of the Saratoga Club House Morrissey had mastered the art of pillaging money from gamblers at night. He needed to figure a way to do it during the day. No question, the five thousand dollars he won on the black mare in California resonated with him as he came East. Hotaling writes, "So the roulette wheel in John Morrissey's head stopped at this idea: take the biggest resort in the land and add the biggest sport, horse racing. The result? A Saratoga race meeting of the highest order."

In August 1863, right in the heart of the Civil War, Morrissey got quality horses to compete instead of leading the cavalry charge. With the help of Commodore Vanderbilt and W. R. Travers (the same Travers whose race is Saratoga's feature, whereas Morrissey has a petty state-bred turf race named after him), he launched the first meet, a four-day meeting at the Horse Haven track under the conifers on Union Avenue. A front-page story in the *Saratoga Republican* on August 3, 1863, read, "The races, which are to come off this week over the Saratoga Course, promise to be among the most exciting and interesting that have taken place in the U.S. for several years."

An ad in *The Daily Saratogian* read:

Running Races!
AT SARATOGA
The Summer Meeting, over the Saratoga Course, will be held
on
Monday, Tuesday, Wednesday & Thursday

August 3d, 4th, 5th, 6th.
Two Races each Day!

First Day—First Race: Sweepstake for 3 year olds, Mile Heats, $200 entrance; $50 forfeit; $300 added, &c. Closed with 8 entries.

Second Race: Purse $300; Handicap, Dash of 2½ miles, for all ages

Second Day—First Race: Purse $300; Dash of Two Miles, for all ages

Second Race: Handicap; Dash of 2½ miles, $40 entrance; $20 forfeit, $400 added. Forfeit to go to second horse, if three or more start. Closed with 5 entries.

Third Day—First Race: Sweepstake for 3 year olds; Dash of Two Miles; $200 entrance; $100 forfeit; $300 added. Closed with 5 entries.

Second Race: Purse $400; Mile Heats, Best Three in Five, for all ags, &c.

Fourth Day—First Race: Purse $500; Two Mile Heats, for all ages, &c.

Second Race: Purse $200; Dash of 1 ¼ miles, for all ages, &c.

Races to commence each day, at 11½ o'clock.

Cards of Admission, $1.00

For particulars, see Posters and Bills of each day.

All sections of North and West, and some portion of the South will be represented by their best horses, and Canada will also contend for some of the various purses. Excellent racing is anticipated.

JOHN MORRISSEY,
Proprietor.

Another publication would write, "These four days of racing at Saratoga must have laid the foundation for a great fashionable annual race meeting at the Springs, like that of Ascot in England, where the elegance and superb costumes of the ladies vie with the beauty of running horses."

Lizzie W, a mare, won the first non-sulky race for thoroughbreds. The Old Gray Mare, Lady Suffolk, won the first-ever race at Saratoga. The first four days, were a success, and the cornerstone, at least in principle, was anchored for generations to come.

∾

At age forty-six John Morrissey tried his hand at politics, marrying his celebrity with a campaign that got him elected as a state senator in 1875. It was said that he was no great orator but fought for his Irish folk and his constituents like they were his seconds in a makeshift boxing ring at Boston Corner or Long Island Point.

Perhaps it was the incessant blows to the head that rained on him as if he were a snare drum, but at barely fifty years old he was suffering from ill health. In addition to that, in 1875, his son, John Morrissey Jr., a baseball-loving youth, died of kidney failure. It was said he never quite recovered from that loss.

After Morrissey won reelection in 1877 he soon became ill and was, at one point toward the end of April, said to have passed away. He suffered a stroke on Sunday, April 28, 1878. While at the Adelphi Hotel on Broadway in downtown Saratoga Springs, he lay in bed. At 2:00 p.m. he was said to be "gradually losing his strength. He has not spoken a word since receiving a paralytic stroke on Sunday. He does his best to make his wants understood by those attending him. In answer to an inquiry whether he had hopes of recovery, Mr. Morrissey replied in the negative by shaking his head." Despite his morbidly prophetic comment, he had regained some movement in his paralyzed hand, a hand that was at one time so powerful. It was also said that he might regain his speech. He never did.

∾

By Wednesday morning, May 1, 1878, reports leaked that he was at the point of death, but he merely had a restful night of slumber, nothing out of the ordinary. During the day he even sat upright in a chair, eating liquid foods. His breathing was less labored.

That lasted just a few hours as the cloud of pneumonia slowly gathered in his lungs.

∾

By 5:00 p.m., Dr. Grant, who was by Morrissey's side during the days after his stroke, found "the Senator wrestling, at last, with death." Morrissey's body was clammy and wet from perspiration. His heartbeats mellowed. His breaths were abbreviated and shallow. However, he still possessed the strength to grasp the hands of those who were present to witness his final minutes.

Father McMenomy held Morrissey's hand, and Old Smoke motioned for the window in his quarters to be lowered. At 7:30 p.m., with the sun just beginning to set, he closed his eyes. One last quiver, an aftershock after the earthquake, pulsed, and, then, relaxation.

People on the streets of Broadway looked up to the window of Morrissey's room. Mr. McCaffery, of the Adelphi, stepped out of the piazza and said to all listeners, "He is gone."

༄

The New York State Senate issued a telegram to Mrs. Morrissey, Susie Smith, the daughter of the ship captain. Lieutenant Governor Dorsheimer appointed a committee of three to prepare arrangement for a send-off worthy of the name Morrissey.

Mrs. John Morrissey, Saratoga Springs, N.Y.:

We have been appointed a committee to prepare resolutions expressive of the feeling of the Senate upon the death of Senator Morrissey. Receive our sympathies upon your bereavement and please inform us at what time and where the funeral will take place.

Hamilton Harris
Wm. H. Robertson

She responded in kind that her husband's remains would be "taken on the 12:40 southbound midday train to-morrow (Friday) to Troy, and that the funeral would take place from St. Peter's Catholic Church in that city on the following (Saturday) morning between 10 and 10:30 o'clock. The remains will be interred alongside those of his son, the late John Morrissey, Jr., whose funeral took place on New Year's Day of 1877."

༄

Just after his death, Morrissey's remains were placed in an icebox by Undertaker Holmes and rested in the south parlor on the second floor of the hotel, the floor where he passed.

The face of John Morrissey was pale and painful but looked "natural and composed" all the same.

In the newspapers over the days that followed, Morrissey's life was reviewed like an Oscar-winning movie. It was all praise for a life lived to the brink and, certainly, on the edge of reason and, at times, sanity.

On May 3, 1878, his body, which retained the massive physical prowess when he was in full health, was placed in a casket, draped with a black cloth, with silver-plated extension handles that ran the entire length of the casket. A raised shield bore this inscription:

JOHN MORRISSEY
Born Feb. 12, 1831
Died May 1, 1878

Hundreds of people paid their respects at the Adelphi Hotel before it was time for him to be ferried off to his final resting place. At 11:00 a.m., Morrissey's wife asked a local quartet from a church choir to sing "Nearer, my God, to Thee," which was one of Old Smoke's favorite hymns.

Mrs. Morrissey was taxed by the ordeal, having spent her nights crying between bouts of caring for her dying husband. Her family tried to peel her away from her husband, but there she remained.

Every rail station along the way to Troy was packed with people paying their respects and uncovering their heads. "The world knew the worst of his life, and yet trusted implicitly in the man," wrote the May 1, 1878, *Daily Saratogian*.

At 10:00 a.m., on the day of his funeral, throngs of people could be found at Mrs. Morrissey's old home on River Street in Troy. On Second Street, in the vicinity of St. Peter's Church, the street was blockaded. The police roamed the area to ensure order and to ensure that the entrance to the church remained free of traffic.

There was no end to the number of politicians who, whether friend or foe, spoke only of the goodness of John Morrissey. His generosity was recognized and celebrated by people in all towns, cities, and villages, and "his purse, unknown to the world, was always open to the poor."

While the Senator still breathed, "not a great while ago, a stranger from a distant place solicited a subscription from him for the purchase of a bell for a church. Upon being asked why he came to him, the stranger replied that he knew from his character that there must be moments in his life when he thought of other than worldly things."

Morrissey's demeanor was said to have changed. It was related that he told the stranger to go no farther with his subscription book. And so the bell in that unnamed village, in the belfry of the church that "rings the hours of worship," was the gift and resonant voice of John Morrissey.

12

The Triple Crown Assembled

At 5:30 a.m., August 11, 2009, assistant trainer to Steve Asmussen, Scott Blasi, aboard his pony, handed his windbreaker to Barbara Banke, wife of Rachel Alexandra's principal owner, Jess Jackson. He traded it for a vest. Rachel Alexandra awaited her first serious workout since winning the Haskell Invitational, where she garnered such headlines as "Rachel Alexandra beats boys again, gallops to Haskell Crown," "Haskell Invitational: Rachel Alexandra proves she's quite a gal," "Alexandra the Great outruns boys again." She spent a mere weekend down in New Jersey, leaving at 4 a.m. on Friday, July 31, and she was back in Stall No. 1 at Barn No. 65 in Saratoga by Sunday night.

Adjectives fall short in regard to Rachel Alexandra. Pundits pour it on, saying she is in "a league of her own among her contemporaries, and belongs with Seattle Slew and Cigar when you talk about history. She is a horse of the ages," said Jerry Bailey, Hall of Fame jockey. "I've watched her work here, and your eyes are telling you that she's going 1:03, and then you look at a stopwatch and it's 1:01. She just does things easy like all the great ones do."

There is no unnecessary motion in her stride. Her legs stay within her boundaries. Every contraction unifies to move her forward without a fiber in her bones straying from her mission. That morning the Oklahoma Training Track had many onlookers who pressed their belly buttons to the rail. Horsemen on the track pulled their ponies to the outside because it seemed that within racing circles they too knew when someone special was on the track, that if they failed to watch they may never see it again in their lifetimes. People yawned, yawned with fatigue, yawned with boredom, waiting for Rachel Alexandra. When that filly with the torch blaze and the melted-chocolate coat set foot on the track, it was as if an alarm clock went off.

She swelled with her own sense of self, entered the track on Blasi's lead, and broke free, galloping to the east, arcing to the north, and straightening out to the west. Her exercise rider lengthened her stride, and a choir of stopwatches beeped. The necks of spectators pivoted smoothly, following Rachel Alexandra's body, which was cruising like a Jet Ski without the noise and chop. She curved around the far turn and hushed by, her hooves dimpling the track as she straightened out, her hind end thrusting forward through the air. Rachel Alexandra ran in the face of hundreds of eyes, and into the fiery east.

❧

Kensei, Rachel's stablemate, worked the day before Rachel Alexandra and sizzled over the dirt. He proved to be worthy of the most quality races at the Spa (Saratoga Race Course). It was almost as if he had trained with a chip on his withers, trained as if to say, "Look at me, am I not worthy?"

❧

Summer Bird and Mine That Bird were set for the Travers which, at this point, was three weeks away. Summer Bird galloped over the grass at the Oklahoma Training Track. Why, no one was sure. His trainer, Tim Ice, said he was experimenting. Then again, perhaps Summer Bird's feet were sore.

Mine That Bird acted like the class clown, a horse whose attitude added to his charm, whose attitude landed him in detention, whose attitude got the girl. Even his trainer, Chip Woolley, had the biker-boy appeal, a rogue figure belied only by his ever-present aluminum crutches. George Smith, Mine That Bird's exercise rider, fit right in. There was always the sense that these three didn't belong, that they were outcasts. Smith, while aboard Mine That Bird on their way to the track, said, "Am I going the right way?" After coming back off the main track he said, "Aw, it's beautiful."

The two "Birds" were separated by only one stall in the Stakes barn, a stall used for storage, the "Preakness Stall," a buffer between the Derby winner and the Belmont Stakes winner. When Mine That Bird wasn't playing with a blue cone or chowing out of his black feed tub, he'd crane his neck to the right to see Summer Bird, a colt who shares the same sire, Birdstone, once trained by Hall of Famer Nicholas P. Zito.

Summer Bird was a bull. He resembled 2007 and 2008 Horse of the Year, Curlin, with his reddish coat and white wooden stake blaze.

All involved looked forward to the prospect of a Travers containing the three Classic winners. Ice, eyeing Summer Bird, noted how good he looked, how strapping his colt stood while staring down the cameras. "He looks good," Ice said. "Unfortunately, we're not in a beauty contest, we're in horse racing."

❧

The buzz of the meet's beginning vanished. Now the talk was whether Saratoga could sustain the momentum to carry the curmudgeons through the grind of the middle weeks, to see who would run in the Travers and, more importantly, to see where Rachel Alexandra would be placed.

The meet plodded on with the right mix of energy and competence, Charlie Hayward's game plan since the spring. He sat in his usual chair in his usual spot across from Paul Vandenburgh. The two discussed the OTB situation, both the mudslinging from Nassau OTB and the bankruptcy of the New York City OTB—the particular branch that was hammered in the *New York Times* editorial.

"Little unrest in the racing world," Vandenburgh said, "you've got some dustups with the OTBs."

"I think it's the same issues," replied Hayward. "Unfortunately it gets personal. Anybody will tell you that, they know that the contract was broke. New York City OTB is in fiscal crisis. I think it's unfortunate that in the efforts to seek solutions it gets personalized."

And later on at the huddle, things were going so well that it was frustrating. First, people were talking and Hayward tried, in vain, to get it to stop, "Okay," he said. Conversations finished on their own accord, "Okaaaay, guys," he continued.

The "Huddle" started with two passive responses meant to quell or dispel any disgust from the CEO.

"Same, all moving forward," one said.

"Good," said another.

"Jesus!" Hayward yelled

"Three things," Dan Silver said, "Today I'm meeting with Neema Ghazi and Ed Lewi to try and get Commentator to the track. I suggested the day of the Woodward, which is a Saturday, but Nick wants to do it on Sunday after the Woodward. We were thinking of providing him with a large, edible key to the city that he may eat or not." This was greeted by nods of agreement. "Hal thought I should share this story," Silver continued. "So, as many of you know, my roommate for the summer is none other than Sam the Bugler. I walk in to see that it looks like Sammy gained forty pounds overnight. Apparently it's his identical twin brother. We played poker and I looked from one side to the other. It was literally the eeriest thing of my life. It was like the *Twilight Zone*. I was waiting for the music to start."

"Mr. Silver," Hayward started, "anything else you'd like to share?"

To this, everyone laughed.

❧

With three weeks gone, eighteen days of racing logged in the annals of history, Calvin Borel sat in his supersized blue robe in his sandals, smoking a Marlboro Light. His feet were chipped and weathered, his face had lines that cracked his face, but the eyes, the eyes still rented space to the twinkle, and it was the twinkle that looked out from Borel's windows.

Just four racing days earlier Borel, aboard a filly named Snap Happy, trained by Dallas Stewart for Dogwood Stables, got his first win. Borel and Snap Happy looked so comfortable, so steady, and when he called on her down the lane, he was able to draw clear. Borel and Snap Happy were coupled with another Dogwood horse, a filly ridden by his longtime friend, Robby Albarado, also a Cajun boy. They galloped their horses side by side, almost as if it were planned that the two should be together curving around the turn.

Borel is older than Albarado by seven years, and Borel was a peer on the Cajun circuit while Albarado was earning his stripes. Albarado has known Borel for twenty to twenty-five years, riding for Cecil, Borel's brother. Albarado, in essence, grew up with Borel's family. The two are incredibly different, from how they present themselves to their very nature. Albarado dresses like a man heading to an upscale restaurant with a tie-less button-down shirt, blazer, designer jeans, and shoes shined such that a white sparkle glows back. Borel fancies a polo shirt and jeans, a ball cap, and dirt roads. But their respect for each other is immeasurable. The past few years proved that. "He's simple, he don't complicate situations," Albarado said. "He's great with outside track people, he's comfortable and not intimidated. He can talk to a sixty-year-old lawyer, the Queen of England, and President Bush, then talk to a five-year-old kid on the rail. He's not lost by words, grooms, and owners."

In 2007 it was Borel who, aboard Street Sense, defeated Albarado and Curlin in the Kentucky Derby. Two weeks later, in the Preakness, the two battled, rubbed flanks, but Albarado and Curlin were the ones who nosed out Borel and Street Sense at the wire, spoiling a Triple Crown bid. Months later at Saratoga, Borel and Street Sense ran in the Travers and were the prohibitive favorite, but Albarado was aboard a long shot named Grasshopper. The two knocked heads down the entire homestretch before Street Sense and Borel edged away by a length. The photograph at the wire shows Street Sense with his ears pinned back, and Borel, holding onto the reins with just his right hand, looks back to his left at Albarado, who holds his whip out as if to challenge him to a duel. This image would be used as the 2008 Travers logo.

"He stands alone," Albarado said, "his work ethic, his demeanor, and passion for horse racing, he knows the horse's physical ability. He was born to ride racehorses. He don't have the book smarts other jockeys and trainers have. What he lacks in education, he makes up for in talent."

Both are relatively tall jockeys, standing at 5' 6", so making weight is a challenge, yet another common tie the two have. "Every day is an experience with Calvin," Albarado said. "There's no enemies of Calvin Borel. If you're his enemy, you're a bad person. When we retire, we'll probably go our own ways. He's very approachable: 'Ask me a question and then go to work.'"

So far this year, 2009, Albarado said that if Borel wasn't on Mine That Bird, then he wouldn't win the Derby: "He has a knack for staying on the fence. Patience, there's nothing like him."

Earlier in the week Albarado won on a filly with a ton of zip, but she was undoubtedly green, even hit the fence once. "Calvin said, 'Let her hit the rail, she'll do it once and won't do it again.' So that's what I did. You know what? She did it again. That time his logic didn't work."

When Borel won that race aboard Snap Happy, the audience cheered for Borel, because when Calvin Borel wins, so do they. Borel and Albarado continued to gallop, both in the same Dogwood silks, as if they were teammates in this game, and, in a way, they were.

Little did the two know at the time that they would meet under the shadow of the wire in a matter of weeks for another stretch duel that would define a year and a legacy, and be even closer in margin than Street Sense and Grasshopper were just two years ago.

Borel's tract in his forty-two years was out of Dickens, a true rags-to-riches narrative. Walking back to the jocks' room after winning his first race of the meet he was met by the usual herds of autograph seekers and some who just wanted to blurt, "Way to ride!" But in the courtyard of the jocks' room are a basketball hoop and an Equisizer, a miniature wooden horse on which jockeys warm up, as well as a few benches where Borel often sat, watching jockey Alan Garcia, Saratoga's 2008 leading rider, shoot hoops or watching jockey Shaun Bridgmohan play with his kids. Then Jean-Luc Samyn, a French journeyman rider, also in a robe, went up to Borel and said, "If you're the owner, would you want all these people going by?" He was pointing to a story on Rachel Alexandra and how people on the backstretch walk by her stall to say they saw the champ, that they got a glimpse of greatness. Borel smiled, because that was why he was in Saratoga. He had some good horses coming up, but to ride five, six, seven a day like the other riders, he had zero interest in it. "Me and my agent are close by her," Borel said. "You know, chill out, it's been a long, long year."

It was hard to fathom that it was three months ago that he won the Kentucky Derby, then the Preakness, and finished third in the Belmont. He won the Mother Goose and then the Haskell. What was next? He hadn't a clue and hadn't a care.

That wasn't entirely true, as his cares revolved around the horses and, of course, Rachel Alexandra. Borel reflected on his first memories as a boy when he galloped horses at his father's farm, from that moment when he was three years old when his parents brought home a little grey pony named

Charlie. It was then that his laser-like focus locked on horses. It was the only diploma he cared for. His brother Cecil rode, and, likewise, so did Borel. Borel made a name on those bush tracks, and when he turned fifteen he recalled: "I knew I was gonna ride. It was just a matter of time before I quit school at St. Martinville Junior High."

Not all visions take you through the Ivy League, and he was lucky that the only schooling he needed was the university of the racetrack and to be bilingual in English and Equine. "God knows how I got to the ninth grade. I knew what I wanted to do. I didn't like school. My brother went to my mom and said, 'He's got potential if I keep him going. He'll make it.'"

Borel's favorite quote is, "Son, you can be anything or do anything in this life that you want to—you just have to work for it is all."

His father had a sugarcane farm, what Borel simply called canes. That was how they made their money. Borel galloped twelve to fifteen horses in the morning before school and finished them off after school as well. His father did the canes; horses were a pastime.

Borel's brother kept him on the straight and narrow, telling him: "You're going to be on top or bottom. You'll make $20,000 this week, $20 the next. It will not last forever." Borel added, "He told me to save it, live by your means."

Borel lived with his brother for twelve years and took care of his money when he had it. His brother would hand him fifty or sixty dollars a week for fun and spending. "He was a like a second dad," Borel said. He shook his head, thinking of some of the younger riders he has seen come and go. "If they had someone like my brother . . . I've seen a lot go. It's sad, in my view."

Cecil's mantra was, "I've been there, so let me help you, but it will be my way." Everything from money management to buying a car, Cecil kept his little brother straight and on the horse. Borel remembers that the first seven years were the hardest. It was during that time that he had that incredible fall where he broke his ribs, caved in a lung, took out his spleen, and was in intensive care for eight days, in a coma. He said he saw the light.

Borel said he loved a rider who was aggressive, so that was why he loved Laffit Pincay Jr. And, no doubt, it was where he learned to ride through seams as wide as a textbook if it meant getting his horse to the wire first. "He helped a horse meditate, then be aggressive," Borel said. "Everybody is friends, but you get in that gate, you gotta win. I learned a lot from Laffit Pincay, learned a lot from him."

He always had his parents' blessings, and they watched their youngest son Boo Boo ride every night until the day they died. "They got to see me win the Derby," Borel said. "I wish they could've seen the second one."

❧

In the paddock Charlie Hayward's wife, Betsy Senior, chatted with Hal Handel and Bruce Johnstone, a man of Peter the Great stature and a voice to match. Johnstone used to train horses and now is in charge of the grounds crew, making sure the track is safe for the horses. Senior asked him about the phenomenon that horses that come to Saratoga get fat and lazy. Was it true that they tend to gain some weight at Saratoga? And was that a product of the horses being able to relax? Saratoga has such broad appeal because of its pristine racing area, and because it is a racing culture in which horses can feel turned out to the farm without actually being turned out. He also relayed information about how a trainer can tell how a horse is feeling, such as knowing its temperament, if it's shuffling around in its stall, where the horse sleeps, and so on. "People ask me, 'Wouldn't it be nice if they could talk so you wouldn't have to do all that?' I say, 'If they're smart enough to talk, then they'll be smart enough to lie.'"

Handel, who spent some of his mornings checking out Mine That Bird and Summer Bird, said that trainer Chip Woolley would bare his teeth at Mine That Bird and Mine That Bird would stretch his neck out, pin his ears back, and bare his Chiclet horse teeth right back. He's a rabble-rouser, like the Italian patriot Garibaldi, Johnstown said. "He's nothing much to look at." Neither, for that matter, was Garibaldi.

13

Enshrined

Fog cloaked the morning at the main track where the water vapor delayed its exit from the grounds and chose instead to paint the sun's beams from sky to earth.

The Philadelphia Eagles signed former Atlanta Falcons quarterback and dog fighting financier, Mike Vick, on Friday, August 14, 2009. That was the watercooler banter this morning, and in a business where the animal should be king, it was natural that people around the track spoke about it.

Charlie Hayward, armed with his coffee, sat down at a table with two radio hosts, a man and a woman. One deejay said, "We have a celebrity guest with us, Charlie Hayward. There's a buzz around Saratoga this year."

"First and foremost," Hayward started, "we're blessed to have horses that were winners of the Triple Crown races, Rachel Alexandra, Mine That Bird, and Summer Bird. The weather is hugely important. Attendance is up, handle is up."

"You look dapper," the woman said, "dressed like a real CEO."

"This is not my natural garb on me," replied Hayward.

Mine That Bird's trainer, Chip Woolley, drove by on a golf cart after watching his horse gallop around the track. Hayward pointed to him and alerted the deejays, matter-of-factly, that the winner of the Derby just drove, as if to illustrate that the game's best just meander around at their own leisure.

Hayward concluded his appearance with them and went to the other side of the building for another radio spot with Rodger Wyland, host of the show "Big Board Sports." The concern, or, rather, the attention was on Rachel Alexandra. "I should point out," Hayward said, "what we do know with Rachel Alexandra is that she's nominated to three races at Saratoga: the Alabama, the Travers the following week, and the Personal Ensign. Kensei won the Jim Dandy, he's owned by Mr. Jackson. They're not gonna want to run an entry. The next week is the Woodward. I think if you want to win Horse of the Year, she'll have to beat the older boys. She's also nominated for the Pennsylvania Derby. We're hopeful, but you can't tell. We'll see what happens. It's up to Mr. Jackson."

"Is there a timetable in the near future?" Wyland said.

"Don't know, the way we look at it, we respect their privacy, and let them make that decision on their time frame. The Travers, that race will take care of itself. The Woodward is on the fifth. It's usually slower that weekend. It would provide a lot of juice for that weekend," said Hayward.

But as Hayward neared the midway point of the meet with no definitive decision on Rachel Alexandra's appearance, he was, admittedly, concerned that whatever the decision, it would be too late for them to do anything with it or about it.

∽

Hayward, Hal Handel, and Dan Silver walked down East Avenue to the Humphrey S. Finney Pavilion for the Hall of Fame induction ceremony where, among others, three-time Kentucky Derby winner, trainer Bob Baffert, was to be enshrined.

It was just a few days ago that this very pavilion was host to the Saratoga Yearling Sale, where baby horses were paraded before an audience of hundreds for dollar signs with two commas.

The ruler of Dubai, Sheik Mohammed bin Rashid al Maktoum, was on the grounds for the sale in humble attire: jeans and a snug, white, long-sleeve T-shirt. He paced the upper tier of the pavilion with an entourage walking in his wake. The sheik perused the artwork on the walls and pointed a finger at ones he liked, while a man in his company wrote the number down. His presence at this sale indicated that perhaps he would bid big dollars to help the flailing horse sale business. Many of the horses he paid top dollar for were horses stallions at his Darley Stable. The sheik smiled while his bloodstock agent outbid D. Wayne Lukas for the sale's topper, a Storm Cat colt that gaveled for $2.8 million. He purchased twelve yearlings over the two-day sale and spent $11,850,000. This sum accounted for 23 percent of the entire sale's gross income. Amazingly, the twelve horses he bought were only 7.5 percent of the entire yearling population of 160 horses. Twelve horses for 23 percent of the entire kitty? "I had fun," he said. He even outbid Nick Zito on a colt out of Bird Town.

Hard as it was to top Sheik Mohammed, a scandal within the pavilion did grab more attention and distracted the audience from the incessant drone of the auctioneer. A man with a waning hairline sat in the front of the pavilion and flicked up a bid of $1 million for Hip 151, a King Mambo filly. This aggressive bid squashed any competition, and he was promptly awarded the horse. The consignors, Denali Stud, those who raised and sold the horse, were elated for having just sold their filly for $1 million. Fasig-Tipton officials came over to him to sign the slip for the horse.

When horses sell for a million or more, it draws the attention of reporters in the room, so like mosquitoes to flesh, they swarmed the bidder. He got up from his seat and waved them off and stomped through people to the exit. Standing in his way was Walt Robertson, chairman and auctioneer. More doughy than officer-like, Robertson held his ground. "I got the best horse in the auction," the man said.

"I hope so," Robertson said. "Let's go to the office."

"Why do I need to go to the office?" asked the man.

"We need your address," replied Robertson. "We need to know how to bill you." Robertson then called for backup by signaling for Boyd Browning, president and CEO of Fasig-Tipton, the man Hayward had met for drinks at the Reading Room before the sale.

"Y'all can kiss my ass," the man said and slithered outside. Browning tried to shuffle his body to block him, but the man made it out and into the parking lot. Browning and Robertson gave chase, but in vain; the man got away.

Police questioned a man sitting next to the false bidder. There was nothing they could do. The filly went back into the ring and sold for $300,000. "They told us he was drunk and had no credit and ran off," said Holly Bandoroff of Denali Stud.

Browning noted, "You continually learn that you think you've seen it all, but you haven't seen it all."

So it was here, in this very space, that the elbow-macaroni shaped pavilion now hosted the Hall of Fame Induction. Hayward and Silver took their seats. Handel left. It was crowded. He didn't like crowds.

⌒

Nick Zito filed in and sat just a few rows back, leaning forward while nearly resting his chin on the chair in front of him. He wore his navy blue Hall of Fame blazer, a symbol of his 2005 induction into the Hall of Fame, a baby-blue shirt, and a caramel tie.

It was hard to imagine that in 1972, when he had just a two-horse stable, that he could ascend the ranks and be a two-time Kentucky Derby winner.

Tim Poole, a former trainer of a "B" string of horses at Monmouth for his father, George Poole, who trained a number of horses for C. V. Whitney, was Zito's top assistant. When George parted company with Whitney, so too did his son. Poole trained his own string at Garden State Park, but when the track burned down he quit training and assisted Bob Reinacher. Nick Zito saw that Poole was unhappy. This was the late eighties, and Zito had just landed Giles Brophy as a major client.

First came Thirty Six Red for Zito and then a colt named Strike the Gold. Around this time, 1991, it was written that, "Heywood Hale Broun once said it about Casey Stengel: 'He can talk all day and all night on any kind of track, wet or dry.'

"But he might just as well have said it about Nick Zito, who can outtalk anybody all day and all night at the Kentucky Derby, and who also has a good shot at having a horse outrace everybody Saturday on any kind of track wet or dry."

Racing had a new face, someone from whom to grab a sound bite or quote, the forty-three-year-old trainer, with his "firm good looks, curly hair, and theatrical flair" would look up at Churchill Downs' famed twin spires and break out in soliloquy: "What would it mean to win the Kentucky Derby? It's not everything in life. But it means you did something right and accomplished something in our profession. It means we got lucky and split the twin spires."

During the 1991 Triple Crown season Meadow Star, a filly, was one of the top prospects before an injury sidelined her. Zito said he thought she would have added some glamour, "even though I don't think fillies can run against colts."

Zito continued: "But you've got to run against somebody. Vince Lombardi said, 'Don't ever underestimate your opponent.' There are still Derby horses out there. They've all got four legs. There are no free lunches."

Strike the Gold chugged down the center of the track to win the 117th Kentucky Derby. Zito pointed both arms to the sky, his graying hair bouncing, his teeth glowing in the Churchill grandstand. He pointed again and darted down to the track. This was a far cry from the days of making $42.50 a week as a teenage hot walker. "Racing is probably one of the few things left that's close to nature. It's Utopia. It's hard work, and your family life's not the best. But it's the only thing I know now."

Zito has a son, Alexander, and a daughter, Sarah, separated by just two years. It was around this time in the early nineties that his marriage to his then-wife Jan was strained. Add to that that Giles Brophy, one of three owners of Strike the Gold, removed Zito as trainer of his racehorses on January 22, 1992. Zito remained trainer of Strike the Gold, but the ownership disputes and legal battles were an added stressor to Zito's already-hectic life. But winning was a good tonic, and after a nasty losing streak, Strike the Gold won the Nassau County Handicap at Belmont Park, and Zito shouted, "New York, this is for you!"

His marriage was in tatters, and he was living alone, but he was violently drunk on this win. "I'm like Billy Martin. Look at what I do with what I've got. I'm not one of those fair-hair trainers that get an unlimited supply of two-year-olds. In my barn, out of a crop of six two-year-olds, I got ThirtySixRed. In Strike the Gold's crop there were four. How's that? It's not a lot, is it? If you see me next year in the Triple Crown, you're gonna see someone who's like Billy Martin and Company. I mean, I get good horses. But Billy Martin, Earl Weaver, they won with teams no one gave a chance."

In June of that year, Stephanie Diaz, a freelance writer for *The Blood-Horse*, charged Zito with second-degree assault at Zito's Belmont Park barn. She claimed that Zito had struck her in the face with a magazine. She had been writing a series of articles, barn diaries, of Zito's string, his recent celebrity throttling him to the front pages of the *Racing Form* and *The Blood-Horse*. Glenn Miller, Diaz's attorney, said, "She needed to buy a gift for a friend whose child was being baptized, and she asked Zito, 'What kind of gift do you bring for a baptism?' and he said, 'Don't mess with my kid.'"

Diaz recalled that Zito was "a raging Lothario who hit on anything with a skirt or breeches."

The strain of training horses had nearly broken Zito's family, and he was living apart from them. "I don't want anyone to say anything about my kids," he said. The weight of Triple Crown, of smothering owners, of winning, was a tremendous gravity on his spirit. Zito maintained, "I was looking after my horses and she called me over and said she wanted to ask me a personal question. She said, 'Are your kids baptized?' I said, 'Don't get personal,' and I waved my program in front of her face, and she said, 'You're going to get in trouble.'"

Zito denied Diaz's charges that he sexually harassed her as well, which Miller claimed in an interview, but not in the formalized complaint. "This was a young woman doing her job," said Miller, "She is a victim of a person who feels he can do anything to her anytime, anyplace. She put up with it for several months. He made lewd comments. He touched her in front of other people."

The following day police questioned Zito at his barn, where he denied the charges and went so far as to hire criminal lawyer, Frank Yannelli. The case fizzled.

Two years later Zito won the Derby again with Go For Gin, with Chris McCarron aboard, and when he won Zito kissed the palms of his hands and shot them to the sky. He lost the Preakness two weeks later, and said, "I can't say God bless America, but thank you, Maryland, thank you everyone anyway. I want to be a good loser."

A year later he lashed out at jockey Julie Krone for riding Suave Prospect too wide in the Kentucky Derby. Five weeks later, Zito put Krone on Star Standard for the Belmont Stakes, and she rode to a valiant second-place finish. "She really proved herself as a jockey today," said Zito. "She's a real cowboy here, she gets over. And that's Post 12. That's hard to do. And look, she made the first turn. That's what I wanted her to do. That's what she did."

Through the mid-nineties Zito became a brand. "If you cut me open, it would say Triple Crown," said Zito. "Grass is an absolutely dirty word to me.

If you have a grass horse, give it to Bill Mott or Richard Mandella." Friends called him a "survivor." Trainer Claude "Shug" McGaughey said, "Nick is a grinder, he keeps going. If he gets beat up, he keeps fighting back. There's a guy who started with nothing, worked his way up, and now is in the Rokeby barn and has won two Derbys and a Preakness. I was happy for Nick when he won the Preakness, but don't think for a minute that I didn't wish that was me."

Zito's longtime friend and neighbor on the Oklahoma backside, fellow Hall of Famer D. Wayne Lukas, beat Zito's Star Standard in the Belmont with Thunder Gulch. The two sparred on the track with their horses, and it was Lukas who handed Zito the olive branch after he won. That didn't mean that they wouldn't take shots at one another. Zito referred to Lukas as Darth Vader, and said that if there were a popular election held he would "outpoll Lukas." To this Lukas rebuked, "Let's see. He wins the Derby, then we win six in a row." Lukas was referring to his six consecutive Triple Crown race victories.

Soon Zito was four years removed from his latest Derby triumph, the wins stalled and his brash edge tempered. He had another horse whose chances at winning were reasonable, but he went to Kentucky in 1998 for serenity. "You have to go where you find inner peace. I get good vibes in Kentucky. I'm from New York, and I'll stay there as long as Kenny Noe and his people are running the show. I find inner peace in Kentucky. That's what it's all about, isn't it?"

With every year came wisdom and a calm, a comfort, in his skin, so that he was apt to say, "Once again, the good Lord rocked me in his arms." He still maintained an edge, still railed on jockeys for poor rides, but that was, and is, the competitor talking.

Zito's coveted race through the 1990s and 2000s was the Belmont Stakes. He had finished second place five times. Hall of Fame trainer Woody Stephens had won five Belmonts in a row, which made Zito joke, "I'm just like Woody Stephens, only I keep getting seconds. I don't know why it's so hard for us to win this race. But I'm delighted that I have horses whom are good enough to run in this race year after year. I should get on my hands and knees, I'm so grateful."

That was in 2001, but he did get his Belmont in 2004, when he upset Smarty Jones's bid for the Triple Crown. He won it again in 2008, upsetting Big Brown's Triple Crown bid. It was enough for him to intone, "This is a game of dreams, a game of people, and so much romance."

NBC's cameras were glued to his face during the 2005 Kentucky Derby. Zito saddled five horses for five owners and seemed a lock to win his third career Derby, eleven years after he had won it with Strike the Gold, back when he lived life as the "curly-haired youth" at age forty-three. He even thought that if "I don't get No. 3 now, then I'll have to have Secretariat himself. I can't ask the man upstairs to give me a better shot than this. But this is a game that humbles kings. If it doesn't happen, it doesn't happen. Hopefully one of these five will get over the line." Zito harbored the apprehension that great expectations make for great disappointments. He didn't get No. 3.

But all he had to do was look around. Later that same year, in 2005, he would stand on that stage in the Humphrey S. Finney Pavilion sliding his arms into the sleeves of the greatest navy blue blazer he had ever known.

On the stage the day he was inducted into the Hall of Fame, he spoke of how blessed, how lucky, he felt to be a horseman, to do what he loved to do and to do it "over and over." He said, "Some things we do well, some things not so well. No matter how bad we do, with the love that we have for the sport, there's never really a bad day attached to it."

Zito had always embraced the underdog role well and always maintained that, "You have to play the game. If you don't play the game, you can't even lose." And he would chime in with, "All you need is a little change here or there. Let's see if he can work his way back in. This isn't a war or a battle. To me, it's horse racing."

Now, in 2009, Zito leaned forward in his seat the way an eager schoolboy would wait for recess. At the ceremony sat other Hall of Famers, Claude "Shug" McGaughey, H. Allen Jerkens, Angel Cordero, Bill Mott, D. Wayne Lukas, and Pat Day. Zito absorbed his surroundings, at times amazed that he was among this group, truly the game's best. "It's really great that so many come back," he said. "I was sitting next to Pat Day, Lukas, Angel Cordero, Mott in that row. It's really impressive. Shug behind me, Allen Jerkens and his wife, it was tremendous for me."

Zito even recalled the men who helped get him there, the LeRoy Jolleys, the Buddy Jacobsons, and the Johnny Campos. They taught him the fundamentals, "what you gotta do." Zito watched Jerkens and learned. "You learn from all these guys, Frank Whiteley Jr. You look at their students. You pick up stuff from all trainers and develop your own style. I'd be interested. I've won a lot of big races, as you know."

And in 1972, when he had more stress than horses, there were many long days, many doubts. "That's tough, I didn't think I'd make it for a long time. You say that thousands and thousands of times, and at the end of the day. . . . It's sad. Unfortunately, if you go into a losing streak, they get mad." They, of course, were the owners, the ones who sign big checks and demand big results, the ones who sometimes lose sight that these animals are not machines. They have personalities; they have intellect. Horses are athletes, and the trainer's job is to get them fit and cranked for race day, but race day is stressful. The weather could be hot. They could get stepped on. And haven't you ever just not felt like working out?

In recent years Zito has spearheaded efforts to keep horses out of the slaughterhouses, to make sure that retired racehorses have a home after racing. He maintains that, "They are not in our food chain. Not us."

Zito's wife, Kim, shares his passion for horse rescue. One such incident saw a former Zito horse, Little Cliff, fall into a direct-to-kill pen in New Holland, Pennsylvania. Little Cliff even had a sticker on his papers that read, "If this horse needs a home when he retires, please call."

"The tragic part of the story," Kim Zito told *The Thoroughbred Times*, "is that Little Cliff had this sticker on his papers, and that breaks my heart because it proves that there are people in this industry who don't give a darn."

"The horse slaughter issue, in my opinion, it's terrible, No. 1," Nick Zito said. "But I don't like how the horse is being treated. Period. When you think about what the horse has done for our country . . . I don't like it, and we need to do something about it. I'm going to do my part as good as I can. I think the racetracks, what they need to do, is police it as good as they can and to make sure that anybody that is involved in that there's no place for them in the thoroughbred business. I mean, it's not what a thoroughbred's about. It's not what a horse is about. It's not what racing's about."

Zito's grind, Zito's near forty-year commitment to the sport, paid off in 2005, the year he was inducted, and yes, the year he felt like he had finally made it in this game. And it could be that his enduring legacy to the sport will have more to do off the track than on it.

∾

"What time is it?" Dan Silver asked.

"Late," Charlie Hayward replied from his seat in the pavilion. Sitting idly while waiting for the ceremony to begin had many people who had other places to be antsy, Hayward included. Sam the Bugler trumpeted the Call to the Post, and someone blurted, "Everything's alive and well in Saratoga, baby!"

Chris McCarron, a Hall of Fame jockey, gave the keynote address. First a video of his career highlights played, showing him at his induction ceremony crumbling in tears: "So many wonderful things happened to me; only horse racing would do this to me," he had said. McCarron watched the screen, and in 2009 he had less hair, no tears, but was still dedicated to racing.

He relayed a story about getting the mount on eventual Kentucky Derby winner Go For Gin. While in the jocks' room, McCarron got a phone call. He picked up and listened to the voice on the other end, " 'This is Nick Zito, I'm looking for Chris McCarron.' " McCarron paused, because normally a trainer would call the agent. " 'Bailey took off Go For Gin. I want you there.' "

" 'I'm there,' " McCarron said.

Then, back at the lectern in the 2009 ceremony, he said, "Can you believe I paid my agent 25 percent for that?"

Then Mike Kane, director of communications for the Hall of Fame, stood and announced all the living members of the Hall of Fame who were in attendance. They then walked up to the stage. "Bill Mott, John Rotz, Pat Day, Bobby Ussery, Shug McGaughey, Jonathan Sheppard, Edgar Prado, Jose Santos, Ron Turcotte, D. Wayne Lukas, Chris McCarron, Allen Jerkens, Angel Cordero Jr., Tommy Kelly—wish him an early birthday, he turns ninety next month—Carl Nafzger, and Nick Zito.

"Ladies and Gentlemen, I say this every year," Kane continued. "Before baseball, before basketball, before football, there was horse racing. These are our legends."

With this everyone stood, and the sound of hands on hands drowned the pavilion in waves.

❧

Radical Sabbatical, the horse Charlie Hayward owned in a partnership, was on the card for this diamond-sharp day. The horse had long legs and yolk-colored tiles for teeth. Alan Quartucci, the racing manager for the syndicate, stood by the horse while the trainer saddled him. "I like our chances on the cutback," Hayward said.

"I like him going long," Quartucci said. Hal Handel asked, "What's the price, Charlie?" "Five to one," Hayward replied.

Don Lehr and Betsy Senior joined Hayward, Handel, and Quartucci, while Radical Sabbatical warmed up. Jockey Rajiv Maragh strutted from the jocks' room and stood near the horse.

"That's your horse?" Lehr said.

Pinching her fingers with invisible salt, Senior said, "That much."

"Doesn't matter," Hayward said with a smile, "the more you own the more it costs you. We got a shot?"

"Wide open," Lehr said.

"Who we have? Maragh?" asked Hayward.

"How much has your horse raced?" Lehr said.

"Seventeen times," said Hayward.

The group sauntered down the horse path, under the awnings, and then up the stairs, the weight of their feet creaking the floorboards of the grandstand. They were soon seated, watching the television screen.

"The horse does have a shot," Hayward said. "The two is really being bet."

"Too much," chimed Lehr.

"He's a hanging dog, though."

"That's what I thought, but there's slightly lesser competition here."

"Non-threes are always tough."

"I have money on the one."

"Should be laying second or third, you think?"

"The six should be the controlling speed. If he gets loose, it's over."

And with that the race started, and Hayward and Lehr kept a keen eye on the fractions of the race. Hayward's horse was the three, and he noticed that Maragh had taken hold of him early. "Twenty-three and two, that's good," he said. "Let's get forty-six and four." He then peeked over Senior's shoulder like a young boy at a parade craning to see the grand marshal. "Wow, forty-six and four," he said. "They're goin' fast. Radical's coming!" Maragh hustled Radical, letting out the reins, "C'mon!" Hayward yelled, "C'mon!"

Radical Sabbatical steadied and finished third. Coming down and speaking in a level tone, shoulders curved, Hayward said, "He ran good. The hanging dog didn't hang. The six did."

"He had a clear trip outside. Your horse always runs a race. He's a very consistent horse," Lehr said.

"He was a little farther back than he wants to be."

"A lot farther."

"Racing here is a different dynamic than on the Belmont turf course. There's two turns here."

"He was only beat a length."

"It doesn't matter. He could've won."

"It really is a longer race."

"Because of the two turns?"

"Yeah."

"Alan says he wants more," Hayward said, pointing to the replay. "He's coming here at the end."

Then, pointing to the replay, Hayward said, "Alan says he wants more. He's coming here at the end."

After the races that would follow, Hayward traveled down to the Saratoga Room where he darted for the popcorn and, with closed fist, funneled the kernels into his mouth.

14

Out of the Fog and into the Fog

The butt end of Week 3 saw Nick Zito, Calvin Borel, and Charlie Hayward reach the halfway point of the meet. Zito flatlined at six winners, and Borel had ridden so few horses that the curmudgeons in the press box even took notice. And Hayward still hadn't a clue where Rachel Alexandra planned on running.

Toward the end of Week 2 Dan Silver mentioned that Summer Bird looked "ouchy." This raised concerns about his soundness and his commitment to the Travers Stakes in two weeks. "I wouldn't be shocked if there's a change of plans," he said in the huddle. This was troublesome, since he was as close to a sure thing that NYRA had. Rachel Alexandra's indecision was an added bout of apprehension, and now with Summer Bird's feet feeling like he had stepped on a nail, nerves were at a peak.

They would spike ever higher in a few days.

The huddle went on as planned, with the players hitting their strides, riffing on each other with the banter that comes with nearly eighteen days of racing in the books. "We didn't huddle yesterday, so some of you may not know that we were up against the rainout," Don Lehr said in reference to 2008's cancelled card after a deluge wiped out the far turn on the track. "This year we had 23,000, up 81 percent," he said, while rolling his eyes, "but we were up 22 percent over '07. On-track was up 14.4 percent with 3.4, up 7 percent over '07. All-source, that's all good, and the per-cap was almost $150. Last year, the Saturday was a beautiful, sunny day. We were on a yielding turf, miraculously. Thirty-one thousand five hundred, on-track 4.8, 19.6 all-source. That's what we're up against."

"How many betting interests?" said Hayward.

"Eighty-nine with eleven races, four on the turf, yielding, as it was last year the infamous Yaddo that didn't fill and was moved to Sunday, and we had the four overnight stakes," said Lehr.

P. J. Campo tossed his head back then and said, "Obviously. . . . Everyone! Because I never hear the end of it!"

Then Hal Handel looked at Lehr and said, "Gonna take the over on 4.8?"

"I'll take the over on 4.8," replied Lehr.

"Whoopee. Want the over on 5.2?" asked Handel.

"I'll take the over! It's too fuckin' beautiful!" said Lehr, and leaned back as if walking under a limbo bar with his arms outstretched.

"Pat," Handel said, "slow the machines down."

"Happy to do it," Mahony said.

Jerry Hissam, Calvin Borel's agent, sat in a box in the Saratoga grandstand with his hands folded over his Southern-style belly. He had the air of confidence that comes with biding one's time and waiting for success to come knocking. Because of his and Borel's efforts, they sat and waited for success to come and greet them, because the two knew they deserved it. They had been waiting—and working—for it for some time.

Hissam and Borel have been a pair since 1991, eighteen years heading into the Saratoga meet. Hissam never threatened to be a jockey; his build wouldn't allow it. Prior to his and Borel's engagement, Hissam had heard of Borel but didn't work with him. Then, in mid-March 1991, that changed.

Borel only had two winners at the Oaklawn meet down in Hot Springs, Arkansas. He was frustrated; the competitive bull in him felt tied by the balls. The meet was coming to a close when Hissam started to carry around Borel's book for him. Borel said, "You still interested?"

"Sure," said Hissam.

"I'll be back," said Borel, who spoke to his brother Cecil to make sure he was about to make a good decision. So the next morning they got started. "What time do you get here?" Hissam asked.

"I get here around 4:30," said Borel.

"I'll never beat you," Hissam replied.

"If I'm not here when you get here, go to the hospital," Borel said.

Before long, Borel won four races, and they "hit it off and haven't looked back ever since," Hissam said. "We've never had two cross words. The final decision is always mine. My decision is final. We've had a great, great relationship."

Jock agents have a way with their dialogue. You would never confuse Hissam with a jockey, but you will hear him say that he won the $1 million Super Derby in 1991 with Free Spirit's Joy. *You* won? Yeah! If agents book a jock on a horse and the horse wins, well, they win too. That was their first big score together, winning that race at Louisiana Downs with a Louisiana-bred horse, with a Louisiana trainer, and with a Louisiana jockey. Unprecedented.

Then, in 1993, "I dethroned Pat Day," said Hissam. "I won the Arkansas Derby and paid $218. I won the Oaklawn Handicap. I won the Oaks race with Hello America."

Borel rarely gets upset with Hissam, but there were times when he'd pull him aside and say, "You know that sore horse I had in the fifth yesterday? Try to duck him back."

"There's no screaming," Hissam said. "It's a business deal and it ends there. If I do ride him back, there's something else down the road." And Hissam never got in Borel's way, never coached him on how to ride this way or the other. The converse was also true: Borel never told Hissam how to carry his book. So Borel went to work, "thriving on the throttle," working as many horses as he could in the morning and riding seven to eight in the afternoons.

They won races, plenty of races, but this came at a price. They showed up. They were consistent, annoyingly consistent. "I tell younger people to keep showing up if you want it that bad. He'll put you to work. You don't show up, he's not going to put you to work. I'm out here at 5:30, 5:45, seven days a week, walking around talking bullshit. Early on it was fun trying to get established."

The two teamed up for leading rider at Oaklawn and moved Borel's tack to Kentucky in the fall of 1997. Borel, according to Hissam, was the second-leading rider in his first fall at Churchill Downs.

That was a far cry from the days Hissam spent in the Old Waterford Park racing office, now Mountaineer. "I started to go to the races and never left. I didn't know what I was getting into," said Hissam. "I've been to Maine, Michigan, Ohio, Kentucky, all over. After six years some jock asked me to be his agent at Ascot Park in Ohio. Now been an agent for thirty-five years. Right now, we're rolling."

Hissam and Borel burst onto the public scene in 2007, when they won the Kentucky Derby, and Hissam wears a ring (bought for him by Borel) the size of a golf ball to commemorate it. But to Hissam, the curtain had just been pulled back. There they always stood. "The only thing that has changed is that I'm talking to you people. You didn't know us before. Now *you* want to know *us*. Now, we don't work quite as hard. He's forty-two, he don't have to work quite as hard."

Rachel Alexandra has only elevated their already boiling profile. Hissam remembered watching her race at Keeneland when Brian Fernandez sat in the saddle. A Dale Romans-trained horse beat her that day. The owner wanted to make a change to Robby Albarado, to put him on Rachel Alexandra. Instead, Albarado opted for the filly that had beaten Rachel Alexandra. Two days passed, and "Boom, it was ours," Hissam said. "Calvin said she's the greatest horse he ever threw a leg over, bar none, bar none. Fabulous, fabulous animal. I don't have a word in my vocabulary other than great . . . or the greatest."

And regarding the musings that NYRA was planting seeds for a Rachel Alexandra versus Zenyatta matchup, Hissam said that it would be unfair to Zenyatta. That was how strongly he felt that he had the best horse in the country. "Zenyatta's a great mare, but it would be an unfair match race. It would be an unfair regular race."

Whether that would be the case or not, it still didn't stop David Grening of the *Daily Racing Form* from publishing a story plugging the race's potential and possibility.

∽

Charlie Hayward and Hal Handel needed to go on the offensive. Floating in the ether were Rachel Alexandra and Zenyatta, two extraordinarily talented female horses that had dominated racing headlines. If there was a way to get the two together, well, then the story would write itself, and racing and, most importantly, NYRA, would benefit.

Owner Jess Jackson's flirtations with running in the $1 million Pennsylvania Derby with Rachel Alexandra gave NYRA an extra gray hair, but Handel spoke to Jackson and said it would be good to see him run in front of three thousand people instead of three thousand slot machines. To this both men laughed. Hayward said, "He has good cover in Kensei. They want to see how this colt works. If he makes his decision over the weekend, we'll know it's not the colt. It was the money."

As for NYRA's efforts to get Rachel Alexandra and Zenyatta in the Beldame run at Belmont Park, that took some maneuvering. Handel's contact, a consultant with TVG, approached him and said that his client might be interested in putting up $400,000, and that they also worked it out with Youbet. NYRA chairman, Steve Duncker, called Jerry Moss, the owner of Zenyatta, to tell him what their plans were, that they intended to bump the Beldame purse up to $1 million, from $600,000. Handel then spoke with Jackson's agent. All they needed to do was alert the media, but whom?

Two to three days passed, and Handel, as an anonymous source, went, exclusively, to *Daily Racing Form's* Grening, who was one of the most credible and hard-working turf writers in the country, because Grening had the most connections on the backside. Since the piece would be published in the most credible newspaper, it made even more sense to go with Grening. If NYRA went to anybody else, then it could be perceived as a local story, especially to Jerry Moss on the West Coast. Grening wrote the story on a Monday, to be published on a Wednesday.

TVG then gave it lots of attention, with Handel going on the air to talk about it.

Alas, the headline in the August 16, 2009, *Daily Racing Form* read: "NYRA out to set up Rachel vs. Zenyatta."

SARATOGA SPRINGS, N.Y.—The New York Racing Association is attempting to make the dream match up between Rachel Alexandra and Zenyatta a reality.

According to a NYRA source, NYRA is close to finalizing a deal with a sponsor either to create a race or, more likely, enhance the purse of the Grade 1 Beldame on Oct. 3 at Belmont Park from $600,000 to $1 million in hopes of bringing in the two superstar females together.

The source, who spoke on the condition of anonymity, said that discussions have taken place between NYRA and the connections of both horses, and there is interest. The idea is not meant to create a match race, but rather a regular race that draws the two stars.

"We've talked to the owners, we've talked to the trainers. Nobody is saying no," the source said.

John Shirreffs, the trainer of Zenyatta, who is 12 for 12 lifetime, confirmed Monday that he spoke with NYRA racing secretary, P. J. Campo, about the race and said, "It's something to consider."

. . . The 3-year-old Rachel Alexandra, who has won her last eight races, including a six-length score in the Haskell Invitation last out, is not being pointed to the Breeders' Cup, so a race on Oct. 3 at Belmont could fit into her schedule. However, her owner, Jess Jackson, has yet to announce where Rachel Alexandra is running next, so getting him or trainer Steve Asmussen to project two races down the road is not easy.

"It would be extremely exciting to get them together," Asmussen said.

Hayward and Handel were both pleased with the story. "The good news is neither of them said yes, but neither of them said no," Hayward said. "Dave Grening did a good job with the story. It was good he got Shirreffs in the story. On Ray Paulick's website *The Paulick Report*, it said, 'Rachel v. Zenyatta. . . . No one's saying no.'"

"That's what you want," Handel said.

"That's what you want," answered Hayward.

This was all well and good, even satisfying, but there was the pressing matter of ensuring that Rachel Alexandra would run here at Saratoga. Her next workout was fast approaching, and the feeling was that there would be an announcement soon.

That was the hope.

On Monday morning, the fog was thick like ice-glaze on a frozen pint glass. The only figures to be made out from a range greater than fifty feet were silhouettes. The vapor was heated and rested on shoulders and misted the skin. Up above was a thumbnail moon radiating an ivory hue with Venus piercing the sky, keeping the moon company.

Calvin Borel walked up to Steve Asmussen's Barn No. 65 with his Rachel Alexandra hat on. He wore a white polo shirt with horizontal blue stripes tucked into his jeans. He stood with his hand on his hip, watching the filly warm up under tack.

Jerry Hissam drove up in a golf cart. He too wore a ball cap, a black mesh hat with his initials embroidered on it. It was perched atop his head like Elmer Fudd's hunting hat. Borel slid into shotgun with a hand on the roof for support. Both turned their heads to the right and watched Rachel Alexandra walk around the trees with heavy, world-conquering strides.

A crescent-shaped mob of onlookers fixed its collective gaze on Rachel Alexandra. Borel stood and walked over to assistant trainer Scott Blasi's pony and scratched its nose. He patted its cheeks, warm like freshly baked bread. Borel then puckered his lips and blew a raspberry onto the muzzle of the pony.

The fog was on the move, with its cloudiness riding the wind to the east. "Boo Boo," Hissam said, "Calvin, I'm goin' up."

Borel nodded while Hissam turned the key to the ignition, backed up his cart, and purred to the rail at the training track.

Asmussen arrived with his coffee, and both he and Borel ambled to the track, following Rachel Alexandra. In their wake was a gallery of people, like following Tiger Woods down the 18th fairway.

"Kids back in school?" asked Borel.

"Yeah, it must be hot in Texas," said Asmussen. "I saw the Red Sox were in Arlington playing the Rangers. The fans were sweating."

"Chicago?" asked Borel.

"No, Texas, they were sweating," replied Asmussen.

The shapes of horses, gray against gray, bucked into the fray. Blasi, on his pony, led Rachel Alexandra with her rider, Dominic Terry, aboard. She bounced on her toes when Blasi let them go, posing for the cameras. She rose to the moment, so aware of herself. Rachel Alexandra then disappeared around the turn, cloaked in mist. Into the fog she vanished, into thin air.

A clocker got on his walkie, "He just turned her loose in front of me."

Rachel Alexandra vanished. There was no way to know just where she was, somewhere on the other side. Then she fluffed the dirt, her cadence swift; she burst through the fog with curlycues of vapor spiraling behind her. Collected, she bounded across the earth with winged feet, her breathing a whisper. Watches beeped.

"1:00 and 2, but I might have been a little slow," Asmussen said.

"1:00 2/5," said the clocker.

"Maybe not," said Asmussen.

Rachel Alexandra was breathtaking, with one onlooker saying, "It's like she's not real."

She bounded back to the barn with her tongue flicking. Reporters gathered around, and Asmussen amusingly said, "Is training my other horses getting in your way?"

He went on to say that as of this morning no races had been eliminated. He thought her work was impressive, loved her energy level, loved how she cooled out, loved that they considered her an obvious Saturday horse. "The discussion of Rachel and Kensei begins in earnest now," he said.

On the cover of an issue of *Saratoga Special* was a picture of Rachel Alexandra bursting through the fog with a headline that read, "Where to?"

༄

Later that morning Dan Silver received a phone call from Mine That Bird's trainer, Chip Woolley. It seemed that Mine That Bird was having some health issues.

Rachel Alexandra's work, while a fantastic athletic move, led to no conclusion as to her next race, and Mine That Bird's health was in question. The summer that began with so much hope seemed to be unraveling halfway through the meet, and there was nothing anybody could do.

Nothing at all.

Week Four

15

Fragility Illustrated

Chip Woolley worried. He peered through an endoscope threaded into the nose of Mine That Bird and down into his trachea. Just this morning Mine That Bird was fine during his penultimate workout for the $1 million Travers Stakes, a race that was to be held August 29, 2009, just twelve days away.

Mine That Bird showed no signs of discomfort, but like all of Woolley's horses he "scopes" them before an upcoming race. This is a routine procedure where a veterinarian inserts an endoscope into the horse's nose to examine the throat. The camera shows the fleshy, cartilage-ringed trachea and reveals whether there is any blood, mucus, or deformities. Like a magician who pulls a strand of spaghetti out of his nose, the vet pulled the scope out.

What they saw discouraged the hell out of them.

On a shimmering morning, Dan Silver paced outside the Stakes barn while a dozen reporters waited. On the far end of the Stakes barn Chip Woolley leaned on his crutches, the brim of his Stetson angled toward the ground. The click of his crutches grew louder before he parked himself, a tripod standing in front of a crowd. The camerapeople hit their "Record" buttons. "Um, after Mine That Bird worked, we scoped him and he had an entrapped epiglottis," Woolley said. "It was enough that we're going to take him to the city and do surgery on him. The doctors think he'll be good for the Travers. It's somewhat day-to-day. We will not run him if he is not 100 percent."

His voice was low and muffled, dejected. It lacked bounce. After Mine That Bird's third-place effort in the West Virginia Derby, Woolley shipped his gelding straight to Saratoga Springs. He was the misfit horse, the one who didn't belong, the underdog, the uninvited one. Yet on May 2, 2009, he crashed the party.

Mine That Bird was an unknown, a horse that was purchased at auction for $9,500 at the Fasig-Tipton Kentucky October Sale in 2007, a horse who ran in Canada and won a prestigious juvenile race, the Grade 3 $232,100

Grey Stakes. It ran his win streak to four for trainer David Cotley and jockey Chantal Sutherland. In that race Mine That Bird was intimidated but was kept toward the front of the herd to stalk the leaders. Mine That Bird would be awarded the Sovereign Award for Canada's Champion Juvenile horse.

Mine That Bird was soon purchased for $400,000 by Mark Allen and Dr. Leonard Blach. He went from Canada to California, from Cotley's hands to Hall of Fame trainer Richard Mandella, who only trained him for a few weeks before the 2008 Breeders' Cup. Mine That Bird finished dead last, and it seemed that this Ford Escort of horses had peaked at the young age of two. Still, he had a nice go of it while he raced.

Allen and Blach shipped Mine That Bird to their home base in Roswell, New Mexico, to his new home track of Sunland Park to a trainer who, in 2009, went into the Kentucky Derby with one win from thirty-two starts and a broken ankle.

∾

Mark Allen was frayed around the edges, like someone who rode into town bareback on a bull. His coal-black leather jacket was blistered, and leather strips hung from the shoulders. His beard was spiny like a sea urchin. When he was twelve years old he mucked stalls, mainly with quarter horses. Allen has both thoroughbreds and quarter horses in training at his Double Eagle Ranch.

Dr. Blach is a veterinarian who breeds about four hundred mares a year. These two, that trainer, and that horse made for an unlikely grouping to try and slay the game's elite in Kentucky.

∾

To qualify to be one of the twenty horses to start in the Kentucky Derby a horse has to be in the Top 20 of graded earnings, that is, has to have enough purse money earned from any graded or grouped race (the rankings being 1, 2, or 3). Going into the Kentucky Derby, Mine That Bird finished second in the Borderland Derby and fourth in the Sunland Derby, both at Sunland Park. He showed little ability to take on the best three-year-olds, but he had the earnings from his Grade 3 win in the Grey Stakes as a juvenile. There were grumbles that horses like Mine That Bird shouldn't be allowed on the graded earnings list, that his presence kept other horses out, other horses with more ability, more worth, and more talent.

Why not? That was the sentiment. So Chip Woolley put Mine That Bird in his trailer, threw his crutches in the front seat, and turned the key. People wanted to write the story that he threw Mine That Bird in the back of a pickup truck, feeding the horse McNuggets, and rolled into Louisville honking a horn and firing shotguns into the air. Woolley said that he actually had a "super nice van."

As far as the horse was concerned, the comments were not flattering.

It mattered not. Mine That Bird would finish a pole ahead of Dunkirk in the Kentucky Derby, a horse who cost $3.7 million at auction. In terms of yearling auction prices, that's 389 Mine That Birds.

∼

Hal Handel, among others, loved to see Mine That Bird at the Stakes barn. Mine That Bird, dressed in his golden Kentucky Derby saddlecloth, would gallop onto the track. The saddlecloth was, by now, a mustard-colored badge of honor.

Woolley insisted that there wasn't more he could relay. The disappointment and the worry in his voice said more than he ever could. "It's enough to take him down there," said Woolley about the surgery, "We could do it here in the stall, but he'll be in first thing tomorrow. We'll haul him down, then bring him back up."

When Woolley's horses are two weeks out from a big race, he has them scoped. There would be nothing quite like discovering that your horse has a blocked windpipe the day of a race. Watching Mine That Bird come off the track, Woolley thought he looked like a plane, like nothing hampered him at all. Woolley, while looking down at his watch, was impressed at how fast Mine That Bird ran his final eighth, eleven seconds and change.

They scheduled an appointment at the Ruffian Equine Medical Center downstate where the hands of Dr. Patricia Hogan would attempt to clear Mine That Bird's throat.

Just a few weeks ago people hoped to see the matchup of the Derby winner, the Preakness winner, and the Belmont winner in line at the starting gates for the Travers. Now to get one of them there would be a stretch.

Summer Bird's feet ached. Who knew where Rachel Alexandra was headed? And now Mine That Bird needed surgery. "If he's not ready, he won't run," said Woolley. "We'll move on to backup plans."

∼

P. J. Campo and Charlie Hayward exchanged words about the weather, Rachel Alexandra, and Mine That Bird outside of Campo's office. "Mr. Jackson got in late Tuesday night," Campo said. "Entries have to be taken today for the Alabama."

The Alabama is a prestigious race for three-year-old fillies, right up alongside the Kentucky Oaks. With no word on Rachel Alexandra, many trainers were held hostage. If Rachel Alexandra ran, then many would have ducked for an easier spot. If she skipped, then it created an opportunity for others to win without running against a monster. Campo needed to fill that race, and without a commitment from Jackson, he was treading water. Campo couldn't, in good faith, call a trainer and get him to commit his filly when Rachel Alexandra abstractly hovered over their shoulders. Which is why Charlie Hayward planned on doing something he had always vowed never to do.

∾

Hayward maintained that Saratoga is Saratoga, and that to court connections by bumping up a purse is a shallow way to draw the best horses. This track has the highest purses of any meet in the country, but when put in the same "race bracket," certain races like the Jim Dandy versus the Haskell Invitational, Saratoga versus Monmouth, the lines aren't so blurry. The Jim Dandy's purse is $500,000, run at 1⅛ miles, a table setter for the $1 million Travers that would occur four weeks later. The Haskell is $1 million, run at 1⅛ miles, and also occurs four weeks before the Travers. The extra $500,000 bumps all shares up 100 percent from the Jim Dandy for running the same distance and not having to travel too far for it. The only drawback is that the Jim Dandy gives a horse a race over the same surface as the Travers. But is that worth sacrificing an extra $500,000? Summer Bird planned on running in the Travers and prepped in the Haskell. Mine That Bird planned on running in the Travers and prepped in the $750,000 West Virginia Derby. The allure of Saratoga alone is not enough when other tracks are willing to purge their purse accounts to bump up for a marquee name. Hayward felt he had to bend.

For Hayward, sure, it was about Rachel Alexandra, but it was more about clarity, to give Campo some clarity. Hayward heard what Jess Jackson said publicly, that "the purses are a little low" for the Woodward and Personal Ensign. It was Hayward's feeling that the $1 million Pennsylvania Derby at Philadelphia Park was an outlier, an escape valve, used as a negotiating tool. Campo already expressed his frustrations during the huddle the day Rachel Alexandra breezed in the fog. "She worked five-eighths. Hopefully we'll know tomorrow," he said. "At this point, it is what it is." They would *not* find out the following day.

Hayward believed, or liked to believe, that Jackson would not take Rachel Alexandra to Pennsylvania. Calling Jackson's bluff at the risk of losing the filly would be devastating and something Hayward could not live with.

Hal Handel went to Campo and asked him what he would do. Would he increase the purse to the Woodward?

"Begrudgingly, I would do it," Campo said.

Handel brought this to Hayward, and then Hayward confirmed with Campo to "get a little color and insight." Campo and Hayward walked to NYRA chairman Steve Duncker's office and talked strategy about who would talk to Jackson and how to talk to Jackson. Since Handel had orchestrated the Beldame promotion with TVG, Hayward thought it best that Handel speak with Jackson. Handel called Jackson's agent and said, "We want to talk directly with Mr. Jackson about the purse for the Woodward. Why don't you have him call me?"

The message was that the purse for the Woodward would be bumped from $500,000 to $750,000. Handel's feeling was that they couldn't be presumptuous. They had to feel threatened by the Pennsylvania Derby. "So we talked to the trainer, we did everything we were supposed to do," Handel said. "Fortunately we have a nice relationship with Mr. Jackson from Curlin. I think he thinks that we try to showcase big horses and stars. I think the fact that went so well last time helped, like we had the credentials with him. I think that's a lot of this."

When Handel had Jackson on the phone, he pounced; he didn't want to make Jackson ask for the money. "We'd love to have you and we'd be happy either place she runs. If she's interested in the Woodward, we're prepared to make the Woodward $750,000 if that helps your decision making. The earliest you can tell us would help us with a bunch of things," said Handel. To this, Jackson said, "I'm very grateful. That's very nice of you."

Handel knew that they couldn't rush him. They must respect the meticulousness of his decisions. In other words, he wasn't someone you could call ten times and hound. There would be no negotiations; rather, NYRA went on the offensive. Handel said: "Listen, we hope you're going to consider the race. We're going to increase the purse to seven-fifty. We didn't make him ask for it which was the right way to do it."

Both Handel and Hayward worried that this could set an ugly precedent, that they would raise the purse for any star. But Rachel Alexandra, in their minds, was different. "You do something like this once every ten or twelve years," said Handel, "If someone says either you do 'X' or I run somewhere else, you let them run somewhere else. I think she transcends things right now. I think we're very comfortable with it."

In so doing the hope was that it would attract more than two or three horses, that there could be a field of seven, eight, or nine who would gladly finish second to Rachel Alexandra, maybe even charge late and beat her.

"More confusion and less clarity made it more difficult for P. J. to do his job, so that's really, why, begrudgingly, I was supportive of increasing the purse," Hayward said.

Campo's job starts earlier in the year, taking stall applications for an upcoming meet whether it is at Aqueduct, Belmont, or Saratoga. For Saratoga, this process takes place starting on June 1. Then he must carve out the racing conditions and publish the Condition Book. Campo writes the parameters for the race, its conditions.

For example:

ELEVENTH RACE   **STAKES**

The 140th Running of
THE SHADWELL TRAVERS
Grade 1
$1,000,000 (Up to $70,000 NYSBFOA)

FOR THREE YEAR OLDS. No nomination fee. $10,000 to pass the entry box. All starters will receive a $5,000 rebate. The purse to be divided 60% to the winner, 20% to second, 10% to third, 5% to fourth, 3% to fifth and 2% divided equally among remaining finishers. 126 lbs. Any horse that competes in both the Jim Dandy and the Shadwell Travers will have their entry fee waived for the Shadwell Travers. Starters to be named at the closing time of entries. Trophies will be presented to the winning owner, trainer and jockey.

Nominations Close Saturday, August 15, 2009

ONE MILE AND ONE QUARTER

Stakes races are drawn up in such a manner, while the claiming races and allowance races have far less detail. Once Campo has written the book, he then has to fill the races. Trainers see the Condition Book, take a look at their stock, and find races suitable for their horses.

Campo starts his morning on the backstretch at 6:00 a.m. by making himself available to trainers. He asks them what they think of the track, namely, its condition. Since Campo works closely with track maintenance chief, Glenn Kozak, and his people, they are able to tinker with the dirt as a chef does with spices. Anything racetrack related—jocks' room, placing judges, paddock judges, clockers, gap attendants—is under Campo's jurisdiction.

What gives Campo headaches is when he writes a card for a day that only has nine or ten races. In the book, there were thirteen or fourteen races, and oftentimes those races fill, but he can run only so many. So some races get pushed back to another day. There is then a surplus of twenty to thirty horses whose trainers wanted them to run on that day. The phone lights up and Campo must explain why he did what did. "Every day is a puzzle you've got to fit together. Those are a lot of the complaints," he said.

This Saratoga meet was unique in that two of the best horses, Rachel Alexandra and Kensei, on the grounds were owned by the same man, Jess Jackson. Add to that that Jackson waits an inexplicably long time when deciding where to enter his horses and it leaves Campo's puzzle without its most important pieces. Said Campo, "These weeks have been very frustrating for me because obviously when you have a set of connections with a lot of pieces of the puzzle and everyone is waiting to make their decisions, it just puts everything on hold. You can't plan. You can't plot. You can't try to get guys in races where they might belong because they're waiting for someone else's decisions. I'm a big planner. I like to have everything set in stone, put to bed. I'm not a fly-by-the-seat-of-my-pants type of guy. It makes things difficult for me, and it's frustrating because obviously you try to put on the best product every single day; some days are better than others. When you have those obstacles in the way, you have to adjust, take a deep breath, and hang on, and hopefully it works out for the best."

Never far from Campo's thoughts were the disaster scenarios, those circumstances where nothing works out as planned. In this case the expectations before the meet were incredibly high. "The complete disaster was Rachel doesn't run at all, Mine That Bird comes up with a minor issue, and Summer Bird supposedly was not training up to everyone's expectations," said Campo. "Those are your three Triple Crown winners a week ago. I'm saying to myself that the last two weekends are going to completely fall apart. You go from having every Triple Crown winner training here wanting to run, *supposed* to run . . . now nobody could run, and, believe me, that did cross my mind."

So when Hal Handel discussed raising the purse for the Woodward, it got Campo's attention. "I think it was a win-win," he said. "If she runs, she deserves to run for more money. I think it will attract a bigger, more quality field. The extra money does help. If she doesn't run and the money's there, you might even have a bigger field. I think that was a win-win situation when we sat down and discussed it. It's not something you do late in the game a lot, but hers definitely warrants doing it. She's a superstar. She's more than a superstar. Having her here on Closing Saturday makes such a huge difference, such a huge difference. It's going to be exciting."

That was, of course, if Jackson took the bait.

16

For Clarity's Sake

Mine That Bird went under. He would only be under for a few minutes while Dr. Patricia Hogan cleaned up the entrapped epiglottis. Dr. Hogan threaded a small hook with a blade as thin as an atom and cut away the excess flesh. Mine That Bird's epiglottis had developed a growth that kept closing over his windpipe. When she cut away the flesh it was as if there was a new throat.

The Kentucky Derby winner seemed fine.

∾

On Friday, August 21, 2009, three days after his surgery, Mine That Bird walked to the track to jog around the oval. He had scoped perfectly and would be tested today, albeit a minor test.

"Give him a leg up, let's go!" urged Chip Woolley.

George Smith bounded on Mine That Bird and walked out of the Stakes barn and into the Saratoga paddock. Half a dozen reporters trickled behind him with notebooks under their arms and pens in their ears. Mine That Bird strutted with his ears pointed forward, internalizing the scenery of towering oaks and pines.

In the stone dust of the horse path Mine That Bird stamped inverted "U's" as he embarked to the main track. Horses were scattered in every direction—some jogging, some sprinting, some standing. It was a thoroughfare, and George Smith put on his pinto's left blinker and walked onto the track.

Mary Ryan announced, "The nominations for the Shadwell Travers came out a few days ago and twenty-one three-year-olds were nominated for the Mid-Summer Derby. Rachel Alexandra is among the twenty-one nominees. Entries, I believe, will be coming this Wednesday." Then she saw the yellow saddlecloth from the Kentucky Derby, and with a smattering of applause from fence flowers, she said, "Remember, he's had a few days off after *minor* throat surgery."

Smith trotted Mine That Bird clockwise around the main track, in no hurry, as if the two were delivering the mail. They made another lap with the same sense of calm and slid down the path back to the paddock. Mine That Bird bucked a little bit, and Woolley, sitting with his broken ankle on the dashboard of a golf cart said, "He enjoys his time out. He don't want to go home."

Mine That Bird walked around the Stakes barn for several minutes and ducked into his stall. A vet scoped him, and Woolley saw that his throat looked "Perfect. It's smooth, if you laid it out flat. He's happy. He came off the track bounding, playful, all you can ask for now."

Woolley worried not about Mine That Bird's fitness but whether the throat would become inflamed or develop ulcers. He would use a liquid and flush it over the horse's throat to keep infection at bay. The circumstances upset Woolley. He understood that he had a superstar in Mine That Bird, a lovable whippersnapper of a horse that had moxie. So when he went under the knife, Woolley's stomach churned, so much so that he had stopped eating. "I feel a little better," he told reporters, "maybe my appetite will be better tonight."

∽

Later, Charlie Hayward reclined in his office chair with his phone pressed to his ear. On the other line was Chairman Steve Duncker's secretary. "I might try to contact him on his cell. We just heard from Jess Jackson."

∽

It was a short conversation, nothing more than a cordial thank-you, because NYRA had offered to beef up the Woodward should Rachel Alexandra run there instead of the Travers, or in Pennsylvania.

At the huddle, P. J. Campo alluded to the coming weeks, the final thirteen to fourteen racing days of the meet: "We're getting ready for next weekend, getting ready for an awful big week."

"You still don't expect to hear from Mr. Jackson until Monday?" Hayward said.

"I'm going to make things miserable for Pennsylvania with an overnight stake. We'll try to use thirteen or fourteen three-year-olds this week," Campo replied.

Back in Hayward's office he thought of the good news, good news for the time, but outdoors, lightning popped over his head and thunder shook the frames on the walls, including the picture of the great filly Ruffian, in her No. 3 saddlecloth, the one Hayward saw every day of the meet, a specter of greatness a dart's throw away.

∾

The following day the color pink was everywhere: ribbons on lapels, stripes on shirts, and ties with inverted conical knots. Today, August 22, 2009, was Alabama Day for three-year-old fillies, and they would run in the spirit of breast cancer awareness.

Hal Handel, with a pink tie in his hands, walked out of the administrative building with his wrists loose and flopping, standing on the stairs a few tiers above the rest of the huddle. "You look good in pink," he said to Bob Polombo, who smoked a cigarette and huffed under his breath. "How about Polombo? Oh."

"You questioning my manhood?" Polombo said.

"I'll leave that up to you," said Handel, as he stepped down, waving his tie like a gay pride banner. "Yoooohooooo! If you walk into certain bars with this, you ain't walkin' out."

"Heeeeyyy, got any daiquiris?" Polombo said.

Handel, looking at the huddle, saw that there were several groups of two to three people. "What a dysfunctional company, four separate huddles," he said.

The weather looked promising, though in the early hours the track looked like melted chocolate ice cream. Summer Bird, Tim Ice's trainee, was scheduled to have his last serious workout before the Travers. He had told the NYRA press people that he would be working out when the sun was up, after 8:00 a.m. But with the track reduced to slop, he snuck his colt out before the sun awoke. "We start early around here," Ice mused. He called an audible, an old trick trainers use to keep reporters off their backs. For the past few weeks reporters had walked past Ice and on to Woolley. Ice stood tall, dressed in his ball cap, T-shirt, jeans, and boots, smoking a cigarette and holding an extra-large coffee from Dunkin' Donuts. In the grassy interior of the Stakes barn he let Summer Bird graze while he hung on to a shank—a six-foot-long leash for horses—that was threaded through Summer Bird's halter. Summer Bird was just the opposite of Mine That Bird. NYRA's Bruce Johnstone had said that Mine That Bird "wasn't much to look at." He was ratty, spunky. Summer Bird was the picture of size and stamina, with his chestnut sheen and crackling white blaze. They shared the same sire, but perhaps one of the mares was sleeping with the milkman.

Ice lacked the distinctive features like Woolley's crutches, Stetson, and handlebar mustache, or D. Wayne Lukas's stable pony and leather chaps. All he did was finish sixth in the Kentucky Derby, win the Belmont, and finish second to Rachel Alexandra in the Haskell. Ice bided his time like a Sumatra Tiger crouched in the brush.

∽

After the second race Charlie Hayward presented a check for $10,000 to the Breast Cancer Research Foundation, a pink check with the routing number 121000298. He turned to Saratoga Springs Mayor Scott Johnson and said, "Lot of rain heading south of here."

Television cameras recorded the smiles, with Hayward on the left side of the check. Framed in their viewfinders, Hayward had a stern yet sympathetic countenance.

Hayward walked back to his office and overheard someone say, "Yeah, Rachel Alexander, she won the Belmont." Funny, the confidence folks have with their own facts.

∽

The smells of the track are abundant. With a sweeping pass of the grounds, popcorn and cotton candy hit one's nose. Mustard, pretzels, sausage with peppers and onions, and even stale Heineken, poured down a sewer. There were French fries and the heavy cream of Ben and Jerry's, as well as Dippin' Dots, the ice cream of the future.

And on today's card there was a six-way photo finish giving fans a thrill—and perhaps a merchandised photograph—that at any time and at any race they could see something special, that there was never a shortage of space under the wire.

In the paddock prior to the Alabama, Betsy Senior looked at her *Daily Racing Form* and said, "I'm not betting." Then she got a look at the Tote board and rethought, "3–8? That's a good bet."

Heading down the path from the paddock to his box a fan yelled out to Hayward, "Lose the politicians," a comment alluding to the mess in Albany that always postponed the groundbreaking for VLTs. "Bring them all to the track and gimme a big gun!" yelled Hayward. "I'll do life, but it'll be worth it!"

∽

In the grandstand paced Liz, a waitress with caramel skin and a crème brûlée smile. She flipped her tray around like a yo-yo and pocketed $100 just for walking by some high rollers. One such group owned a filly named Careless Jewel, who was approaching the starting gates for the Alabama. They ran up a significant tab, and Liz was by their side the entire time.

In two minutes, Careless Jewel would win the Alabama, gate to wire, by ten lengths.

❧

"We won the 'Bama! We won the 'Bama!" the owner yelled in the Saratoga Room.

Looking on were Hal Handel and Charlie Hayward, both with flutes of champagne. Hayward, munching on popcorn, smiled after each and every race, reliving the experience through replay after replay. He felt the energy. "By ten lengths, you gotta add ten lengths!" said Hayward. "You're gonna have some fun with this filly, I'll tell you that."

Standing by the door was Liz, in her white blouse and black shorts, her tray hanging by her side. She needed to make sure they didn't leave without paying the bill, a day's worth of drinks and food. The owner finally signed the tab and she thanked him. He hugged her. On the tray was a $300 tip.

17

The Fog Lifts

There could be no more waiting. Today, Monday, August 24, 2009, was the day that the racing world would find out just where Rachel Alexandra would race. NYRA did all it could do. It was a cool morning, better suited for windbreakers and long-sleeve T-shirts. A thin veil of fog hastily found its way to the clouds.

It had rained the night before and turned both tracks to soup. Rachel Alexandra and Kensei had spent their training time on the Oklahoma Training Track, but this morning it was too muddy, so the schedule was to have them work out at the now-sealed main track across Union Avenue.

A sign outside trainer Steve Asmussen's barn read:

Restricted Area

**Do Not
Enter**

**No Patrons
Allowed**

This was always the mood, but the sign made it official.

Asmussen arrived at 5:25 a.m. and was ready to send Kensei with his assistant trainer, Scott Blasi, to the main track. Dominic Terry got a leg up and walked beside Blasi and his pony. Asmussen roared his Escalade and then purred down the road to the main track.

It was dark with a layer of haze that made it tough to see across the pond of the main oval. Blasi barked up from his pony to Asmussen standing a few tiers higher in the grandstands, "It feels pretty good, Steve. It sounds pretty firm."

Horses breezed by and smacked the mud. The sound was uncomfortable, almost unnatural, like sprinting over pavement instead of grass.

Kensei whipped down the lane, slapping his hooves over the dirt highway. Asmussen swiveled his neck to watch Blasi shift his weight and gallop his pony around the turn to catch up to Kensei.

☙

Jerry Hissam and Calvin Borel sat in their golf cart outside the Restricted Area of Barn No. 65. Hissam stood and polished the windshield. Borel asked Amy Kearns, Rachel Alexandra's bodyguard, "Is she gonna work over here or over there?"

"I don't know yet," she said.

Asmussen appeared and said, "She's gonna go to the main track."

☙

Rachel Alexandra had never set a hoof on the main track, but there she was at the top of the lane with Blasi leading her out. The great cartoonist Pierre Bellocq drew a portrait prior to the Preakness Stakes of a Western saloon scene. All the horses and their connections tossed drinks around and then kicked them back. Then the piano music came to a halt, no more sharps or flats. In burst a pistol-wielding, hair-raising, bone-chilling, show-stopping, bipedal form of Rachel Alexandra. She had arrived, and the world be damned if it didn't take notice.

The fog still rested on her withers, yet her form came through, that distinctive torch blaze an apparition. Asmussen's ocean-blue saddle towels and the halogen-light white of the cotton on the horse's yoke shone through the haze. All eyes turned and faced her. She seemed like she was ten feet tall and three thousand pounds, and when she walked it registered a 5.9 on the Richter scale.

Blasi let them go and she skipped across the dirt and around the clubhouse turn, easily gaining speed. Blasi watched as his virtual daughter straightened out down the backstretch. He looked at his phone and clicked his stopwatch. Asmussen, up in the grandstands, leaned on the rail and started his watch with Jess Jackson's wife, Barbara Banke, on his wing. Calvin Borel joined them with his fiancée, Lisa Funk.

Jerry Hissam watched from ground level when Rachel Alexandra rocketed home, all by herself, the sound of her hooves a golf clap compared to the fraternity-paddle hooves—including Kensei's—that were heard just a few moments ago. Hissam watched, a bit worried: "Slow 'er down, son, slow 'er down." But that was just her, her own cruising speed, and her own comfort and relaxing clip was a full-on sprint to other horses. She made speed look like as smooth as chocolate truffles.

Borel came down the stairs and stood by Hissam. "Shew!" Borel said, shaking his head, the corners of his mouth curled high onto his lined face.

"That says a lot of words!" said Hissam. "Shew!"

∾

Rachel Alexandra's shoes clopped on the tar, leaving clods of dirt behind that marked her trail. Terry said to Asmussen, "Beautiful."

Then to the reporters, Asmussen said, "Once and only once, please."

Barbara Banke took to the forefront, speaking on behalf of her husband, saying that a press release would be coming shortly. Asmussen cut in, "I discussed it with Jess. Kensei is going to the Travers, and with that Rachel Alexandra is pointing to the Woodward."

18

A Good Guy

The sun was beginning to set on the Saratoga meet. On the final night of Week 4 Charlie Hayward was to be presented with the "Good Guy" award by the New York Turf Writer's Association at Saratoga National Golf Club.

Through towering doors angelic piano music filled the recesses of the room. The floor tiles were colored like beach sand, and the beams resembled Oregon redwoods. A staircase wrapped around the left side of the foyer, at last leading into the banquet hall, where a silent auction was in progress. Items included cigars, *Daily Racing Form* books, a gift certificate to the Wishing Well restaurant, and a Kendall-Jackson bottle of Curlin wine, with a minimum bid of $100, a $300 value.

Tasteful ceiling lights hung like stalactites. Ornamental swans stood static with wings fanned out. Sesame-seed rolls and room-temperature florets of butter sat on the tables, awaiting diners.

Outside, on the patio that overlooked the golf course, the air was comfortable and cool. The clouds, which smeared the sky, gave the appearance of being accidentally laundered with a red T-shirt.

Beggar's purses and other hors d'oeuvres were passed around on trays and served to trainers, jockeys, owners, and the myriad racetrack people on hand. Men whose work attire routinely consisted of Hawaiian shirts and loose khakis found it in them to wear a blazer and tie, but with the same loose khakis. Wedding bands glowed and diamonds shimmered on the fingers of those resting their limbs on the balcony, looking out over bamboo trees and the bubblegum sky.

More people walked in and stood at the rail of the balcony overlooking the entrance. It was like a scene out of *The Great Gatsby*, pampered elite summoned to be seen.

Charlie Hayward and Betsy Senior arrived and stood by the bar in the banquet hall and had a drink. A man walked up to Hayward and said, "For a tough guy you get the nice guy award."

While Hayward spoke, Senior reached into her handbag and revealed a thick Popsicle stick with Hayward's head on it—only his head had a jockey's helmet on top of it, courtesy of Photoshop. Several of Hayward's colleagues kept these tucked away.

When Charlie Hayward was president of Little, Brown, he turned its professional division from a flaccid branch into a profitable one. By 1996 its sales topped $40 million. Once it was profitable, Time Inc. sought to sell the division, this after Hayward resuscitated it. A spokesman for Time Inc. said that the division, which employed 150 workers, "was no longer a good fit," despite the fact that the division had kept the company afloat. Hayward thought of the 150 workers under him, how they were used and then promptly disposed of. His resignation, at age forty-four, shocked the New York publishing community. Hayward's motivation was said to be a "major difference in opinion." In fighting for himself, he fought for the others as well. Though he would land on his feet, the 150 workers under him might have had a harder time. Hayward's staff was said to be "totally devastated" by his sudden resignation.

Larry Kirshbaum, the new chairman of Time Warner Trade Publishing, said, "I'm very sad that Charlie is not staying. He's been a good friend and comrade these past five years. I wish him the best because he is the best." It was even reported that Kirshbaum had begged Hayward to stay.

Hayward's employees presented him with a book of *Bartlett's Familiar Quotations* (incidentally, published by Little, Brown). Cheryl McLean, head of human resources at Little, Brown, wrote the following as part of the gift to Hayward:

Charlie,

In just the short seven or so months that I've known you, you have become to me an inspiring model of servant leadership; you have demonstrated that rare balance of business acumen and compassion; and you have lived out the values of fairness and integrity. There is no better legacy to leave. I shall miss you greatly, and I shall remember you always.

Cheryl

Bill Phillips, editor in chief, wrote:

Charlie,

"The true teacher defends his pupils against his own personal influence. He inspires self-trust. He guides their eyes from

himself to the spirit that quickens him. He will have no disciple."
Bronson Alcott, father of Louisa May [noted Little, Brown author],
impecunious forger of daughter's note, and author of the perfect
description of the finest teacher I've known—you.

Your devoted student,
Bill

From Michael Pietsch, the current editor in chief:

Charlie,

If this were a book of our teachings on the biz it might need to be
bound in brown paper instead of red leather—but it would be *read*.

Thanks for making L.B. so exciting a place to work, and for all
you've taught. I'll miss you.

Michael

⌒⌣

Hugs and kisses were abundant and candlelight flickered guests' reflections in
glasses of water. People started to file into the room to sit at their assigned
tables. Charlie Hayward sat up front with his NYRA huddle, this time at a
roundtable. Hayward would be sharing the award with trainer Larry Jones,
who trained the ill-fated filly, Eight Belles, who broke down after the 2008
Kentucky Derby. Alan Garcia won as top jockey, Curlin won as best horse,
and Jess Jackson won as top owner.

Bill Heller, author of *Graveyard of Champions*, presented Hayward with
his award. As Hayward was called to the podium, his entire table put the
"Charlie Hayward heads" in front of their faces and waved them around like
a dozen jack-in-the-boxes. Hayward smiled. It was the kind of respect that
had always been shown to him, the kind that people at *Daily Racing Form*
and at Little, Brown illustrated in notes, the kind of respect when he saved
the franchise. Sure, he was an executive, and, that being so, many executives
are looked at with disdain, as if they are in some way better than all who
hold them up. But Hayward seemed different, even though he makes over
$400,000 a year, has a beautiful house on Fifth Avenue in Saratoga Springs,
drives a Volvo, and wears slick suits—underneath it all, he was motivated to
perform, a skier who looked to get down the mountain faster, yet he was no
different than those who populated the peanut gallery.

"In all seriousness," Hayward began, "I tell you, to share this award . . . Larry Jones is not a good guy, he's a great guy. To share this with him . . . I'm a good guy because I have great people working for me. I came through this business in the *Racing Form* and spent twenty-five years in publishing, so I've developed a great appreciation for the written word."

It seemed to the outsider that Hayward choked up. Betsy Senior knew how important the award meant to him, so perhaps she understood. She knew he wanted to tie in his publishing background. She knew he wanted to thank his staff and his team that pulled through to make it all possible. Senior thought that there was still a "ton of gratitude for those who got the franchise."

As Senior sat there, waving her Charlie Hayward "head," she thought that this award didn't surprise her. If he won five good guy awards, it wouldn't surprise her.

Week Five

19

One Tough Throat

Peculiar, on the same day that Rachel Alexandra's connections gave her the go in the Woodward Stakes, a story by Ed Fountaine ran in the print edition of the *New York Post*. It was not formally announced that she was running until 6:30 a.m. Monday morning, which meant that the edition went to press Sunday night.

> SARATOGA SPRINGS—The guessing game is finally over. Rachel Alexandra will make her next start in the Grade 1 Woodward Stakes here on Sept. 5, the final Saturday of this meet, and the New York Racing Association will raise the purse from its current $500,000 to an as-yet-undisclosed amount, probably $750,000, according to a NYRA source.
>
> Hal Handel, NYRA executive vice president and chief operation officer, said yesterday he could not comment, either to conform or deny the report.
>
> "Hopefully we'll have something to announce [today]," Handel said.
>
> The spokesperson for Jess Jackson, owner of Rachel Alexandra, did not respond.
>
> In the Woodward, at her preferred distance of a mile-and-an-eighth, "Alexandra the Great" will face older male horses for the first time after beating 3-year-old colts twice this year—in the Preakness and the Haskell.
>
> Some of the greatest thoroughbreds of all time have won the Woodward in its 55-year history, but it's never been won by a 3-year-old filly.

Yet "Rachel" will be odds-on against a nondescript field of older horses while carrying 118 pounds to their 126, getting a five-pound break for being a 3-year-old and a three-pound break for being a filly.

Hal Handel sat at his desk and minded his work when he was jarred by Charlie Hayward. Hayward stomped into his office with a rolled up *New York Post* in his hand and said, "They ran the story last night." "How the hell did he get it last night when they decided it this morning?" asked Handel. "They announced it 6:30 this morning." Hayward replied, "This was printed yesterday. 'Guessing game is finally over where Rachel is going to make her next start. . . . The Woodward purse is going to go from 500 to 750.'"

"How the hell did he get it last night when they decided it this morning?" asked Handel.

"They announced it 6:30 this morning. This was printed yesterday. 'Guessing game is finally over where Rachel is going to make her next start. . . . The Woodward purse is going to go from 500 to 750.'"

"Someone talked to him last night. I know two people who didn't."

"It says, 'Hal Handel couldn't comment to either confirm or deny the report. Hopefully we'll find out something else today.'"

"So he ran with it anyway."

"He must have gotten it from somebody."

"Who would talk to him?"

"It had to be someone from their camp," Hayward said, referring to Jess Jackson.

"That's possible," said Handel.

Dan Silver walked in behind Hayward and saw the story in Hayward's hands. "I have no idea where that came from," Silver said.

"What?" asked Hayward.

"Are you talking about Bossert's thing today?"

"No, I'm talking about Fountaine."

"That's what I meant. It said a NYRA source?"

"It said . . ." and Hayward motioned to the article.

"I think it said a NYRA source," Silver said. "Maybe that was Bossert's. One of them had an article today that said . . ."

"Well," Handel interjected, "they're both pissed off about being scooped on the Beldame."

Hayward read from the article, "'Purse probably boosted to 750 according to a NYRA source.'"

"It wasn't me," Handel said. "Fountaine walked up to me in the paddock and I said I wasn't going to comment on it. He said, 'Does that mean you're denying it?' I said, 'I'm not commenting on it.'"

"What did Bossert write?" Hayward said, turning to Silver.

"I think Fountaine's what I meant," Silver said. "I just saw that today that he had said the horse was coming to the Woodward, and that was before anything was said."

"The decision is done," Hayward said, "she's running in the Woodward."

"Where did he get that from?" Silver asked.

"And they announced it this morning after the horse works," Handel said.

"The only person who could have definitively know wouldn't have been us," Hayward said. "We didn't know."

"Jackson's camp," Handel said.

"It must have been," Silver said. "Like I said that note I got from the father's exercise rider two days ago. They must have told someone something."

"Remember we heard that they booked the hotel already," added Handel. "We knew that. Maybe Fountaine felt that he needed to get in front of one."

"Take a shot," said Hayward.

"And take a shot," said Handel.

"Right. It's interesting. Why print the facts?"

"Why start *now* is the better question."

❧

It being the week of the Travers, it was time for Mine That Bird to show something, to show that he could bounce back from his surgery and be a contender. When he walked around the shed row of the Stakes barn, all that could be heard was the scratching of a spring rake on the gravel. Summer Bird, wearing his Haskell Invitational blanket, walked around the barn as well.

Like a storm cell approaching from the Southwest, Mark Allen, the gruff part owner of Mine That Bird, arrived for this workout. His black garb and black hat cast an ominous pall over the morning, as if he were an undertaker.

Jamie Theriot, a regular rider at this Saratoga meet, and a Cajun jock from the mold of Calvin Borel, rode Mine That Bird for his workout. He started Mine That Bird slowly and let him loose down the lane, galloping out strong. It was exactly what trainer Chip Woolley wanted, and needed, to see.

❧

Trainer Nick Zito saw good things from his colt, Our Edge. The past two workouts suggested that this horse was as sharp as any of the 1,800 horses in any stall on the grounds. Over the Oklahoma Training Track, a track known to be deeper and to produce slower workout times, Our Edge blitzed over the surface. He blasted a half-mile work in 46.70 seconds. A normal work over a fast track is 48 seconds. His following work was five furlongs, or five-eighths of a mile in 59.55 seconds. Both workouts were the fastest out of any other horse breezing on those days. This left no question who would go to the front in the Travers.

Following a Saturday workout, the next day Our Edge walked around the barn. Zito surveyed him and said: "This is kind of a roll of the dice. I think the main thing is that this is a step up, but the horse is working great and he's coming off three wins in a row. All of these horses are very good. We're going to try running in the big race. There is racing after the Triple Crown. Everybody forgets that . . . it's silly."

∿

Chip Woolley clicked along, his body moving like a pendulum, as he left Mine That Bird's stall with Mark Allen behind him, cloaked in black, a shadow. Allen's attendance felt troubling, as if he were policing Woolley, to dictate his terms and to ensure that they were carried out. He may also have wanted to see Mine That Bird work, since it was his most important drill of the year, all things considered.

"He scoped good, the doctor was happy with the way he looked," Woolley said. "He worked real nice. I told Jamie I was looking for forty-nine; he let him go right back at the wire. He looked pretty sharp."

Woolley swayed on his crutches. His Kentucky Derby belt buckle glimmered, and his Super Bowl-style ring for winning the Derby matched the buckle. "As of today, he looked good. We'll scope him again tomorrow at 7 to 7:30. He looked good striding past the wire. He's gotta come first."

It was queer that Woolley said that they would scope him again, this after he was scoped after the surgery, then scoped after this workout. To scope him again the following day to see if having scoped him caused irritation seemed superfluous. It was as if they were using Mine That Bird as their own voodoo doll, pricking him in the throat as an "excuse" not to run him.

In 1985 Hall of Fame trainer D. Wayne Lukas sent Tank's Prospect to the gates after this surgery and won the Arkansas Derby. "It worked for me, but they're all different," Lukas said. "If there are no complications, it'll heal after forty-eight hours."

There were no hidden agendas: Woolley and Allen wanted to run Mine That Bird in the Breeders' Cup Classic on November 7, 2009, and perhaps there was a rift between the two as to the avenue by which to arrive there. Woolley had been at Saratoga for a month, and he had to think that if Mine That Bird won the Travers at a distance (the same mile and a quarter that he won the Derby at) then he should certainly relish that it would lock up the Champion Three-Year-Old title. Should he not run, then the door would swing open for Summer Bird and others. Still, Woolley came back to the same point, with Allen standing at his back: "Any doubt at all, we won't run him. I'll tell you more in the morning."

The sun hung beams in the air and sliced through the pines by the administrative building. Entries and the post draw for the Travers were on today's slate. For many involved, today was an exciting day, one that signified that one of the country's premier races from its premier track was fast approaching.

From fifty yards away, NYRA press officer, Dan Silver, took ground-punishing strides from the paddock, imprinted his feet on the dirt with heavy heels, and stepped up to the administrative building. Someone asked, "How'd he scope?" Silver turned his back, threw his hands in the air, swung the door open like an action hero, and disappeared.

Silver, two minutes later, peered around the corner, his voice hurried, "Mine That Bird is out of the race."

Charlie Hayward and Hal Handel walked the grounds before the gates opened like two Gregorian monks. They expressed their disappointment that Mine That Bird would, in fact, skip the Travers. The disappointment went beyond losing his star power; he was the Derby winner, an underdog, an unpleasant, hard-knocking gelding with a chip on his shoulder. He was *American*.

"They have this horse here for a month," said Hayward.

"I think there may have been a divide between the owner and the trainer," said Handel. "It's been discussed that there were problems with his running style. You get owners like that, and they turn into geniuses. We've seen that before."

"It was a mistake to run that horse in that bull ring at Mountaineer," said Hayward.

Handel replied, "They said he lost something like fifty or sixty pounds after that race. He came up here and put it all back on. It's just a shame. He's great, got great charisma."

P. J. Campo looked as if his soul had been stripped from him. Hal Handel approached him and gave him a high five. "Good luck," he said, and rubbed Campo's freshly buzzed head.

Hayward said, "With that, I'll start with Mr. Silver."

Despite the morning's proceedings, despite all that furrowed his brow, Silver said nothing. Hayward looked at him understandingly: "Mr. Campo?"

"Yes! . . . Well, let's see how this morning has been," said Campo. "Mine That Bird is not running in the Travers as of 8:30, and there's a possible hurricane on Saturday coming up the East Coast. Other than that, it's been a great day."

"Mine That Bird is parading next weekend," Silver said, regarding Mine That Bird's presumed plans to be the grand marshal at Ruidoso Downs in New Mexico the weekend following the Travers.

"After hearing Mr. Campo, I suggest we have Bloody Marys at the breakfast and prepare for a hurricane," said Handel.

∽

The day was fraught with hurdles. Mine That Bird was a kick, two kicks, to the proverbial groin.

Prior to the post draw for the Mine That Bird-less Travers, there was a breakfast buffet at the At The Rail Pavilion. Handel filled his plate with food and sat down: "Now you see why racing secretaries age fast. Drown our sorrow in food. Sometimes you just have to eat."

John Ryan, senior vice president and chief administrative officer, said, "I'll go and say, 'Can I have your tie, belt, and shoelaces?' "

Handel laughed. "Do it with a straight face. He could use a pick-me-up. When you're doing that and you have the Derby winner snatched up . . ." Handel shook his head and forked the food on his plate.

∽

Underneath the oaks of the paddock, the Post Draw lacked the energy that having the Derby winner would have provided, but it was an event for those who still had a shot at winning the race. Dan Silver emceed the event, calling up horses' names one by one with a post position assigned. "Warrior's Reward," he said.

To this Charlie Hayward leaned and whispered to Hal Handel, "That's my horse." Then, when he realized Calvin Borel would be riding Warrior's Reward, he added, "They really stiffed Calvin this meet."

Borel, up until this point, had less than thirty mounts, nearly unheard of for someone of his profile. Borel's brother, Cecil, and even his agent, Jerry Hissam, thought there might be some prejudice, but the reality was, and is, that New York trainers have their jockeys, and they have unwritten bonds that say that John Velazquez rides first call for Todd Pletcher, Alan Garcia for Kiaran McLaughlin, and Kent Desormeaux for Bill Mott.

Borel's eye was glossed in blood, as if he'd been bare-knuckle-punched. It turns out that an extension cord whipped him in the eye when he opened the door to his place. He saw a doctor to make sure it wasn't infected. He shook his head and said, "I always get hurt when I mess around with the house. I can ride a horse, but I'm accident prone."

Hayward saw Chip Woolley enter the paddock hobbling in on his crutches, his eyes hidden behind black lenses. Hayward said to Handel, "Can you send them a rent check? Isn't the stakes barn for horses who run here?" Handel broke away and approached Woolley, extending his hand and condolences: "Charlie was asking who do we send the rent bill to." Charlie hustled up to Woolley and shook his hand. Woolley said, "It's a bummer."

P. J. Campo watched him enter the paddock the entire way, eyeballing him with the bottled rage of a husband who just discovered his wife's lover trespassing on the davenport. His face instantly looked sunburnt. Listening to Woolley spout excuses, Campo said, "It's all an act. It's a fuckin' act."

Hayward and Handel came back to Campo. Campo said, "He's taking one for the team."

"He had a chance," Hayward said.

"Of course!" exclaimed Campo.

"It's something," Handel said, "there's never a straight road, is there?"

And the three walked down the horse path, united in mood and temper.

•

20

The Travers Stakes

Tropical Storm Danny loomed five hundred miles south-southeast off of Cape Hatteras, with maximum sustained winds of 60+ mph. The storm lumbered at a speed of thirteen miles per hour. The projected path would buzz up the East Coast and not even clip New York State. There seemed to be some wobble room that Saratoga's most popular day would be dry.

In the infield of the main track a flock of seagulls flew into the wind to the eastern side of the lake. They seemed suspended in midair, a near-ominous act of witchcraft.

Charlie Hayward's voice became raspy, his coughs violent.

Nick Zito's Our Edge was ready. Zito thought that he had his work cut out for him, but, as he was wont to say, that's why they run the races.

Maxine Correa, the exercise rider with the strawberry-blonde hair, loved Our Edge. She thought him to be "wonderful, very pleasant to be around." She said he was "an all-round cool horse. He doesn't do anything bad, loves to train."

She breezed and galloped his father, The Cliff's Edge, who finished second in the 2004 Travers behind Birdstone, both Nick Zito trainees. The Cliff's Edge lost his shoes on a muddy track at Churchill Downs in the Kentucky Derby that same year.

Zito conversed with Robert LaPenta, the owner of Our Edge. LaPenta's Da'Tara shocked the 2008 Belmont Stakes by wiring the field, defeating the heavily favored Big Brown, spoiling yet another Triple Crown bid. The first time Zito played spoiler was in 2004 with Birdstone while defeating Smarty Jones. He and LaPenta talked about the upcoming race and about what it takes to keep a horse sharp for so many weeks, to get him to peak after nearly six weeks on the shelf. "Like I said, it's what we're supposed to do," said Zito.

For the time, Zito pre-knotted his ties and hung them in his truck, along with his shirts and sweater vests, which hung from dry-cleaning hangers. The fighter was wrapping his wrists.

∽

On the day before the Travers, Charlie Hayward approached P. J. Campo, and spoke with a rasp: "Sounds like we might get rain tonight. Are we trying to stay on the turf if we can?"

"We'll do everything possible," Campo said.

"We did good yesterday," Don Lehr said. "It was a very good day. I was concerned that we had only 12–13,000. We had 16,537. It surprised me. We were only down 11 percent. Today is shaping up okay. The lots are full. The tables are full. We did almost 23,000 last year, one-day carry, 4.2 on-track, 15, almost 16 all-source."

"You want the over?" Hal Handel said.

Lehr shot him a sideways look, "Uh, no."

Smiling, Handel said, "Thought I'd ask him."

"It looks like the tropical storm will have no effect on us," continued Lehr. "We'll get some rain tonight. It will be cloudy, but it will clear up by mid-morning. We're really dodging some bullets."

∽

Bullets, millions of them. Tropical Storm Danny bucked his northeast trend and brought his wrath inland, threw a ball at a target, and dunk-tanked Saratoga Race Course. Only Saratoga Race Course wasn't surfacing. While Saratoga drowned in water, streams dripped from the eaves, and puddles ballooned. Still, the people came because, after all, it was Travers Day.

Mud, tents, umbrellas, ponchos. Steam swirled from one's breath. It was a nasty day, but as NYRA handicapper Andy Serling's Twitter feed read, "What's a little rain anyway? It was worse in 1987 when Java Gold won the best Travers I ever saw and who remembers that weather?" And with five major stakes on the card, there would be ample opportunity in the Saratoga Room to drown one's sorrows with champagne and to eat cheese, chips, and popcorn.

Charlie Hayward glued his frame to his bed the night before. He had eaten a heaping plate of spaghetti and was lying low. Hal Handel had to take over the huddle for Travers Day, since Hayward stayed in to nurse his cold, something Betsy Senior saw coming from furlongs out. Still, Hayward planned on arriving later in the morning.

"It's time to 'muddle,'" Handel said, referring to the rainy, muddy conditions. "We'll start with our most senior member."

"I have nothing to add," said Bob Polombo.

"That's very helpful. Way to start Travers Day," replied Handel.

Campo, with a look of frustration, looked at the Tote and saw that the odds were incorrect for Race 1. "The board is screwed up. I don't know who fixes that."

"That's an auspicious way to start the day," Handel said. "It's going to be that kind of day. There's a lot that we are not in control of today, so we need to control the things we can: bathrooms, ATM machines, *help* people. They are going to be wet and miserable. Do what we can for the people here, make the tents secure, all of that stuff. It's easy to feel sorry for ourselves."

"We're staying ahead of the game," said Kim Justus, director of Guest Services.

"We're pumping water, sweeping puddles, trying to control what we can, like you said," Kevin added.

"We had a perfect day last year," Don Lehr said.

"How do you feel about today?" asked Handel.

"8.2 (on track) and 37 (off track)," Lehr replied.

"Wow," said Handel.

"I have no prognostications," said Lehr.

"The people will look at us," Handel continued. "Customers identify us whether they hate us or not. Everyone, today we can walk with our hands in our pockets and say, 'Woe is me.' We'll take some blows. Today it's about attitude. Let's try and enjoy today. If you're asked, it's about horse safety. If the track is sealed, tell them why it's sealed. We don't want the casual fans thinking we're doing anything improper. If you're depressed, go have some champagne."

∽

Prior to Race 3, with the ever-present backdrop of rain, it was announced that Nick Zito's Our Edge would run with two bar shoes. This was a peculiar announcement, but Zito insisted that Our Edge had won all his races in bar shoes so he figured it was best to leave well enough alone. Still, a bar shoe, which has a metal bridge between the open spaces of the horseshoe, is meant to protect the vulnerable part of the hoof. Over a fast track the bar shoes could work, but over a muddy track they might be disastrous. A man approached Zito and asked him about the bar shoes. "You just hope they like it," Zito said.

∽

At 11:45 a.m. Calvin Borel rested in the jocks' room, face down, getting a massage.

∽

Charlie Hayward, with a phlegmy cough, a raw throat, and feeling run down, shared an umbrella with Hal Handel in the paddock. Hayward, reflecting on when Mine That Bird won the Derby on a muddy track said, "Mine That Bird would've liked this track."

Handel made a comment about a German horse in the upcoming race, Salve Germania, that it had a zero shot at winning the Grade 2 Ballston Spa on the turf.

Hayward and Steve Duncker went up to the chairman's box in the front row at the wire. Race caller Tom Durkin said a horse "sashayed" in the race, and Duncker turned to Hayward and said, "C'mon, Hayward, you gotta give him some love for that!"

Bombing down the lane, Salve Germania won at 24–1.

Hayward said, "24–1 shot wins? Nobody Pick 6."

"Nobody Pick 6," Duncker said.

"That eight was flying," said Hayward.

"I think I'm presenting," Duncker said.

"You better get your ass down there. How's your German?" asked Hayward.

"*Ich bin ein Berliner*," replied Duncker.

Back in the Saratoga Room, Hayward and others sipped from flutes of champagne, with Hayward saying, "Hal was denigrating that horse, denigrating! Wasn't he?" Then, in a moment reminiscent of blitzkrieg, the door to the Saratoga Room swung open. It was Handel. "Salve! Germania!" he exclaimed.

~

The deluge regressed into a drizzle as Calvin Borel headed out to the paddock for the 140th running of the Travers Stakes. Warrior's Reward, the runner-up in the Jim Dandy, waited for Borel in the paddock. Fans yelled to Borel from the fences, rooting him on and tossing out Rachel Alexandra anecdotes.

Kensei, Rachel Alexandra's stablemate, had his mane tied in knots so it looked as if ants had crawled in a line up his neck. It was time to see if it was worth running Kensei instead of Rachel Alexandra in this spot. *Daily Racing Form's* Dave Grening asked, "Why would you run your second best horse in this race? It's like trying to win a game with your second string."

Tim Ice, trainer of Summer Bird, saddled his strapping chestnut colt. He ran well in the mud at Monmouth, so the feeling was that he would like this track. Mine That Bird's absence promised to give Summer Bird more attention, possibly respect.

There was a field of seven horses heading to the gates, with Nick Zito's Our Edge saddled and ready to roll the dice.

"Should be a fine race," Hal Handel said, while watching the horses in the paddock. "Hope they get home in one piece."

❧

The apron swelled with a focused energy on the starting gates. All the horses lined up. The crowd of 34,221 came to a head. The gate blasted open.

Nick Zito's eyes fixed on Our Edge, watching him with the rest of the field blurred in the background. Something was off. Our Edge, taken to the lead by Alan Garcia, took an awkward step in the slop. Zito watched with unease, chewing his gum. On the far turn Zito turned his attention from his television screen and saw that his horse had been eased.

❧

Meanwhile, the race went on, with Kensei taking the lead with three-quarters of a mile to go. No sooner had he struck the front did Summer Bird soar off the turn, three paths from the fence. Under Kent Desormeaux, Summer Bird straightened and widened by two lengths ahead. Still widening, he broke through the wire three and a half lengths in front to win the $1 million Travers Stakes.

Hold Me Back closed for second. Charitable Man clopped in behind Quality Road. Warrior's Reward, with Calvin Borel, flattened. Next came Kensei, the heralded stablemate to Rachel Alexandra. And last of all was Our Edge, who did not finish.

Hal Handel, watching the race in the NYRA box, yelled, "Rachel destroyed that horse, destroyed him, and he just won the Travers. How *GOOD* is Rachel?"

❧

Trainer Tim Ice's feet, clad in dress shoes, the cuffs of his slacks perfectly tailored, sank in the mud. His horse, like his sire, won the Belmont Stakes and the Travers Stakes, the thirtieth horse to do so.

All those mornings, ever since Summer Bird and Tim Ice took up residence in the Stakes barn, he and his horse were passed over. Summer Bird was even dubbed "The Other Bird." Ice had stood in the courtyard of the Stakes barn with Summer Bird's shank while the horse tugged at grass, minding his business, and Ice puffed on a cigarette or sipped his extra-large cup of Dunkin' Donuts coffee. "Whatever you guys want to call him, 'The Other Bird,' he's won the Belmont Stakes and the Travers," he said.

His words were spoken like a man who had gotten his redemption in the best way possible: between the lines, where actions roar and words flutter to the ground with lifeless intent.

❧

Nick Zito was back at his barn thirty minutes after the race. On his patio table, which had beaded up with water, were an open bottle of sparkling Saratoga water and a soaked cardboard coffee cup sleeve from Uncommon Grounds. Zito walked an uneven line around his barn. Our Edge had grabbed two quarters, meaning he chunked the quarter part of his hooves, the inner part, similar to the arch of the human foot. He also lost his front shoe. "Bar shoes, tough, tough," Zito said. "He wore them his last three times. When the track gets muddy here, it's the worst."

The replay streamed from his office, and Zito and Maxine Correa watched it. "He probably lost it leaving the gate," Zito said. "Here's the replay. He lost it leaving the gate! Poor horse. Poor horse, both quarters."

"He looked so good, acted so great," Correa said.

"Look how bad the track is. Saratoga is the most insane thing. Like he was wearing combat boots. Right there he could have lost it, he's not comfortable," said Zito. Then, on the replay, that awkward step he took, Zito finally saw it. "That's where he lost it!"

Then Zito put a hand on Correa's shoulder. He considered her a second wife. Zito marveled over what a good wife and mother she was. Correa wore a black dress, and her hair, normally balled up under a jockey helmet, was wavy and shoulder length, like vines of ivy. "She looks different, huh?" Zito said and smiled.

Zito walked down the backside of his barn, gesturing as if he were throwing a rock to skip across a pond, his head hanging. Our Edge was bathed by an entourage of trainers, grooms, and a vet, and after getting hosed off, his ears were pricked and alert. "How's it look, doc?" asked Zito.

"Not bad," replied the vet.

"I'm happy, knock wood," said Zito, as he tapped his knuckles on a nearby tree.

Zito thought about the bar shoes and how they're great on a fast track, that you train with them, but wouldn't want to race with them. But what about Our Edge's other races? He had run so well, had won three races with them, so Zito kept using them. Today, the mud, the circumstances, the track, it sucked that boot right off his hoof. Zito, as if he himself had been injured, walked unsteadily back to his office, the bottom of his blazer swaying.

"Aw, shit," he said.

21

Comings and Goings

The morning was cool and light with the fog exiting the premises as if it were chased away by the police. It was Rachel Alexandra's first work since the announcement that she would tackle older males—and history—in the $750,000 Grade 1 Woodward Stakes in five days. It seemed that even with the meet five weeks old, and with only one more to go, it was finally taking shape. So much hinged on Rachel Alexandra being in attendance, tacked, and in racing form.

Assistant trainer to Steve Asmussen, Scott Blasi, escorted Rachel Alexandra to the Oklahoma Training Track and watched her break off. Blasi was one of many watching her train on this Monday morning. Hundreds of spectators and members of local and national media outlets lined the rail like cookies on a tiramisu. All squinted to watch Rachel Alexandra, ridden by exercise rider Dominic Terry, as she entered the first turn. With dozens of other horses jogging, galloping, and breezing, it was difficult to pick out Terry's checkered sleeves, as they were the only sign that the horse that was being watched was, in fact, Rachel Alexandra.

At the top of the stretch, photographers peered through viewfinders, panning around the final curve waiting for the horse's stylish body to come into view. One had to be sharp to pick her out, since she moved with such swift ease that she hardly made a sound, as if she traveled at the speed of her tympanic waves, Rachel Alexandra, noise embodied. She was not breathing hard. Air came in through her nose as gently as it went out, yet she clipped along as if her hooves were winged like Mercury. But there she went, on her orbit around the track, straightening out down the lane, her massive hind quarters like two boulders married at a narrow axis. She skimmed over the dirt, to the delight of many admirers on the rail, running into the eastern sky strewn with fish-fillet clouds of a most electric pink.

As reporters and photographers meandered back to trainer Steve Asmussen's barn looking for insights only horsemen can provide, a mile away an exodus of sorts was being planned by another horse and its connections, a horse whose hopes were every bit as high as Rachel Alexandra's.

❦

Sad. It wasn't supposed to be like this. But when Mine That Bird, the winner of the 2009 Kentucky Derby, developed an entrapped epiglottis two weeks before the Travers Stakes, there was a collective groan that so often comes when hinging one's expectations on the health of a thoroughbred racehorse.

On Tuesday, September 1, 2009, at 2:30 a.m., Mine That Bird's connections planned to put him on a trailer and ship him out as anonymously has he had entered racing lore some four months earlier.

The morning air was so cold it pinpricked the skin. The moon was startling, both in its brightness and size, the roads were barren, save for the rumble of cars and semis on the nearby Interstate, and, overhead, the street lamps buzzed, hard at work.

At the Stakes barn, dirt crunched underneath a pair of bike tires as two NYRA peace officers stood guard, like they did every morning and evening. One woman expressed her sadness that Mine That Bird, whom she called "Minor Bird," would be leaving. He left quite the impression on those he touched, because he was the horse who "wasn't supposed to win." Mine That Bird had such spunk and attitude, often pinning his ears back before taking a snap, a bad poker tell tipping off that he was sitting on a full house. Woolley, who had no horses at Saratoga besides his Derby winner, bore his teeth at Mine That Bird, and Mine That Bird bore right back. The two were wed in the Church of Underdogs. Both were rough around the edges, Woolley a former bareback rodeo rider, Mine That Bird always having to prove his ability.

The Brook Ledge horse van purred, breaking up the tranquility of the morning. The driver, thankfully, cut the engine, restoring the mood. Soon, Mine That Bird would be heading south to Newark, New Jersey, where he would be FedExed to El Paso, Texas. From there it would be another van ride to New Mexico's Ruidoso Downs to be paraded in front of the hometown crowd.

The air was not just cool, but cold to the skin, a reminder that the leaves would soon be changing and that apples would be ripe for picking. The courtyard of the Stakes barn showed elastic shadows. Blackened trees lined an off-black sky pricked with pinholes of light. A ghoulish horse with milky eyes tugged at its hay bag for a midnight snack. This horse was the only one awake, 2:45 a.m. being early even for these chronic early risers.

But now, strangely, both Woolley and his assistant and exercise rider, George Smith, were absent. In a matter of moments, Mine That Bird was to leave, but where were his handlers?

A truck bearing allegiance to the Philadelphia Eagles sped up and backed into the elbow macaroni driveway of the Stakes barn, and out poured

Woolley and Smith. "Tell me you got coffee going. Please," Smith said as he hustled to Mine That Bird's Stall No. 9, tucked into the far corner. Woolley, with alarming pace, sped as fast as he could on his crutches. They clicked with such cadence that they sounded like chattering teeth.

The scene resembled a prison break where the guards threw up their hands and said, "Why not?" Smith, filling a wheelbarrow with supplies, balanced as best he could and swiveled like a drunkard as he loaded the truck. He called back to Woolley, "I left those papers on that bucket."

Woolley's crutches leaned against the far wall as he disappeared into the stall, hopping on his good leg. It was at this point that all the horses—a dozen or so—woke and stirred. There was the newly minted Travers winner Summer Bird, Mine That Bird's neighbor, snacking on hay. One horse whinnied and was soon joined by others, a farewell chorus for the Derby winner.

Woolley, still hobbling, threaded a lead shank through Mine That Bird's halter and let him out of his stall. Mine That Bird stood in the corner. His shadow against the far wall amplified his pinto frame, the outline of his body etched in sharp precision.

Smith filled the wheelbarrow with one more load and followed his own path to the trailer that had since roared back to life at the turn of a key.

Woolley leaned his armpits onto his crutches and cinched Mine That Bird to his right side. Mine That Bird, the horse with so much spunk and attitude, walked kindly by his trainer almost as if he were walking Woolley and not the other way around, like a friend pushing a wheelchair. And in some ways, no statement could be truer. After all, before the Kentucky Derby, Woolley was 1 for 32. Mine That Bird finished second in the Preakness, third in the Belmont, and third in the West Virginia Derby.

So the pair took abbreviated steps, with Mine That Bird's head darting around. Horses in neighboring stalls stuck their noses out to get a whiff of the figurative cologne of roses once draped over Mine That Bird's withers four months earlier.

The Derby winner left an impression. Mine That Bird's footprint differs from that of any other in the country, maybe in the world, in that it is accompanied by the circle of a rubber stub from a pair of crutches.

The trailer's ramp slammed down, slanting into the trailer's cavity like a tongue, as Smith stood inside, awaiting his roommate, ensuring that all four of his legs would be safe and comfortable.

A garden hose hissed, filling up a bucket of water for Mine That Bird. Smith handed Woolley the papers to sign, and Woolley, in passing, exchanged a few words to a peace officer. Two NYRA security trucks were parked in waiting to see off the Derby winner.

Woolley, assisted by his crutches, walked to the other side of the van and climbed into the cab without a word to anyone. A red light cast a raspberry film over his black cowboy hat, as if he were in the hold of a submarine, the light somehow reflecting an inner anger over his stay in Saratoga that was, in essence, unfulfilled. Someone said, "And so it's over."

The driver shifted the trailer into gear, easing away from the Stakes barn and brushing up against the low-hanging branches. The gears clunked as the trailer stopped at the blinking red light at the intersection of Lincoln and Nelson Avenues.

It turned left onto Nelson, at first moving slowly and then picking up speed. In a lot of ways, it was similar to Mine That Bird's running style: slow early, explode late.

High above an immense population of stars shimmered across a violet sky. Light years below went the trailer, its red taillights shrinking before it bent out of sight on its way south to New Jersey. There went Mine That Bird, leaving Saratoga Springs as anonymously as he had entered the sport, another star shining without the light of day.

Week Six

22

The Rachel Show

Rachel Alexandra had, at last, taken the stage in full for her soliloquy. Broadway, from south to north, starting at the chimney sweep's van that read "For Christmas consume less, save more" and "Why Not Give Up War for Lent?" all the way to the would-be construction site for the new Saratoga Springs City Center, was flagged with Woodward promotion. Namely, it was all Rachel Alexandra. The flags slanted and whipped in the wind displaying a drawing of her face and that distinctive torch blaze. Another flag read, "Run Like a Girl." Saratoga Springs had caught the fever.

In the window of Saratoga Saddlery leaned a framed photograph, the size of a second grader, of Rachel Alexandra working out. The shot was a close-up of her bowed head, her mane cascading like the flowing locks of a Hollywood starlet, her nostrils huffing fire, her amber eyes ringed in red. Through the window, on a nearby wall, one could view a painting of Calvin Borel. The two, even in the artist's renditions, were paired, two kindred spirits, human and horse.

As was customary, Charlie Hayward started his week with coffee and a radio spot with Paul Vandenburgh. Vandenburgh's complimentary breakfasts, his view of the horses that were training, and the eastern sun's beams illuminating his table would soon be traded for his studio in Albany.

Hayward, with five weeks in the books, noted that, despite some strong days, the meet, overall, in terms of all-source handle, was down 5 percent. Ever since the beginning the feeling was that they would be down 10 percent, and his rationale was to manage expectations so that if they had a stronger-than-forecasted meet then they would look that much better. He mentioned that they had "started with a roar," but that was due to the soft numbers they were up against. Still, Don Lehr often pitted their numbers—should they have been up against the softer kind—against the record-setting year of 2007, when

Calvin Borel won the Travers aboard Kentucky Derby winner Street Sense. "But we've got Rachel Alexandra for the Woodward on Saturday, and that could be our biggest day," said Hayward. In many ways this was an exhalation of relief, the wedding cake topper of a pastry six weeks in the baking. For months, since June, when she last ran against females of her own age in the Mother Goose, the question was whether NYRA could get her to run at Saratoga in the summer or Belmont in the fall. The Beldame at Belmont against Zenyatta was still a possibility, but that would be the icing—Rachel Alexandra at Saratoga Race Course would be the cake.

"Let's talk about Rachel Alexandra," Vandenburgh said. "The New York Racing Association made the decision to spend a lot of money on this event."

"Yeah, we got banners through town, her own website, we've got special events each day. She's really captured the imagination of people," replied Hayward. "Sandy Frucher, president of the New York City OTB, said he wanted to bring his two favorite girls to see Rachel Alexandra. My wife has talked to people in town who are not track people, and they want to see the filly."

"Everyone here sees the promotion of the filly," replied Vandenburgh.

"She's beaten fillies by twenty and nineteen, she's defeated the boys— Mine That Bird in the Preakness—and beat the boys again in the Haskell, said Hayward. "She's really going for Horse of the Year against the older boys. It's never been done. She's the real deal."

"Talk to me about the promotion. Was it your decision to really promote the last week [of racing]?" asked Vandenburgh.

"We looked at the calendar and we knew we were in trouble with Labor Day being so late. This week is really for Capital District fans. The Kentucky and city people have all gone home," answered Hayward.

"This week, you've got something going for you, it's sunny and eighty degrees from the first three days of the week," said Vandenburgh.

"I think we can run the table with the weather right through Labor Day," answered Hayward.

"How bad a day was Saturday?" Vandenburgh asked, about the Travers. "The teletheater had a big day, so people were saying, 'We don't want to get wet.'"

Answered Hayward: "I was worried when at first post the place was empty. Later in the day it filled and we had 34,000, by far our lowest Travers in thirty years. But they were 34,000 happy people."

"I know it's late and Saratoga should have closed on Monday, but now you have an extra week. Because of the strong promotion, is this week in jeopardy?" asked Vandenburgh.

"No," replied Hayward.

❧

Saturday, September 5, 2009, would be dubbed Rachel Alexandra Day. The red carpet had been rolled out, so to speak, as much as it could be rolled out at a horse track. Out on the Jumbotron in the infield was video of Rachel Alexandra's latest workout, an easy half mile to sharpen the saw. Jenny Kellner, who works for NYRA's press department, had brought a digital video camera to film Rachel Alexandra's workouts. The videos were then posted on "Rachel's Sandbox" so people who needed a fix could watch her train.

NYRA held a press conference with trainer Steve Asmussen and his top assistant, Scott Blasi. Blasi was cut straight out of Asmussen's mold: a horse loving, straight talking guy. Usually Asmussen handles the press because, after all, it was his brand, his letter "A" on the sign outside Barn 65. Blasi, it seemed, was more comfortable with the horses. Because he was the top assistant and the one in charge of Asmussen's best horses, he often found that he was on the fringe of the spotlight, whether he liked it or not. It was a small cost to be able to train a filly like Rachel Alexandra. He related: "I've never seen anything like her. . . . If you see her, you love her. I think she has that effect on people when she walks in the paddock. Anybody who gets a chance to be around her can feel that sort of dominance and brilliance."

Blasi traveled the globe with two-time Horse of the Year Curlin, venturing to the Middle East, to Dubai [United Arab Emirates], where Curlin was positively smashing in winning the $6 million Dubai World Cup. There Blasi trained him, essentially, by himself. He has Asmussen's trust. Blasi, as an assistant, trains the country's best horses and he bonds with them, forms friendships with them. He spent twenty-two months with Curlin and never left his side. When Rachel Alexandra is ready to leave and become a mother, Blasi will have spent close to seventeen months with her. "I mean I love her. I want to keep her racing and keep her around as long as I can. That's my job when she walked into my barn, her day-to-day care."

When Curlin left his barn after he finished fourth in the Breeders' Cup Classic—his worst finish in sixteen career races—Blasi lost a friend. "There is definitely a void," he said.

Watching that screen, watching her breeze by with an audience of people wondering what went through the mind of a trainer, Blasi thought that she was strong, that she was cocky, that she was willing to do their bidding, to answer the call of her coaches, like a well-conditioned athlete with the team's best interest at hand.

Nice and easy, that was how she looked, well within herself. Asmussen expressed, as he so often prefaced his comments when talking of Rachel Alexandra, how blessed he and his staff were to have talent like hers in their barn. When he watched Rachel Alexandra win the Kentucky Oaks, before he was her trainer, he couldn't believe what he saw. Asmussen is tremendously demanding and driven, but that is what one would expect from the 2008 Champion Trainer and one who would, sure enough, be the Champion Trainer of 2009.

Curlin won the Woodward in 2008, and that weighed heavily on Asmussen's mind. "To run her in the race that Curlin was fortunate to win last year, we understand what a tall order it is for her," said Asmussen. "We hope she gives the fans the show that they're expecting."

∾

Trainer Nick Zito put the Travers to bed and geared up with two horses to take aim at Rachel Alexandra. He had 2008 Belmont Stakes winner Da'Tara, a likely pace threat, and Cool Coal Man, a graded stakes winner. Both came in training well. If you're going to try and commit a form of regicide, you might as well have two bullets in your chamber.

∾

The Woodward Post Draw drew as much, if not more, than the Travers draw. Calvin Borel squatted and picked at the grass, accompanied by Rachel Alexandra's exercise rider, Dominic Terry. The two huddled, as if talking strategy over a touch-football play, the pair drawing plays in the dirt. It had just been announced that Borel would be back on the Travers-defecting Mine That Bird for the Goodwood Stakes and the Breeders' Cup Classic in a few months.

Terry, when not working, that is to say when not riding horses, dresses like a Southern California vintner, with striped, button-down shirts, collar undone, jeans, black shoes, a blazer, and black shields for sunglasses. "Where are you staying?" Terry asked Borel.

"Got a home by the police station," Borel said.

"Downtown?" asked Terry.

"Yeah, in a corner, nice and quiet," replied Borel.

Borel stood and Terry sat down on the stairs of a nearby camera tower.

Charlie Hayward stood by Borel, who was accompanied by his agent, Jerry Hissam, "How about the weather?" Hayward said.

"Aw, it's unbelievable," said Borel.

"Looking forward to Saturday?" Hayward asked.

"Yeah," replied Borel.

"So, you're back on Mine That Bird," inquired Hayward.

Borel smiled and said, "Yep."

"I was excited to hear that," said Hayward.

"Everybody was excited to hear that," interjected Hissam.

"Good luck Saturday," Hayward said.

"Thank you very much, sir," Borel replied.

Tom Durkin, who was emceeing the event, called Borel up to the podium. Borel scampered to the mike. "What is it about her that makes her *so* much better?" Durkin asked. "Does she just cover more ground with her stride? Does she have a bigger heart and cardiovascular system? Is her jockey that much more superior? I mean, what is it that makes her *so* much better than her contemporaries?"

"I think it's her jumpin'," said Borel. "She jumps so far and covers so much ground, and just keeps it on. Going a mile, or a mile and a quarter, and she keeps jumpin'."

"Now, in the Preakness, correct me if I'm wrong, but I thought that she was getting a little tired at the end. I mean, she doesn't win by twenty that day, but she did win the Preakness," said Durkin.

"Yes, sir, she did have a lot on her plate," Borel said. "She moved from one barn to another in seven days. Steve got her and had to get used to her and everything. It was a big step for her, running against the boys for the first time. Leaving the 13-hole, she stumbled a little bit. I kind of used some of her to get her over, but she overcomes it."

Asked Durkin: "Does she take direction well? She's got such great natural speed. What about your connection with her in terms of communicating to her, when to go, when to stop, but she's just so naturally fast that you don't want to take that out of her."

"I think that's why I get along with her, answered Borel. "I just let her do her thing. If she runs away from there, I just talk to her and she comes back to me."

"You talk to her?" asked Durkin.

"Yes, sir, she listens on command," Borel replied.

"Oh, really? Unlike any woman I've ever known. What exactly do you tell her to do? This could be groundbreaking here," said Durkin.

"I don't think she's a woman!" Borel answered.

For now, after being snubbed for the entire meet, Calvin Borel was the star again, the star again at everyone else's convenience. After throngs of reporters gathered their quotes, Borel turned his back and walked, with his abbreviated strides, out of the paddock and toward the jocks' room.

On a morning that had more chill than boil, Hal Handel worked on his golf swing, sans club. He took a swing at an invisible ball and watched its invisible flight. "Christ, it feels like winter out here," he commented.

Handel patted Charlie Hayward on the back and said, "We've sold over five hundred tickets."

"Those were seats that would not have been sold otherwise without Rachel," Hayward said.

P. J. Campo added, "Rachel will be in the paddock today. Can we get some extra security in there? It would be helpful."

Today Scott Blasi planned on schooling Rachel Alexandra in the paddock, meaning that they planned on escorting her through the paths and into the saddling area to get her acclimated. This way it would be habit, just another place to go en route to another race. The Asmussen camp alerted everyone to create as big a stir as possible, to make it crowded and noisy and disruptive, the way NFL teams practice with an overly loud sound system to simulate crowd noise.

Neema Ghazi, a well-groomed man with a neat goatee, prim suits, and a gentle voice, opened *Daily Racing Form* to show the ads on the front and back of the *Form* alerting people that Rachel Alexandra would be going for history. "I hope this is not lost on Mr. Jackson and Ms. Banke." Then he spat his guess for the attendance: "36,272."

"That's the number?" Hayward said.

"That's my number," answered Gazi.

"That's a good number," replied Hayward.

"*Sports Illustrated* and *The Boston Globe* sent people," Dan Silver said. "It should be a well-covered event."

"We knew we were light yesterday," said Don Lehr. "On-track was off 23 percent, but all-source was only down 3 percent. We have a double-carryover. Today's card is impossible as far as I'm concerned. It would be nice to get a carry into Saturday."

"You're becoming quite the optimist lately," Handel chimed in.

"Becoming? The meet's almost over!" exclaimed Lehr.

"This Saturday with the filly, she is a serious animal," said Handel. "What she's trying to do hasn't been done in 100 years to give you some context. You have to give Jackson credit. They're really shooting high."

"She'll be 2–5," Silver said.

"That's too much," said Hayward.

"Will you be trying to get out of that race?" asked Handel.

"It's too late to get out of that race," replied Hayward.

∿

Amy Kearns, Rachel Alexandra's security escort, had her hair straightened, and it bounced when she moved. She wore a maroon polo shirt, the colors of Stonestreet Stables, tucked into her khakis. Her boots were scuffed and her expression hardened. As the "bodyguard" to Rachel Alexandra, Kensei, and others, she had zero tolerance for disturbances: camera flashes, gawking eyes, people. She was the grand marshal of a parade that would lead Rachel Alexandra from Barn No. 65 to a stall in the paddock.

Insects let out shrilling cries, a buzz echoed by its fellow species from other trees and telephone poles. They trilled a summer chorus.

Scott Blasi came out of his office and donned a Rachel Alexandra ball cap with letters that were electric, illuminating. His eyes hid behind black shields, and his white shirt, tucked into Smurf-blue jeans, hugged his framed.

Juan Gonzalez, wearing freshly washed jeans and sand-colored boots, walked Rachel Alexandra around the trees. He too wore a "Rachel" ball cap.

Blasi and groom Jose Espinoza fixed two shanks to Rachel Alexandra's halter, with Blasi on her left and Espinoza on her right. She wore white bandages around all four ankles. Her mane was tightly knotted with fourteen "teeth," like that of a hedge trimmer. With her ears pinned back, she was hosed down. The water spilled over her body as if she had just surfaced from a pool.

Steve Asmussen had arrived with Barbara Banke and her friend, Peggy Furth. Blasi and Dominic Terry exchanged a few words, while Gonzalez cradled under his left arm, as if it were a football, Rachel Alexandra's saddle.

A golf cart escort arrived, did a U-turn, and led the way. Kearns walked with militant strides twenty yards in front of Rachel Alexandra, who left a dotted trail of drool that looked like wasabi dressing. It was another fifty yards back to Asmussen.

The caravan threaded through Barns 55 and 59, 54 and 58, 50 and 49, 47 and 44, and then by 47, until they crossed Union Avenue and stomped onto the stone dust horse path. The horse's ears pricked, her head held high.

Then came the comments:

"That's Rachel Alexandra. That's why there's all the police."

"This is Rachel right here."

"She's not as tall as I thought."

"She's gonna be the morning-line favorite."

"What horse is that?"

"That's Rachel Alexandra."

And then the applause, always the applause.

Down the path she went with Kearns, turning her head to the left, staring down any would-be offenders. Blasi's face was stern, businesslike, the way a batter stares down an opposing pitcher. At the gate of the paddock stood dozens of photographers popping off shots, dragging their shutters, like the skittering of crabs. Blasi led her counterclockwise, and as if she were a magnet, she pulled them into her orbit like flecks of iron. High above it looked like a mist of gnats in pursuit, and all she did was bat her tail to swoosh them away.

Blasi and Espinoza threaded her into Stall 12 of the saddling area, spun her around, and stood her still.

Hall of Fame trainer D. Wayne Lukas mused, "I thought they were coming to see my two-year-old maiden!"

Race caller Tom Durkin came over the PA system and said, "Schooling we call it. Rachel Alexandra, America's most famous horse."

Steve Asmussen, removed from the mob around Rachel Alexandra, a mob that was twenty people deep, said, "Crazy, isn't it? This is what schooling is for. This is why we announced it. Think what it will be like on Saturday with people screaming."

Rachel Alexandra looked inquiringly at all the people around her hovering, staring, the scurrying-crab shutters clicking. Her lip chain made her drool, so Espinoza toweled her mouth off. She gnawed at her bit like a wad of Big League Chew.

Blasi's face relaxed. With the back of his right hand he stroked Rachel Alexandra's rippled chest, feeling the baked-bread warmth of her skin on his knuckles, the micro-hairs smooth as hot cocoa. Repeatedly, his hand coaxed relaxation from her throatlatch to the heart of her chest. The river of her hair's current skimmed below his chapped knuckles.

With her saddle on, she walked around the paddock again, and Charlie Hayward watched her, watched her with the grin of somebody in the presence of his favorite ballplayer. He thought of the scene, hundreds of people crammed into this paddock to see her.

Saratoga Race Course calmed for her. At last she exited the paddock, a horse that could freeze rivers and shake down mountains.

And, again, the comments:

"She looks pretty nice."

"Oh, my, God, there's one cop in front and two behind."

"She's got a butt like a colt."

"She's big, huh?"

"She looked at me!"

"She's beautiful. I love her. She looked at me."

Cars and trucks halted when she approached Union Avenue. She clopped across all four lanes and onto the path that would lead her back to Stall No. 1 at Barn 65.

23

The Orphan

Lotta Kim could fly and she had the precocity to boot. In her athleticism she showed her owner and breeder, Dolphus Morrison, glimpses of being special, that she was a filly that could take him places he had never seen. So she was saddled three times, and three times she lost. The races lacked the punch, the killer instinct, to cap off the contest, but that would come. Still, they believed. Then, in her fourth race, she broke through to win the Tiffany Lass in New Orleans. Lotta Kim had arrived.

Shortly after the race, less than a week later, Lotta Kim went to the track for a gallop. A loose horse running from the other direction without guidance and without control screamed in her direction. The bone-crushing collision slammed Lotta Kim down in a mangled heap.

Her rear end was torn. It took 278 stitches to mend her.

She would never race again.

❧

Dolphus Morrison never saw a better-looking horse. The horse in his crosshairs was Medaglia d'Oro, a horse that he thought had as perfect a conformation that one could want in a sire, one that put the stud in stud. "He had that Classic look," said Morrison.

Medaglia d'Oro won the Jim Dandy and Travers Stakes at Saratoga and, according to his trainer, the late Bobby Frankel, "I remember taking him to the paddock for the Travers, and believe me, he looked like a man among boys."

Morrison thought that there were no words to describe Medaglia d'Oro, nothing that could verbally describe or announce why he thought this sire had everything he ever wanted. Morrison walked up to the horse, standing 16.2 hands tall, and he just felt his class. He knew he had a winner, a horse whose rhythm was said to "make music."

❧

Early in the morning, January 29, 2006, Lotta Kim was about to deliver her first foal. It was a filly, and the filly was large, that much Dede McGehee, of Heaven Trees Farm, knew. The delivery was not promising; in fact it was tight and difficult, the kind of delivery that can threaten not just one life but two.

Lotta Kim delivered the foal, but failed to ease into motherhood, to care for her foal. The foal was hard to get out, but they extracted it like a molar. Within the hour this robust, strong filly was up on her hooves.

Lotta Kim produced little milk and showed little interest in the foal that she had carried for eleven months, sired by Medaglia d'Oro. "It hurt her, it scared her," recalled McGehee. First-time mothers often reject the idea of motherhood so vehemently that they can cause physical harm to their foals. McGehee thought that some old tricks of the farm would get Lotta Kim to accept that she was now a mother, and that without her help, the foal would die in the hay. The foal kept at her, kept trying to nurse at the milk-less teats. McGehee saw that no urging on her part would work, so, to save the foal, she separated it from its mother. She then ushered Lotta Kim into a separate stall away from her foal. If she threw fits and tantrums, indicating a biological longing for her foal, then there was a chance to salvage this relationship. Instead, Lotta Kim paid no attention, as if her delivery were a painful inconvenience and nothing more. "That's a *bad* sign," McGehee said.

Soon a nurse mare was brought in. "I remember the nurse mare was such a bitch," recalled McGehee. "We called her Lotta Bitch. She hates people, but she'll take really good care of the foal. Most nurse mares are so kind and so happy to come to a place, and they get a lot to eat and get taken care of. This mare, she didn't like me, she'd bite you in a second." But, McGehee added, "She's a good mother."

As a precaution, Lotta Bitch was kept tied and supervised while with the foal. They graduated to being free in a stall, then a small paddock, and then a larger paddock, and then they were incorporated into the herd.

The foal was keen on running around the field, cutting in and darting. As McGehee watched her, she saw that she was big, strong, forward, and attractive. "We knew she was a nice foal."

This foal would soon be named after Dolphus Morrison's granddaughter: Rachel Alexandra.

∽

With minimal hollering Rachel Alexandra and her buddy, with whom she was paired, were weaned. Left to their own devices, the majority would wean themselves in the field.

Morrison is, by his own admission, a commercial breeder first and a race breeder second. When he looked at Rachel Alexandra, he knew he had a nice foal, but he also knew he wanted cash, so he nominated her for a weanling sale. Since she was Medaglia d'Oro's foal, he figured she would bring a good price. But her sire was a late bloomer, with most of his success coming at age four and five. With an eye on quick runners and the three-year-old Classic races, owners are seldom willing to wait. Before sending her to the sale, Morrison saw that she had minor osteochondrosis, a cartilage-related orthopedic condition. It was not severe, but her body was scarred in a way that would fail to bring top dollar.

As a yearling, Rachel Alexandra was sent to Diamond D Ranch in Lone Oak, Texas, to be broken. There, Ed Dodwell and his son Scooter (who, at this point, handled most of the operations) prepared the yearlings for racing or sold them when they were two years old. They work with the yearlings for three months, acclimating them, through various steps, to the saddle. Next the horses, with a rider, are taught to jog and gallop on the training track. X-rays are taken of the horses' knees and ankles, and their makeup is monitored.

Most horses have an independence problem—too much of it. Ed Dodwell said that the horses "want to go into business for themselves. They obviously want to not follow through on what they've been asked to do in either galloping or breezing, getting gate broke and so forth." But with time and patience they work through the hiccups. Rachel Alexandra toed the company line, not wasting a single calorie on inefficiency. Of the eighty horses that the Dodwells broke, from 2007 to 2008, Rachel Alexandra was in the Top 5.

The Dodwells evaluated Rachel Alexandra and knew "she was as good as you want one to be, so we gave her thirty days off at the paddock and let her start remodeling and came back with her."

She looked so good that Ed, Scooter, and Morrison discussed putting her in the two-year-old training sale at Calder. But as they got closer to the time to put up the entry fee, Scooter and Morrison thought that they might not get exactly what they wanted in the sale, so since she was training well, they figured they should hang onto her. She proved to be above average, and she followed in step with Dodwell's philosophy of letting the horse take charge of itself, to come into its own skin.

Rachel Alexandra went to the track and started breezing half miles, mesmerizing the Dodwells. Over the years, out of the hundreds and hundreds of horses they broke, one constant has surfaced for the two-turn horses: they don't get tired after a breeze. Whether the distance is three-eighths, a half mile, or a mile, the two-turn two-year-olds don't fatigue on their program, and Rachel Alexandra was no exception—she never got tired. "You had to think that this is a two-year-old in the beginning half of the year," said Ed Dodwell. When Morrison saw that Rachel Alexandra's 80 percent effort surpassed every other horse on the track, he said, "We thought we'd better race this one. We changed our mind pretty quick."

For every hurdle put in her way, she cleared it by a dozen lengths, and this made them raise an eyebrow. The feeling was you better not sell this one, not yet, because she just might be something special. "Of all the times in the world when we need a hero, it's right now," Ed Dodwell said. "It's unbelievable that we have been a part of the hero."

∾

She wasn't quite a hero yet. First she went to the barn of Hal Wiggins, a gentleman of the backside. When she dropped into his hands he noticed immediately that Rachel Alexandra had "the best disposition of any horse I've ever had, and she came to me from a farm that we've been doing business with for over twenty-five years."

The two-year-olds arrived at Wiggins's barn, and the Dodwells told him "she was extremely fast. They didn't tell me how good she was, but they said she was fast. She came to the barn with expectations of being a decent horse."

So on May 28, 2008, Rachel Alexandra made her debut at Churchill Downs and ran the worst race of her life, finishing sixth and running a Beyer Speed Figure of 51. The comments read "No menace, inside." It wasn't what one would call a promising race, but she would win her next race, and with a speed figure of 85. Perhaps all she needed was experience. In her second graded Stakes race, the Grade 3 Pocahontas at Churchill Downs, jockey Brian Hernandez Jr. finished second to Sara Louise with Robby Albarado up. After the race it seemed that Rachel Alexandra had the potential, but it was time to try a different rider. The first call went to Albarado, but he turned it down, choosing instead to stay aboard Sara Louise for a rematch in the Grade 2 Golden Rod, also at Churchill. That was when Calvin Borel got the mount.

Rachel Alexandra scared Borel. She took these deep inhalations, as if prompted by a stethoscope-bearing doctor. Borel thought she was ready to fire up. She took several breaths, her lungs ballooning and then slowly deflating. Her expression calmed. Her ears pricked forward. Borel soon realized that she was preparing herself. Rachel Alexandra is the only horse that Borel has ridden that performs this pre-race ritual.

She had never been on the lead in her prior races, and Borel sent her from the gate. She won by four and half lengths over Albarado and Sara Louise. A marriage had been forged between Borel and Rachel Alexandra at the end of her two-year-old season. Wiggins sat back and watched the fireworks.

In his own modesty Wiggins draped the credit on Rachel Alexandra's shoulders like a blanket, because, he said, "I'd like to take credit for her. I'd like to think it was something I did, but I really don't. I think it was just her. We trained her just like the rest of the horses and she was just so much head and above the rest of them."

Still, Wiggins didn't know just how special Rachel Alexandra was. Leading up to her three-year-old debut at Oaklawn Park in the Martha Washington, he was about to see a metamorphosis. Rachel Alexandra won by eight lengths under wraps. She broke a stakes record in the win, and this was the eyebrow-raising effort that Wiggins knew he had when the Dodwells shipped her to him. Wiggins wasn't even sure if he had his filly fit for the race, since she had spent time resting for what would be an aggressive three-year-old campaign. "I think it was at that time I knew I had something special."

Looking at Rachel Alexandra, Wiggins knew she was big, but especially big in the hindquarters. That was where she got her tremendous drive, that lift. Wiggins has watched slow-motion video of Rachel Alexandra running and has marveled over the ground she covers with each stride, going close to 30 percent farther than any competitor per stride. "At the end of the race, she's got so much left because she does it so easy," said Wiggins. The horse took fewer strides to cover the same distance.

The comments for her next two races—the Fairgrounds Oaks and the Fantasy—read: "Eased up final 1/16th" and "Took command easily." It seemed that, as Wiggins had noticed, she was smoother than Kentucky bourbon. Then, on the day before the Kentucky Derby, she exploded onto the scene with a $20^1/_4$-length romp in the Kentucky Oaks. Down the lane she widened, and widened; as the camera panned it receded its zoom farther into its cavity and still had trouble enveloping her winning margin. The comment read, "On own, easily."

Dede McGehee was there to see the Oaks. She had on her sombrero-size hat and her yellow-green jacket. Her eyes hid behind the brim of the hat as she smiled, almost maniacally. One of her foals did the unthinkable. "I got all weepy. They're our children. You may not own them, but they're still partly yours."

But as with any such performance, the phones began to ring. Let it be known that any such athletic feat such as the one Rachel Alexandra performed in the Oaks would attract bidders of the highest order. And while the champagne bubbles tickled their throats, phones rung off the hook.

∼

Dolphus Morrison received ten phone calls a day, some as late as midnight. "I'm not interested in selling," he said. But the calls kept flooding in. Morrison was closer to the end of his life than the beginning, and how often would a horse like Rachel Alexandra come along? So why not enjoy her for who she is because, she would hand out joy and triumph like they were after-dinner mints.

After four days passed, Morrison got a call from Jess Jackson, the California vintner of Kendall-Jackson. "Would you be interested in selling Rachel?" he said.

"She's really not for sale," said Morrison. "At this point in my career I've got a pretty nice horse. You work your butt off to raise one like this all your life. I don't really want to sell her."

"Well, if you were going to sell her, what would you just *have* to have for her?" inquired Jackson.

Morrison gave a ridiculous figure, a number that even a billionaire like Jackson would scoff at. "Well, I can't pay that," said Jackson. "I don't think I could pay that."

"Well, I don't think you'll ever own her," replied Morrison, and the two of them laughed.

They hung up their phones and went about their business when Morrison got another call from Jackson. After some thought, Jackson said he would pay Morrison his ludicrous figure. Early reports pegged the amount at $10 million, but a *Sports Illustrated* story, published in late 2009, stated the number was closer to $4–$5 million. Jackson and Morrison signed a confidentiality agreement, so the world may never know.

∾

Trainer Hal Wiggins went about his training. Just because Rachel Alexandra made history didn't mean he could rest on his laurels. This was to be Wiggins's final year training horses, and he had just had the biggest one—and the biggest horse—of his life. The year was half over, so he put his head down and got back to work.

That same Tuesday night when Jackson spoke with Morrison, Morrison called Wiggins to tell him that he "had something in the works and that they would be by the next morning," "they" being the new trainers of the filly. Since it was Jackson who bought the filly, "they" would be Steve Asmussen and his assistant Scott Blasi. Both Wiggins and Asmussen had stalls at Churchill Downs, so Rachel Alexandra would only have to walk a few yards, nothing more.

Wiggins thought that if they were to sell the horse it would be after a race like the Kentucky Oaks, a race so visually impressive, so effortless, that it was only natural for her to get this sort of attention, a supermodel walking into a classroom full of nerds. Wiggins was still celebrating the win, still marveling over what Rachel Alexandra did. Though it made sense for Morrison to sell the horse, it caught Wiggins off guard. The euphoria clouded his vision and quickly faded.

There she was, Rachel Alexandra, in Stall 17 of Wiggins's barn. It was Wednesday, May 6, 2009, and they had just vetted her out, meaning Jackson's veterinarians inspected the filly for any physical problems. Wiggins kept to his word, ensuring that his barn still ran effectively. To the best of Wiggins's knowledge, negotiations were still in progress, so Rachel Alexandra was to remain in the barn until Wiggins heard from Morrison.

By the time Thursday morning came, May 7, Wiggins had yet to hear from Morrison, and by this time Asmussen and Blasi came by with a lead shank to escort Rachel Alexandra into their barn and place her under their care. Wiggins said, "I still haven't heard from Mr. Morrison. I'm going to have to hear from him before I let her walk out of the barn." Asmussen and Blasi said they were fine with that. Asmussen went back to his barn, but Blasi hung around, likely talking with Wiggins's assistant trainer, Brett, who Blasi considers one of his best friends.

Because it was around 5:30 a.m., Wiggins knew it would be tough to get in touch with Morrison, but he had to. Finally he contacted him and Morrison apologized for not calling because, yes, they had made a deal, signed papers, transferred funds, and went out to dinner, "It's okay, they can go ahead and take her."

This feeling of detachment wasn't necessarily reflected at the barn. Wiggins gave Blasi the go-ahead and stood back as Blasi went to Stall 17. Wiggins wasn't prepared for how it would hit him until he stood there and watched her, listened to her hooves clop out of his care. His staff felt the same way: Rachel Alexandra wasn't being led out for a bath or a gallop, she was leaving for good. She had the same stall every day since age two, just a baby, in horsemen-speak. Her groom was sad, as were all the others, because sometimes horses are more than horses.

According to Wiggins, she was the horse one worked for and dreamed about and hoped to get. And, at the pinnacle of her achievements, she was led away. It left a void, not only physically, in Wiggins's barn but emotionally. To block it out, to move on, two days later Wiggins made sure to have a new horse put in Stall 17 so his staff wouldn't have to walk by and see it empty. "You just pick up your head the next day and go on about your business," said Wiggins. "You've got to realize you've got to go on about it."

⤳

It wasn't easy for Scott Blasi either, with Rachel Alexandra's hooves clopping to his right. It wasn't easy for him to lead her away from Wiggins's barn. He didn't want to do it. After all, he was close with both Wiggins and his assistant. But business is business. He understood. He had been through it, cared for a horse, considered that horse a friend, and then had it stripped from him.

Blasi remembered when Curlin left his barn after the horse retired from racing. Blasi stayed by Curlin's side for twenty-two months, and when Curlin exited, he said there was a void "when you're used to being such close friends."

Blasi once trained a filly, not of the caliber of Rachel Alexandra, but a nice filly. He won five races in a row with her, and he said she showed flashes of ability. "I know we're talking apples and oranges here," said Blais, "but you get attached to these horses, and when they're gone it's different."

As Blasi walked, he knew that behind him was a staff that felt empty with Rachel Alexandra's departure, even angry, and what was worse?—*he* was the cause. No doubt there was scorn and discord, but at least Blasi understood. He knew that the members of Wiggins's crew were Rachel Alexandra's biggest fans, and that he would do his part to uphold what they began, to keep the legacy in motion. He knew no other way. Blasi was determined, for he still had a job to do. "Believe me, Mr. Jackson didn't steal her, I know he paid a fair price for her. At the same time, everybody talks about what they would do. Mr. Jackson is willing to do that."

Rachel Alexandra's hooves scuffed beside Blasi, her head bobbing, her ears tuning into new frequencies. She couldn't feel it, but there were needles shooting from behind because she was stripped away at the height of her power by the black-and-white world of green. But she was more than a commodity—she was a breathing embodiment of a movement, and Blasi would be damned if he didn't coach her, out of respect for not only him but her previous handlers. Reflecting on Curlin, on the filly who won five races in a row, and how they were ushered away from his hands, he said, "I know how I felt, so when she walked out of their barn, believe me, I know what they felt."

∾

Rachel Alexandra Fever quickly spread down the streets of Saratoga Springs. Broadway's storefront windows were ornamented with Rachel Alexandra photographs and paintings. The streets were dedicated to her, a horse.

There was the photograph, in the window of Saratoga Saddlery, Rachel Alexandra's head the size of Polyphemus, her eyes ringed in fire. The cards were down. No more bluffing. No more posturing. Rachel Alexandra was ready.

It was time.

24

The Cusp

The day before the Woodward, Charlie Hayward sipped his coffee and readied for a guest appearance on radio station Star 101.3. He'd be on with Tom Gallo of Parting Glass Racing, the same man who hosted the monthly meetings every third Thursday of the month. Hayward chatted with Mark Bardack, of Ed Lewi Associates, about the Woodward, namely, how it would compare to when Curlin ran a year ago. Could it be that Rachel Alexandra would draw more than Curlin? The answer was an unequivocal yes, since Curlin was more of a professional, a big name *within* the industry. Rachel Alexandra, aside from being a female horse taking on the boys for a third time, was in *Vogue* magazine and the darling of little girls across the country. She had successfully crossed over into the mainstream, commanding people's attention. "We're going up against 22–23,000 with Curlin?" asked Bardack.

"We should crush that number," said Hayward. "Steve Crist wrote a piece for tomorrow's *Form* about Rachel backing out, dodging the Travers. He cited that the horses in the Whitney and others have won $8.5 million and twice as many graded stakes. He thinks it's hard to get a crowd on Labor Day weekend. I'd be thrilled with anything over thirty thousand."

"It's shaping up okay," said Bardack. "There's a buzz, the Suburban winner, the Whitney winner."

Not to mention the 2008 Belmont Stakes winner, Da'Tara, and runner-up, Past the Point, to Curlin in the 2008 Woodward. Also in the mix was the Grade 1 Stephen Foster winner, Macho Again, ridden by Robby Albarado, Calvin Borel's old friend and under-the-wire rival.

Where other connections saw the appearance of Rachel Alexandra in the Woodward as a deterrent, the people in Macho Again's circle saw good reason to run. He was trained by Dallas Stewart, who at one time trained Kentucky Derby runner Dollar Bill, the same colt who was pulled from Calvin Borel. Stewart planned to skip the Woodward in favor of the Jockey Club Gold Cup at Belmont in the fall.

But when Rachel Alexandra's presence pumped up the purse to $750,000, it was an opportunity, as *Courier-Journal* reporter Jennie Rees reported, to run for extra money and, more importantly, publicity. Macho Again had seventeen owners in the West Point Thoroughbreds syndicate. West Point president Terry Finley said, "How many times do you get a shot to really be part of history? I would hope that in 50 years people would talk about the 2009 Woodward. And he's obviously not outclassed. He's not going to be 50–1. She looks like she's a pretty dominating factor. But we all know it's a different pond, and the pond is a lot deeper in this case. I'm not insinuating she can't swim in the pond, but it is deeper."

Rees wrote that Macho Again "was training like gangbusters," something Stewart echoed as well, "He's on the top of his game," said Stewart. "He's eating better than he ever has. His energy is there. It looks to me like he's put on weight, put on muscle. I'm just looking at my horse and saying he's ready to run. With a horse like Macho Again and these types of races, you can't go ducking anyone. . . . He was taking the rider around there every day, bucking and kicking. I told Terry, 'I don't think he needs to pass this race.'"

And Albarado was primed for yet another clash against his friend Calvin Borel. He was long on praise for Rachel Alexandra. He thought she was phenomenal, dominating, as big physically as many of the colts and horses. "Who says she can't be the greatest?" asked Albarado.

But he wouldn't bow down to her. No. "I can't take my horse out of his running style. He's going to have to come from way off the pace. I'll probably compromise his finish if I do try to keep him closer or try to chase a fast pace. I've just got to let him fall back there, relax, and make one run like always.

"If the pace sets up, I really think Macho Again is the horse to beat."

Robby Albarado would soon get his wish, but would Macho Again hold up his end of the deal?

∾

After Hayward did his radio spot, touting the Woodward and listening to Gallo say "Putting the Woodward on the last weekend really gives a crescendo and climax to the meet. It was fabulous when you had Curlin and I said, 'How can you top this?' Now you have Rachel Alexandra! What a double!" he got to work putting the final brushstrokes on this meet. It was nearly time to sign his name to this painting.

Hayward and his team met outside for one of the final huddles. Hard to believe, he thought, that the meet was near completion, this being Day 33 of 36. Neema Ghazi held the daily program with Rachel Alexandra's face on it, the same design that emblazoned the flags through town. P. J. Campo said, "Hey, boss," as Hayward stretched his arms out and replied, "What a day."

"We learned something yesterday," addressed Hayward, "about the press and photographers and credentials. If that is any indicator of what will happen on Saturday, it will be huge." Hayward was referring to the Rachel Alexandra circus in the paddock. "We had a great day yesterday, as Mr. Lehr will say, and we'll have a great day today."

Don Lehr, to this, curled his lips into a smile that resembled the Grinch's.

With yet another carryover, just over $656,000, Pat Mahony noted that money poured in. "They bet four times the jackpot on that Pick 6. I don't think we'll do that today, but there is a lot of money in there today. I'm sure Mr. Lehr has handicapped the card. So I don't know if we can carry it."

Said Hayward: "17–18 [thousand for attendance], 1.7–1.8. I'd be happy with 12–13 percent of the total handle." Lehr muttered something that only Hal Handel could hear.

"He's going to be low-balling this baby. I can't wait for this," Handel said.

Hayward asked, "Mr. Polombo, how's your cold?"

"You gave it to me," replied Polombo.

"Maria gave it to me!" exclaimed Hayward.

The huddle worked its way around with three "goods" in a row. While "goods" were, well, good, too many signified fatigue or, worse, in Hayward's eyes, laziness. "You guys are getting tired," Hayward said. "Mr. Ghazi, you must have something going on today."

"This is tomorrow's program," said Ghazi. "In the middle Mr. Jackson bought a full-page ad showing his appreciation. If you pull it out, there's a poster of Rachel."

"Show the centerfold," said Handel. "It's like a *Penthouse* centerfold!"

"These are gonna be pinned up in every stall of every barn," John Ryan said.

"And we've got the Commentator on Sunday," said Hayward.

"Big finish, big finish," added Handel.

"Big Brown came out of this weekend two years ago," Hayward said, this, of course, an allusion to his mantra that Saratoga not only attracts stars but also makes them.

Lehr spat out the numbers from previous years, and the numbers from 2008, which were encouraging: "2.8 on-track, 13.3 all-source, nine races, and seventy-five betting interests. Same as today, I believe. Today's card, to me, based on shear numbers, from a handicapping perspective, it's impossible."

"You think it will carry?" Mahony said.

"Does 3.1 interest you?" asked Handel.

"3.1? You mean on-track? Do you want all-source?" asked Mahony.

"We can do all-source if you want to do that. 15.5," said Handel.

Almost before Handel had finished, Lehr spat, "Under! We have no shot."

"That was decisive," said Hayward.

"I'd encourage everybody tomorrow," Handel said, "if you have fifteen minutes to be out there when that horse comes out of that paddock. That will be something you remember for a long, long time. You have to step back. There will be lots of women and lots of young girls all here to see Rachel."

When the huddle disbanded, Handel said to Dan Silver, "It was fortuitous to have a Pick 6 carryover come when it did."

"If we have a Pick 6 carryover tomorrow . . . ," said Silver.

"Don't be a pig. We have Rachel tomorrow. Don't be a pig. At six tomorrow, the world will change. It will be Beldame, Beldame, Beldame, BELdame, Beldame, Beldame, Beldame, BELdame," Handel said.

∽

The morning of the $750,000 Woodward Stakes was calm, like a windless morning at a lake where the water gently laps against the hulls of rowboats. Signs in the shops in downtown Saratoga Springs celebrated Rachel Alexandra, urging her on to victory.

The sky at dawn was breathtaking—the sun a crimson orb, the moon pure white, both awake, the sun to the east, the moon to the west, the earth a fixed point in a cosmic obtuse triangle. Fog levitated between the sun and moon.

By 6:51 a.m., P. J. Campo arrived on the grounds of Saratoga Race Course and Jerry Davis, director of admissions and parking, chirped into his walkie-talkie as people lined up at the gates ready to burst through. A long line of cars waited to turn into the grounds.

Hundreds of programs, in stacks of twenty, were wheeled in on golf carts, and, like a game of Tetris, they were piled hip-high in the kiosks. A NYRA peace officer walked by, speaking into his walkie: "Ten-four, all units stand by." After a few moments, the fans on the other side of the fence pressed as if they could pass through the fence mashed into the iron. "Open all gates, open all gates. Let's go! Open 'em up!"

The masses darted through the gates, coolers tipped over, chairs strapped to their backs as they sprinted to picnic tables to claim spaces along the fences. Davis called it "the running of the bulls."

All this energy, all this hustle, and it was still ten hours until Rachel Alexandra was ready to race.

∽

Pink buttons labeled "RACHEL" were doled out to the earliest risers. It was the same button that Charlie Hayward would pin on his Good Guy Award. It was also the same button plastered on lapels and little girls' T-shirts, one such shirt reading "Fillies Rule, Saratoga 2009."

Horses still trained on the main oval, where trainer Tim Ice stood on a set of stairs. He watched his Travers Stakes winner Summer Bird gallop. Hardly a soul paid him attention, the man who won the Belmont and the Travers. Maybe if he had a set of crutches, a Stetson instead of a ball cap, and a mustache instead of a baby-smooth glean, people would point and gawk. No, they passed him by as they had the entire meet, the entire year. There was a smattering of applause for Summer Bird when he trotted by, so at least one of the two was recognized. Ribbons of cigar smoke curled around Ice's head as he continued to lean on the rail with that air of confidence that comes from accomplishment. In little less than a month, Summer Bird would win the $750,000 Jockey Club Gold Cup at Belmont Park, running 1¼ miles and locking up the category Champion Three-Year-Old Male.

Charlie Hayward surfaced for some television interviews. His team had placed friendly wagers for the attendance figures for the day, the low being around 24,000 and the high being around 41,000. Hayward felt it would be somewhere in between, because Curlin only drew 23,000 a year ago with similar promotion. "It's gonna be special," Hayward told a reporter, "We're thrilled Rachel is here to help us out."

Echoing throughout the clubhouse were race calls and replays of Rachel Alexandra's races throughout the latter part of 2008 and the entirety of 2009. Hayward paused and watched the video of her romping in the Golden Rod Stakes, the race caller calling out Calvin Borel's actions, peeking over his shoulder, "No danger. No danger."

Replays were streamed as if to brainwash those present that she was unbreakable, or perhaps to show that the legends were true, that she never touched the ground, that she was ten feet tall, that she was invincible. Hairs stood on end as if called to an about-face at basic training.

Calvin Borel stood in his blue robe outside the jocks' room palming his butane lighter and cylinder of Marlboro Light tobacco. He thought that once he got out there, he'd try to block out the noise, block out the weight of history, and glide. Focus on the horse, see what's going on, get in the gate, make sure everything is right. Something he had always admired about Rachel Alexandra was that she was not like an everyday horse: *She blanks it, she forgets about it, I don't know what it is. The main thing is to keep her calm and collected. She'll run on ice, on broken glass, she just keeps going. She's like the Energizer Bunny.* With that thought, and the magnitude of the event, Borel said: "It's tough. We're stepping up to the plate. We're just going to put them in the gates and see what happens."

He had seen the past performances so he knew there was speed in the race that she'd have to contend with early on. Nick Zito's Da'Tara was one such contender. Four years earlier, in the Woodward, when it was still run at Belmont Park, Zito's Commentator was flanked by two rabbits, horses that are sent to the front to tire a known front-runner. The trainer was Rick Dutrow Jr., and he ran the two rabbits so that his third horse, the 2005 Horse of the Year, Saint Liam, could close and zip by a tiring Commentator. It worked in that race, but Commentator didn't give up. Now Zito had a rabbit in Da'Tara, and Cool Coal Man might be a contender at the end to lap up a tired Rachel Alexandra.

So Borel thought that perhaps there were two horses that could run with him and Rachel Alexandra, "but I don't think it's her kind of speed. She has so much class. I just gotta save her, take her back, ride off them." He did nothing but commend trainer Steve Asmussen for his handling of Rachel Alexandra. His face bent into a smile. Borel never imagined that she'd be better than when he first started riding her. "He's got this bitch doin' so good!" said Borel. "It's crazy! I can see it in her eyes."

Borel relaxed in the whirlpool and got a massage. With a couple of other horses to ride, he'd get a feel for the track. "It's gonna be fast. It was fast yesterday. *Phew!*"

∽

Jess Jackson came into his box, which happened to be situated next to Nick Zito's. Jackson eyed the bigger picture. He conceded that money was not the major factor when it came to Rachel Alexandra. He emphasized, "If the financial considerations were the primary thing, we would have gone to the Travers. We look to the race, we look to the horse, and we look to the legacy of the horse."

Zito cracked the seal on a bottle of sparkling Saratoga water and leaned forward to look at his television screen. Jackson looked "California," his white shirt unbuttoned and his collar tieless, wearing a black blazer and a wool fedora, the latter to hide the hair lost by bouts of chemotherapy for skin cancer. Zito wore a white shirt with a maroon tie, a navy sweater vest, and a navy blazer. The two coasts were at odds, both in style and horses. No matter the style or competition, Zito thought Jackson was good for the game of horse racing, that, if nothing else, he knew how to promote. Zito even mused that Jackson "made the National Thoroughbred Racing Association look like morons." Many knocked Jackson for his free-spending ways, as if he were the George Steinbrenner of horse racing, this in a sport where Steinbrenner [who passed in July 2010] even owned horses, most notably the post-time favorite for the 2005 Kentucky Derby, Bellamy Road, trained by Nick Zito.

Jackson, who was getting situated in his box, amusingly said, with his clear and articulate air: "Don't let that rabbit get in my way."

Zito had thought all along that, "You gotta run. Like the famous guy told me once, if you don't run, you can't even lose." He pivoted in his chair and peered over his left shoulder. He smiled, but avoided eye contact. "Don't worry about it," Zito said. Zito did plan on sending the rabbit, Da'Tara. It was the only shot he had.

❧

Charlie Hayward sauntered into the paddock, knowing that he didn't have a Woodward Paddock Pass. He didn't see the problem. When he saw Don Lehr, he said, "Maybe they'll stop me."

"That'd be consistent," Lehr said, dryly.

The next race was the Forego, a sprint for older horses. It had twelve horses, and Hayward observed, "When was the last time there were twelve horses in this race?" It was going to be a war, he thought, this being one of his favorite races to watch all year.

Pyro defeated the favorite, Kodiak Kowboy. Coming in third from off the pace was Ready's Echo, ridden by Calvin Borel. Borel had twenty-seven minutes to ready himself for the Woodward Stakes.

It was go time.

❧

Calvin Borel scampered through the crowd, following his escort on the jockey path. People called and clamored for a piece of Borel, but he blocked them out. He had signed hundreds of autographs throughout the meet, when he had little to do except sign photographs, magazine covers, and goggles. Business was far from booming, so he might as well pay back the people who reveled in his glow, his face creased like tree bark. Not on this walk, however. He marched with purpose, the noises and voices smothered by some unseen pillow.

Borel stopped before the counter outside the jocks' room. His contoured bald head was silhouetted against a blinding white wall reflecting the sun. With sinewy arms he tore off his silks as he dashed into the jocks' room.

Twenty-five minutes to post, the clerk of scales got on the mike and said, "Check for the tenth race, checking for the tenth."

Other jockeys, Jeremy Rose, rider of Whitney winner, Bullsbay, weighed in. "Okay! Saddles up!" exclaimed the clerk again.

Alan Garcia, rider of Asiatic Boy, came out, stepped on the scale, and turned to no one in particular, belching out in his Peruvian accent, "Whoa, Rachel! You going to see Rachel?"

Just outside the jocks' room, hundreds of people lined Man o' War Way, the dirt path that led to the paddock from the security barns. Enthusiastic cheers followed Rachel Alexandra, and she absorbed these cheers from a bloodthirsty populace. The screams were deafening, and fathers stood on tiptoe, with daughters sitting atop their shoulders, hoping to catch a glimpse of Rachel Alexandra's chocolate coat. Rachel Alexandra's ears pivoted and flicked. Her eyes widened where the fire burned. She stomped along, entering the paddock the way a prizefighter would enter the ring.

At twenty-two minutes to post, Calvin Borel weighed in. His valet folded his No. 3 saddlecloth with RACHEL ALEXANDRA embroidered on the fringe over his saddle pad and saddle. The valet then dashed out to the paddock to aid in the saddling of Rachel Alexandra. A security guard said, "*Hasta. La. Vista.*"

At eighteen minutes to post, a last call went out to summon all jockeys: Robby Albarado, Jeremy Rose, Edgar Prado, Johnny Velazquez, Alan Garcia, Jose Lezcano, Julien Leparoux, and, finally, Calvin Borel.

Under the darkness and shade of the jocks' room was the last remaining shelter. Beyond the threshold were light and a corridor of people, like rocks on a riverbed. The other seven jockeys filed out, with Borel bringing up the rear.

The comments flew:

"Here we go Calvin!"

"Safe trip, Calvin. Safe trip."

"Give her a good ride, Calvin!"

"Calvin woooo! Woooo!"

"C'mon, Calvin!"

"Macho's comin', Calvin!"

Borel's feet crunched the gravel of Man o'War Way, his wafer-thin boots scuffed across in hiccupping strides. There was Lisa Funk, Borel's fiancée, in a black dress and heels. Borel gave her a peck on the lips. He then found Rachel Alexandra, saddled and nostrils pulsing. Her mane was knotted up in a sawtooth pattern. Trainer Steve Asmussen grabbed Borel by his left leg and hoisted him onto his high tower. There Borel's legs dangled like earrings against Rachel Alexandra's ribs. The horses made one pass around the paddock, and Rachel Alexandra, normally as light as Anna Pavlova, stomped with fury, creating craters in the dirt. The horses made another pass to give the onlookers another chance to see the field but, more accurately, to showcase Rachel Alexandra one more time.

There at the mouth of the horse path that leads from the paddock to the track stood Charlie Hayward. He focused on Rachel Alexandra, the crowned jewel of the meet. He noticed that the atmosphere contained enough energy to power the entire grid of the Capital Region. He saw the digital cameras, cell phone cameras, and all the pink. Hayward knew when he saw hundreds of people in the paddock just two days ago, when Rachel Alexandra schooled, that the volume would be deafening, but he never imagined that it would be like this. He watched as the field of horses was led out onto the track, Rachel Alexandra's massive hindquarters tightening in columns and striations.

Borel scanned the crowd and found the blonde radiance of his fiancée. They locked eyes for just a moment. It was all he needed.

∞

Hayward followed the massive crowd down the horse path, veering off it before he entered the clubhouse. His dress shoes clunked on the wooden floors. He was about to set foot onto the staircase that led up to his box when the crowd let out a collective gasp. Over thirty thousand souls drew that audible breath, making hearts skip and bellies drop. Hayward's head swiveled quickly, looking for a monitor.

Rachel Alexandra had thrown Calvin Borel.

25

Alexandra the Great

Lisa Funk had just been in the paddock next to Jess Jackson and his wife, Barbara Banke, to watch Steve Asmussen saddle Rachel Alexandra. Funk said hello and looked around, absorbing the electricity of it all. All eyes were on Rachel Alexandra, she thought. She soon reflected about the pressure her fiancé must have been under, not only here, but during this past Belmont Stakes when he finished third aboard Mine That Bird. Funk worried. She worried about Calvin Borel. She worried about Rachel Alexandra. Fillies haven't fared well against males, the great fillies in North America. Some of the most storied names in the game have fallen, bridging the gender gap with raw ability. Certainly there was Ruffian, who broke down in a match race against Foolish Pleasure in 1975 at Belmont Park. In 2008 Eight Belles broke both her front ankles in a freak accident after a Kentucky Derby, where she finished second to Big Brown. For males there was 2006 Kentucky Derby winner Barbaro, a name not lost on many, who saw him turn his right rear ankle into bone meal two hundred yards into the Preakness Stakes. His fight went on until he was put out of his misery on January 29, 2007, the exact day Rachel Alexandra turned one.

So Funk walked up to the grandstands and to her box that was ten horse strides past the wire when she heard the gasp. She whipped around and looked for a monitor, anything, to see what had happened. A friend of hers grabbed her by the arm and said, "Oh my God, Calvin fell off!"

"Oh, shit!" said Funk. Her mind raced: Is Rachel running around the track? Is Rachel loose? Her eyes focused on the monitor, and she relaxed. For the time, for this moment, this one worry ceased.

◞◟

Calvin Borel stared straight ahead, focusing on Rachel Alexandra below him, feeling her step over the track, feeling the way her hooves pitted the earth. Then a group of boys surged to the fence and, in a collective energy, screamed, "RACHEL!"

Rachel Alexandra reared, her snout craned downward from a height of some ten feet in the air. The outrider let the leather shank drop so as not to fight her. Her front legs shadowboxed while Borel keenly slipped off her back while maintaining his hold on the reins. He let the slack unthread itself as if they were tethered by something invisible, the way coupled figure skaters know not where they are but where they will be. Borel said in a calming tone, one used to soothe a spooked child, "Rachel." She stood there and didn't move. She looked at Borel, and he felt that she recognized him, that there was nothing to be afraid of, "I guess it's because being around her all the time and they have a saying with a horse that after you're with a horse for a long time." Another outrider got off his horse and leg-upped Borel. As far as Borel could tell, there was nothing wrong with her at all.

That knowledge was unbeknownst to Charlie Hayward and Hal Handel, who were both sitting with their wives in their grandstand box. They were worried, because the threat of disaster loomed. To scratch her would be safe—disappointing, but safe nonetheless.

The first thoughts were of Barbaro breaking through the gates prior to the 2006 Preakness. In that race the track's veterinarian deduced that nothing was wrong and let him race. Rachel Alexandra had never acted like this before, had never been this worked up, and to explode the way she did created widespread doubt as to whether she should be taking on this field of men.

Handel said to Hayward, "I can't remember the last race I was almost afraid to watch."

"Yeah. Me too," replied Hayward.

 ∾

The horses galloped and warmed up around the backstretch. The grandstand had turned to murmurs while above the ceiling fans spun like helicopter seeds forever suspended in mid-flight. "It's all going to be what happens heading into that first turn," said Handel. "Borel has to make a decision. If he gets stuck on the rail, it will be a tough way for her to go."

 ∾

Rachel Alexandra steadied before the gates. She took those deep breaths.
Again.
Again.
Again.
She let the air fall out of her lungs. Her face relaxed. Her ears pricked forward.

Tom Durkin announced, "The horses have reached the starting gate, they'rrrre at the post." Da'Tara walked and snuck into the first post. Bullsbay, the Whitney winner, slotted in next. In went Calvin Borel and Rachel Alexandra into Post 3. Cool Coal Man, the second Nick Zito horse, slipped into Post 4. Robby Albarado and Macho Again went into Post 5 to Borel's immediate right. It's A Bird, the Suburban winner, filled out Post 6. So too did Asiatic Boy in Post 7 with Past the Point, runner-up in this race a year earlier to Curlin, rounding out the field.

"It'd be nice if she won," said Handel, "but I just want her to get around safe."

The horses shuffled a bit on their hooves, their eyes staring at the clubhouse turn.

"This will be nuts," said Handel, "one minute and forty-seven seconds of lunacy. Just be safe." And with that he knocked on the wooden rail of the box.

The horses were all corks in a dam littered with holes. The pressure from behind could be held only so long.

Nick Zito's eyes, from his box just behind Hayward's, were fixed on the gates, his two horses in the number one and four posts.

Jess Jackson and Barbara Banke sat to his left, their eyes also locked on the gate.

Lisa Funk, many strides past the wire, watched her fiancé and Rachel Alexandra.

Charlie Hayward sat with his hands cupping his mouth.

Rachel Alexandra's amber eyes, ringed in fire, stared with eager intent. The sun's light reflected a highlight that curved over its surface. Calvin Borel's hands strangled the reins that rested on her shoulders. The veins in the horse's neck swelled to the surface. Borel tugged at his silks. The assistant starters locked the gates behind the horses, and the starter raised his thumb above the button to blow up the dam.

"There's a lot of people on that apron," said Handel. "Watch this start. It's going to be huge. What will the guys to the outside do? C'mon, baby. It's showtime."

"They're in the gate and they're off!" exclaimed the announcer. The dam burst, and with a few thrusts, *phfff phfff phfff*, the Woodward Stakes launched. Rachel Alexandra cleared Da'Tara and Bullsbay in the time it takes to fold back a newspaper. Borel's body was locked, his arms, his hands, and his legs, and he leaned into the clubhouse turn. Rachel Alexandra was four paths off the rail and safely in the clear. The announcer continued, "So they race into the first turn here. Rachel Alexandra will duel with Da'Tara."

Handel called out, "Wow, she's cookin'. He's got great position."

"They're going quick," said Hayward. "She's on the lead!"

Da'Tara came up to her left flank and pressed her from the inside, while Past the Point coasted to the outside. Nick Zito's other entry, Cool Coal Man, was to the inside in fourth, in a perfect pocket of air. Macho Again, with Robby Albarado sitting chilly, trailed the field some fourteen lengths back. Zito liked the positioning of his Cool Coal Man, liked what Da'Tara was bringing to Rachel Alexandra on the front end.

"Oooh! The first quarter was twenty-two and four-fifths seconds. There'll be no free ride for Rachel Alexandra. They're making her work for every step today. Da'Tara has sent her through a punishing opening quarter mile," said the announcer.

Rachel Alexandra burned the dirt, yet Borel still had her in a hold. It was like he always said, regarding how she could maintain such a high cruising speed, "I believe it's her jumping. She jumps so far. I know Churchill like the back of my hand. The poles that hold the fence up are ten feet apart. When I first started working her she jumps two-and-half, two-and-three-quarters, twenty-five or twenty-seven feet. That's what makes her such a good horse. Secretariat's runs made him a good horse. Jumpin'. Watch the replays."

There was just under a mile to go, and to set a quarter-mile fraction of that speed is suicide in a sprint, let alone a route of 1⅛ miles. "She can't do this," said Handel, "it's too fast."

No sooner had Tom Durkin exclaimed his concern about her opening quarter had Da'Tara receded from the lead. It was still Rachel Alexandra, and Borel knew she was flying, but he looked at her ears and one was forward and one was cocked to the outside, signifying that she was well within herself, that this speed had yet to go full throttle.

The announcer said, "Forty-six and two half-mile. Calvin Borel was able to slow that pace down just a little bit. But they move into the far turn. There's a half-mile to go, Rachel Alexandra still holding that lead."

Past the Point made his move, down on the inside, with Rachel Alexandra's lead only a length. His bid was foolhardy, and he fell back, repelled by her as if a spell had been cast. Asiatic Boy started to lengthen his stride from the back of the pack. But with stronger, more confident lengths, Macho Again swooped around the far turn, only now starting to gather momentum.

Said the announcer: "They're coming to the top of the stretch, and it is still the filly in front. A dramatic stretch drive awaits in the Woodward Stakes."

Out on Union Avenue, drivers could see the torch blaze, the yellow silks, and the maroon "V" soar off the turn. The ground gave way to the thundering herd. Rachel Alexandra's nostrils expelled breaths like a compressed air gun. Borel knew, and Rachel Alexandra knew, it was time to get serious. Borel straightened Rachel Alexandra out—she was still clear by a length. The bellowing roar of the apron and the grandstand was deafening to the ears. Fans jumped and clapped and screamed as the blue saddlecloth on the bay coat blurred by with Borel popping her flank with the whip. Hayward and Betsy Senior and Handel and his wife stood on their toes and craned to the left to watch Rachel Alexandra. "C'mon, Rachel!" Hayward implored, "C'mon, Rachel!"

The announcer said, "Macho Again is making a tremendous run from the back of the pack!"

The grey hide of Macho Again, peppered with a mile's worth of dirt, stormed down the center of the track, his nose even with Rachel Alexandra's right hip. Borel whipped, and whipped, and whipped. Rachel Alexandra's legs curled, thrusted, and extended to the wire, the pair skimming the fence. "Kick away!" Handel yelled, "Let her go! C'mon, Rachel!"

Macho Again's nose was up to Borel's stirrups, and Robby Albarado could just about reach out and touch his old Cajun buddy. Borel yelled back to him, the whip his metronome, "You can't get by me!"

Macho Again was still gaining, swallowing up ground, but Rachel Alexandra felt the pulse of his hooves behind her.

The announcer cried, "Rachel Alexandra! Macho Again! They're coming down to the finish! It's going to be desperately close!"

Borel started to worry. He knew it was up to Rachel Alexandra to dig. It was her race, her legacy, that should she get eyeballed, she couldn't let him pass. There was the core of Macho Again's eyes looking at the fire-ringed, amber orbs of Rachel Alexandra. Her eyes widened. She saw Macho Again, the glint of the sun in her eyes, and as Borel said she would, she dug in. Borel's left arm was fully extended, his head buried between his elbows. His right arm kept Rachel Alexandra to task.

"Here's the wire!" screamed the announcer.

Borel swiveled his head to the right and looked at his friend and the rival who dared to come so close.

And, finally, the announcer screamed, "Rachel won! She is inDEED Rachel Alexandra THE GREAT! Beating Macho Again here and farther back Bullsbay was third. The time was one-forty-eight and one. Rachel Alexandra rrrrraises the rafters here at the Spa!"

Hayward and Handel threw their hands up in the air, and their cheers drowned by the roar of 31,171 fans. They slapped five and jumped up and down, the wind billowing their blazers, their ties flapping and swaying. The grandstand shook, and the pitch and the roar bruised one's eardrums. Rachel Alexandra had brought out the inner child in all.

"I tell ya," Hayward said, "she appreciated that eight pounds."

"She didn't appreciate that twenty-two and forty-six," replied Handel.

Nick Zito looked like a man who had just broken his pencil in mid-sentence. His two horses finished last of all. He threw a rabbit in there, and he did his job. Cool Coal Man was in the perfect spot but didn't fire. He had run twenty-five days earlier. Zito thought Cool Coal Man just bounced; twenty-five days was too short a gap.

After Zito had time to digest the Woodward, he would later say, "She's a freak of nature. She's like—you know what?—you know how the sisters are in tennis, that's how good she is in this port. You know how good they are, you know Serena? You know Venus? How many times they win? She's that good. She's something different. When you see Willie Mays or Joe DiMaggio or Hank Aaron or John Elway or Peyton Manning, Brett Favre, that's what being Rachel is. My greatest compliment with her was when you say 'Ruffian,' that's *enough!* There's nothing else you can say. You're comparing her to one of the greatest—if not *the* greatest—filly of all time. So there's nothing left to say, really. I'm hoping Steve [Asmussen] does the right thing. One more race, hopefully an easy race, a filly race, and that's the end for this year. Sew up Horse of the Year and that's the way it goes."

❧

Funk, sitting past the wire, thought that Macho Again had won. From her angle it looked like Rachel Alexandra was collared. She heard Tom Durkin say that Rachel Alexandra had indeed won, but until it was official, she wasn't about to show a flicker of excitement. Funk watched Rachel Alexandra gallop around the clubhouse and turn; she saw that she looked fine, tired, but fine. She looked to the Tote board and it was official—Rachel Alexandra had won.

Borel trotted back to the grandstand, took his helmet off with both hands, and held it above his head with straight arms, like he were hoisting the World Cup trophy. He then fixed his gaze to the Jumbotron to watch the replay of the race.

Borel's friend, Robby Albarado, could think of nothing but praise. There was never a point when he thought he had her. He said, "You never think you have champions. Champions show different dimensions. She is in a league of her own. No matter what they throw at her, she'll beat them."

Bullsbay's jockey, Jeremy Rose, said, "I got within a neck of her and she just rebroke. She's just too good of a horse. She's awesome; there's no two ways about it."

Everyone stood, and hands were beaten pink from ceaseless applause. Borel waved off the applause that he felt was attributed to him and then pointed to Rachel Alexandra. Borel had been here the whole meet, and on just his forty-first mount had won his second race in thirty-four days of racing.

"Returning to the winner's circle is Rachel Alexandra!" Durkin announced. "And Calvin Borel."

Rachel Alexandra was draped with a blanket of pink flowers, a presumptuous move because if she had lost, they would have been tossed. "The things we do for love," said Handel, looking down into the winner's circle. "She's gonna get a hand going down the homestretch. Watch this. She just . . . that's a race you'll never forget."

Robby Albarado and Calvin Borel met in the winner's circle and shook hands. The two Cajun riders have met many times under the shadow of the wire. Out of Rachel Alexandra's three career losses—all at age two—Albarado beat her twice.

Borel said he never saw so many people crying in his life, and when he saw Funk, she too was crying. "Baby, we won!" Borel said to Funk. "Baby, you don't understand!" she said.

And into the Saratoga Room for the champagne toast, P. J. Campo was already there sipping from a flute of bubbles. "Hoo! She's unbelievable!"

"We are now a part of history," Handel said.

"Now *this* will be a champagne toast," said Steve Duncker, NYRA chairman. "Oh my God! I can't believe she hung in there."

Don Lehr stood with a tiny smile on his face and watched the replay many times over.

Jess Jackson, in a wool fedora, and dozens of others followed him. Jackson thought Borel's ride was perfect. He even recalled looking down into the starting gate and thinking that his filly looked like a three-year-old, thinking those are a lot of big animals that she was running against, but she showed her speed, she showed her class, and she didn't give up. That's my Rachel.

The Saratoga Room broiled with the crowd's heat and swelled with their voices. Glasses clinked—it was a party! Cheers and looks of adulation were focused on the monitors, on the replay of Rachel Alexandra's win.

Calvin Borel came in briefly with Lisa Funk, after he told people that Rachel Alexandra was the reason he came to Saratoga. Winning the Woodward Stakes was a great burden lifted off his 110-pound frame. He admitted it was like winning the Derby. He knew she was good enough, that all he had to do was execute and "not mess it up."

He handed his silks to Funk, and she gave him back his ball cap. By this time, most of the room had cleared. Borel shook hands with those who remained. He grabbed a glass and filled it with white wine and, with a splash, shuffled a few ice cubes in it. Before long he transferred the wine to a plastic cup, turned, and departed, having just made a deposit into the memory banks of thousands who would, without question, let the interest of this lore accrue indefinitely.

26

King Henry V

One day of the meet, on the last Sunday, Charlie Hayward trades in his suit for shorts and a polo shirt, a beer for coffee, and a cigar and *Racing Form* for the weights that bring him down. One day of the meet Charlie Hayward loses the titles and gets back to his roots as a horseplayer with no other worry beyond hitting the first leg of a Pick 3. His buddies from out off town come to visit and buy tickets to sit in the grandstand. Hayward's legs are as pale as Count Dracula's. And, as King Henry V, he drapes himself in commoner's garb, to blend in, but his motive is comfort, not to poll the electorate.

Hayward scribbles notes in his *Form*, "sp" for speed horses, circling gobs of past races to signify that a horse had no business racing in certain company, putting scratches through one horse altogether, circling a bullet drill on the work tab, and slashing a check next to the ones he liked. He circles the trainers and pens "shortens up" in tight letters. There's a science to his handicapping—it's all numbers, it's analytical, and this was how he got into this sport decades ago. Hayward hit the opening Daily Double for $325 and his bet paid out five times the $2 payout. He also hit a Pick 3. Things were good, and he let out a big puff from his cigar.

By most accounts Nick Zito had a decent meet. He won seven races, with $378,740 in earnings, which tied him for tenth in the standings, though well short of twenty wins set by the first female trainer ever to win the Saratoga training title, Linda Rice.

It being the end of the meet, his now-retired horse, Commentator, was honored on the penultimate day. Zito stood in the paddock twirling a chain, waiting for Commentator and talking to Carlos Correa, Commentator's exercise rider. "He's goin' to the winner's circle, right?" Zito said.

Tim Poole, Zito's longtime assistant, said, "It's sad." Poole noted that Commentator looked a bit confused, since this paddock ceremony was unlike anything he had ever experienced. He thought he was going to race. No more racing, just a ceremonial good-bye and a cake baked just for him.

Commentator paraded down the horse path and onto Saratoga's homestretch one last time. Correa galloped him up and then back, down the stretch where he broke his maiden in 2004, the same stretch where he won the Whitney Handicap in 2005 and 2008. Zito watched replays of Commentator's greatest hits and shook his head in amazement. "Remember that one?" he said to his wife Kim.

In the winner's circle a cake in the shape of a key to the city awaited his arrival. The cake contained ½ cup of unsalted butter, ½ cup of firmly packed brown sugar, ½ cup of white sugar, ¼ cup of honey, ¼ cup molasses, 4 cups uncooked oats, ½ teaspoon of salt, ¾ cup Grape Nuts cereal, finely shredded carrots, and 1½ teaspoons of peppermint abstract. Bake at 350 degrees, and twenty to thirty minutes later, voila, Commentator's edible key to the city.

Commentator returned to the winner's circle with his veins pumping, like he was fired up, ready to race. Zito grabbed a piece of the cake and gave him a fistful. With the bit in his mouth, he seemed to have a hard time chewing, but it whetted his appetite for the fruits and pastries of retirement. "It's bittersweet. It was emotional," Zito said, "especially in 2005 for me because I was inducted in the Hall of Fame on the [following] Monday. We came back in 2008 and he almost wins in 2009. He was a tremendous blessing. I thank God for giving me a horse like this. He's a New York horse."

∾

After Charlie Hayward had his day in the gambling limelight without the burdens of his job, it was back to work to close out this 2009 chapter of the Saratoga meet. On his desk, much to his chagrin, was a *New York Post* article from Ed Fountaine knocking NYRA.

Calder Race Course in Florida is famous, or infamous, depending on one's frame of reference, for running lots of races, fourteen-race cards. Due to the overflowing horse population and demand for races, Saratoga ran more races than forecasted. Good for horsemen, but apparently bad for turf writers looking to get to the bar, this according to Hal Handel. It infuriated him, too, to read this:

> **Calder-on-the-Hudson:** Admitting that they overdosed on the number of races last summer, NYRA officials promised this meet would be different, cutting back to nine races on most weekdays, 10 on Thursdays and Sundays, and 11 on Saturdays except for Travers Day.

That went out the window when the meet opened. NYRA will run 365 races this year to last summer's 359.

Some cutback.

Hayward slammed the paper down—maddening, just maddening. Here newspaper reporters are losing jobs around the country covering sports and events that are far more relevant than horse racing. Keep knocking it in this manner and why would a publisher see a turf writer as being valuable to his enterprise? Handel planned on sending Fountaine a Calder T-shirt.

"We didn't have a huddle yesterday," Hayward began. "Rachel Day on Saturday was unbelievable. Most people didn't think we'd get 30,000. There were little girls on the rail, and the race itself; I never heard the grandstand rock like that. Mr. Campo, the day went off without a hitch. The day was just perfect."

"It was a great meet from the racing side, from Glen's crew to my whole department," Campo said.

"We try to run fewer races and we end up running more because of the demand of trainers, two-year-olds, and others, and our friend, Mr. Fountaine, called this meet the 'Calder of the Hudson.' It's fucking insane, pardon my language. We're gonna have a few words in the press box today."

"The Commentator ceremony went well," said Dan Silver. "Nick really appreciated that. I thought it was a nice thing to have."

"This was the best meet I've seen here in four years," said John Ryan, "Thank you."

"I'm done," said Kenneth Cook, vice president of security, "I'm done."

"Great meet," said Hal Handel, "Saturday was a day . . . you'll never see anything quite like it again. I don't think we can do better."

"I agree," said Hayward.

"This was the best meet ever," said Don Lehr, holding his spiral notebook with his numbers and figures. Then looking down at his notebook, "There are excruciating numbers. We were down 2.3 percent for the meet, 1.9 on-track, 1.3 all-source, maybe down a little today, 28,578 last year, 3.4 on-track, 19.5 all-source, eleven races, we have eleven today, 101 last year, 104 today without scratches. These numbers will hold. For what it's worth: congratulations."

All the crates and file cabinets that had been strewn about the administrative building were, at this time, awoken from their six-week hibernation and were out in the hallway ready to be fed with office supplies after their slumber. In a few days racing would begin at Belmont Park for the fall season, but did they have to move so fast? Soon it would be like Saratoga never happened, like it was all an illusion.

P. J. Campo met Charlie Hayward just outside the building where they have their huddles. The two prepped themselves to head up to the press box and give the media one last opportunity to pick at their bones. "Rachel was good," Hayward said. "That made the whole summer."

The two took the escalator up to the second tier and strolled to the narrow staircase that led to the press box. The wood creaked under their feet, and they opened the door. "Ready to roll?" Hayward said.

Immediately, diving head strong into what peeved Hayward the most, quite possibly the most of all that went wrong during the meet, he broached the Calder-on-the-Hudson piece. "Related to that," Hayward said, leaning over to add emphasis, and pressing his fingers together and pointing them at the half moon of reporters, "I think Mr. Fountaine mentioned that we are the 'Calder of the Hudson.'"

"Calder on the Hudson," said Fountaine.

"Good enough. I refer you to it. He made a lot of nice observations. We thought we'd run fewer races than we did, but we ran more. We're actually going to run one more race that we did last year. To Mr. Fountaine's new moniker, we're running one more than they are in Calder today. They're running ten."

"We had 164 turf races," Campo said, "[and] 140 last year. When the races filled, I had to turn trainers away. The horses are there and the population is here."

Someone asked: "What was the worst thing that happened during the meet?" Hayward spoke of the VLTs.

Someone else asked: "What was the second worst thing that happened?"

Hayward spoke of computer hackers bombarding the NYRA Rewards website to keep NYRA customers from using their online accounts.

"You think it was Nassau OTB?"

"That would be giving Dino too much credit," Hayward said, chuckling.

And what was the third worst thing that happened, asked a reporter.

"My wagering activity until yesterday, when I hit the early double and the early Pick 3," said Hayward.

Hayward and Campo exited the press box and creaked down the stairs, "That was okay, right?" Hayward said. "I was making fun of Fountaine and he didn't even know it."

"*What's the third worst thing?*" Campo emphasized, shaking his head.

"That's the mentality," replied Hayward.

Campo and Hayward parted ways, and Hayward said, "It drives you crazy, P. J. works his ass off. "There's never a dull moment."

Hayward told Handel how it went, which is exactly why Handel skipped it. He couldn't take the press box mentality. To some degree the responsible thing was to question authority and to point out weakness and fraud, but there comes a point when that culture of negativity is positively nauseating. "I would've railed those motherfuckers," Handel said, in his always ever-present soothing tone of voice.

∽

One of the horses running in the Hopeful Stakes, a prestigious two-year-old race, was named Overlap. Steve Duncker, part owner of the horse, named it after his friend and racing manager's dating style, which is, when you're ending one, you've already begun another.

In the Saratoga Room, Handel sat at a table with his flute of champagne before him. Hayward fisted popcorn into his mouth with his wife, Betsy Senior, beside him. Apparently Duncker named the horse, "When you're in a relationship . . . ," said Hayward, then he ducked into a private room leaving the sentence to hang on its own. Senior's brow furrowed, and she tilted her head, not that she completely misunderstood, but that she was piecing together the end of the frayed sentence. Handel convulsed in laugher, red in the face. "Does Melinda [Duncker] know about this name?" Senior asked.

On their way to the paddock, Hayward broke off, tangent to the circle, in a sprint, his blazer splaying out behind him like Batman's cape. The rest of the group hardly took notice; rather, they just ignored him and kept moving on to the paddock. Hayward was nimble, recalling the motion that finished the New York Marathon decades ago, darting and weaving his way through patrons, under the banners of stakes races, his marathon stride evident on his executive frame. With his tie curled around his neck, he leapt up onto the stairs of a stage just outside the winner's circle. It seems, in the tumult that six weeks of racing had built, that he had forgotten about his last television commitment of the meet, one he made as they readied to hit "Record" on their cameras.

The gang met back in the Saratoga Room after the Hopeful where Overlap was dumped somewhere toward the rear of the field. Hayward went to the popcorn basket and heaved a few kernels in his mouth and dropped some on his tie. He dusted off the crumbs, with a larger piece falling to the ground. Janine, the head server of the room, watched from her corner with a twinkle. Hayward kicked at the piece several times trying to scurry it under a table, any table, but only topped it with the sole of his shoe. Handel was in hysterics and Janine said, "That's all right, he's the president."

Hayward turned to Handel, "I forgot that I was doing live for Channel 10. I get over there one minute before the hit. Breaking news: Shug McGaughey won the PA Derby."

"Good for them at the casino," said Handel.

Before long, as the shadows grew longer, Handel and Hayward walked back to the administrative building one last time. Handel went inside and grabbed his shoe-shine box and cradled it like a football. Handel slapped it, and it made a hollow sound. "Ready to go," he said. "Great meet."

"Great meet," Hayward said.

And the two shook hands and parted.

∾

Calvin Borel had forty-one mounts the entire meet and won two races. He, arguably, won the two most important of the 2009 calendar year: the Kentucky Derby and the Woodward Stakes. That, however, was in the eye of the beholder.

Borel was reflective in the days after the Woodward. He sat in the courtyard of the jockeys' quarters with his right leg crossed over his left, twirling his butane lighter in his hands. He was forty-two years old and had the weathered lines and cracked skin to prove it. He didn't know what to think of his career. Was it time to hang up his tack? Probably not—not with five thousand wins waiting for him—And not with Rachel Alexandra waiting for him in 2010. But he and his fiancée Lisa Funk owned farm land in Kentucky and planned on raising horses. Borel wanted to pinhook (to speculate in race horses). He'd never be too far removed from horses. It's what he knew—it's all he knew. Rachel Alexandra was the best horse he had ever ridden, and it had only taken thirty years to find her. Maybe it was time to think about retirement, but only once Rachel Alexandra became a mom.

Borel took off his remaining mounts for the weekend and decided to head back home to Kentucky with Funk. They packed their belongings from their apartment by the police station and grabbed their corgi Chloe Bea and hopped into the vehicle. It mattered not that Borel had garnered so little respect in Saratoga. The chips on his shoulders have been calloused by slights of this manner for years. In a few weeks Borel would go on to share the title of leading rider at Churchill Downs with twenty-seven wins. That showed them. After one last pass through Saratoga Springs with the Rachel Alexandra flags still flapping in the September breeze, Borel and Funk hit the highway and turned their backs on Season 141.

∾

As the egg-yolk sun was setting to the west, people flooded out of Saratoga Race Course for the final time in 2009 with the images of big scores, big races, and big memories. The season had ended, but the races still ran laps inside the heads of all who cared to remember.

Star-shaped balloons wobbled into the air, released by careless hands. They floated on and on into the baby-blue sky, with one gaining on the others. It launched into a smear of clouds, a shooting star taking its lovely time to reach a pinnacle unseen by any and all. Onward it rose to the echo of memory, until it was so small, so high, that it looked like a spot of ink.

27

Farewell to the Champ

The photograph of Rachel Alexandra in the window of the Saratoga Saddlery had disappeared. Someone had either purchased it, or Rachel Alexandra had gone out of style, it being past Labor Day. And, like white clothes, Rachel Alexandra would soon be tucked away in a trunk and put away for the winter.

Rachel Alexandra rested for the remainder of the season, her connections finally having found the bottom of the tank with her Woodward Stakes win. She went out to the track for jogs, but she was never put under duress. This much she deserved.

She walked around the barn and then was turned out in a round pen, where she bucked like a bronco, up on her front legs, and flicking her hind end with such force that she could catapult clumps of dirt from her barn to Union Avenue.

The days were warm, and the nights were cool. Rachel Alexandra remained in light training, nothing serious, just enough to take the edge off. She still got a few visitors, people eyeballing her in Stall No. 1 to say they caught a glimpse. Trainer Steve Asmussen thought that it was amazing that this filly has been such a sweetheart, given that Rachel Alexandra had had such a grueling campaign. The plan was to ship her to Churchill Downs in six days.

It was October now, just a month after closing weekend, and the Saratoga backside looked like a ghost town, the barns skeletal. The few remaining horses were like discarded scraps. Most of the horse population had been transported to other barns and tracks closer to the equator. Only five horses remained in Steve Asmussen's Barn 65. All of the benches, plants, and signs were gone. The flowers around the barn's main tree were flaccid.

Rachel Alexandra poked her head out of her stall, her ears pricked, her head bowed low, snacking on hay. The trees were brushed with fine autumnal color, and the sky was a rich and settling blue. Rachel Alexandra gnawed on the door of Scott Blasi's office; her teeth grinded with a metallic scrape.

A Sallee van, like the one Commentator left on, eased up to a ramp. Rachel Alexandra was leaving Saratoga Springs.

Eight members of Asmussen's and Blasi's staff spoke in Latin tones, their life's belongings in bags next to them. They rushed their bags onto the van and grabbed hay nets and horses. A flock of pigeons started and flew off. Blasi said, "Javier, get Rachel's water bucket for her, will ya?"

They were like an army's last line, picking up and moving to the front with their rear secured. Blasi retrieved Rachel Alexandra, the last of the remaining. Her tongue flapped and her shoes clopped on the tar. In her obedient stride she walked beside Blasi and disappeared into the chamber of the van. Behind her, all eight of Blasi's helpers embarked on the vessel bound for Churchill Downs, the site of Rachel Alexandra's Kentucky Oaks triumph.

The van's engine grumbled and its doors closed. Its wheels turned slowly on the axles. The van carried all that was good about horse racing, in its belly a hero. It even caused Ed Fountaine to write: "RACHELMANIA: The Woodward was the kind of race that made you remember why you became a racing fan in the first place." Kind words followed by: "Unfortunately, in a sad reflection of how inept the racing industry is when it comes to marketing itself, the Woodward was not on national TV." Small victories.

Rachel Alexandra's impact on Saratoga and on the culture was encouraging, this sports hero who upheld so many virtues, even when our most cherished and infallible sports stars would come crashing down from their Halley's orbit. That a female horse could beat up the boys was inspiring, truly inspiring. The following are some actual fan letters sent to Rachel's Sandbox:

> Hi, I'm Jayden and I'm Rachel Alexandra's biggest fan. I say that because I made a book about her. It's called "The Famous Filly." It's not published yet. Soon I hope it will be. It's weird though, because I had a dream about a bay filly, she won all the time, she made it to the Preakness. I know my dream came true. I have pictures of her all over my room and on my phone, too. If Rachel ever does lose, I would always be her number one fan.
>
> When I race someone at my school, all I think about is Rachel and how she beats the boys and I run so fast when I think about her. I'm glad my dream came true. I'm also glad that there is a horse that made me different.
>
> From Jayden

Rachel has brought excitement not seen every day at the races. She has sparked the imagination of men and women alike by her grace, power, and beauty. At the Mother Goose and Haskell, which I excitedly attended, she was greeted in the paddock with cheers and picture taking, which did not even faze her calm demeanor. She is a superstar filly who I hope has a long racing career.

Joan
Racing Fan

Dear Rachel Alexandra,

What we watched unfold this summer will never occur again in our lifetime. I am so thankful to have found you on YouTube before the Oaks. Even through video, your star power shined through like a beacon, like nothing I had ever seen in my life. I knew right then and there you were special. I told anyone and everyone that would listen, about you, and when you won the Preakness, people said to me, "that is the horse you were talking about." I said, "Yes, I cannot wait to see what she does next." What I didn't know is that you would electrify this household, the casual fan, this sport and this summer. You have become a household name, and because of you, I flew 3,000 miles to fulfill a lifelong dream to step through the gates of Belmont Park. You did not disappoint. You have never disappointed. You have only made us all smile and cry because you are so beautiful, so perfect, so heaven sent.

Whatever your future holds, I want to say a true thank-you for creating a summer that will float into history as one of the most special horse racing seasons anyone has ever witnessed. And you did it so willingly, so professionally and so proudly. You, most likely, have not finished your story, but if for some reason, you have, I can say that I was there, that I saw you in person, and that I watched you in every race. I can say with a smile on my face, that in the years to come, when your name is mentioned like Ruffian's or Secretariat's, I can smile to myself and know that I was there, in the midst of history. How lucky we all were, to have been there, during the summer of '09.

With love and peppermint kisses . . .

Courtney Cunniff
North Bend, WA

Hey Rachel:

You are the best horse of the World!

You can win the DUBAI WORLD CUP!!

YES YOU CAN!!

Filiberto Rodriguez

Hi Rachel,

I want you to know how much you have done for the horse racing industry. You and Calvin have taken it to a new level! Take care of yourself, eat your oats, and we hope to see you racing in 2010.

Blessings, Carolyn Linder, a Fan

The van came to a halt at Union Avenue and turned left at the intersection where Rachel Alexandra had stopped traffic on her way to school in the paddock two days before she had won the Woodward Stakes, when she drew the eyes of thousands to learn the ropes of the Saratoga saddling area. The van hesitated and jerked as its gears shifted and began to pull away.

The light ahead was green, and the van continued onward, picking up more speed as the on-ramp to Interstate 87 South neared. The mountains to the east peaked like jagged teeth on the eastern horizon, walling off the state of Vermont.

A compact car zipped by the van on the on-ramp to the right, the only time Rachel Alexandra had been passed in eight tries in 2009. From atop the overpass, one saw the van accelerate onward.

The Interstate doglegged to the south against a backdrop of speeding cars but also against the oranges, reds, yellows, and browns of the treetops so crisp against the blue horizon. The van accelerated and merged into the right lane. Its directional winked one last time. Rachel Alexandra, like the final fragile leaf of autumn, at last fluttered to the ground with the van curving around the bend and out of sight.

Epilogue

The Coronation

". . . Rachel Alexandra," finished National Thoroughbred Racing Association President Alex Waldrop at the 39th Annual Eclipse Awards.

Principal owner Jess Jackson stood and raised both arms to the ceiling. He kissed his wife, Barbara Banke, and wrapped his left arm around her. Jackson, followed by his family and the horseman who handled Rachel Alexandra, threaded his way through the tables and up to the lectern.

Jerry and Ann Moss, owners of the magnificent undefeated mare Zenyatta, sat in their chairs visually disappointed. Jerry's lips clamped together. He possessed the look of someone who knows no moral victories.

The clamor died down as Jackson leaned into the lectern and addressed the audience. "Um, I'm almost speechless, because this contest was so close. I don't know the count, but I know either horse, either filly, deserved this award."

Jackson seemed humbled, as if any exhibition of joy might seem like he was gloating. To one's ear he sounded like the gracious winner. "Together Rachel Alexandra and Zenyatta won nine Grade 1 races. Together they conquered four of the best groups of males that were running last year. If you think about their achievements individually or collectively, there has never been another year like this for fillies. I want to thank Jerry and Ann for being so gracious all through the year, and we supported each other. You wouldn't know that but occasionally we talked and we sent congratulations to each other, and I really appreciated the grace and charm and ability of the Zenyatta team, and particularly Jerry and Ann Moss. It couldn't be arranged that they would meet last year. We're hoping that each horse, taking its course, may win their way to an ultimate match, and maybe we can work toward that."

The Mosses remained expressionless. Jerry Moss would later say, "Zenyatta's never lost. She's perfect. Nobody's beaten her on the racetrack. So they beat her by proxy as far as I'm concerned. This doesn't take away anything, from the just enormous job done by [trainer] John [Shirreffs]. I can't say enough about what he and his barn have done. I obviously congratulate Mr. Jackson and Mrs. Jackson. They have a great horse. Someday we'll meet, and we'll decide at that time who is the best. Frankly I wouldn't trade with anybody. I'm looking forward to the encounter."

∾

Oaklawn Park ponied up.

If Rachel Alexandra and Zenyatta met on the track in the Grade 1 Apple Blossom Handicap, then the purse would be $5 million—tied for the richest race in America with the Breeders' Cup Classic.

Zenyatta trained beautifully toward the match, never missing a beat after her own win over the boys in the Classic. With thirteen of her fourteen wins on synthetic surfaces, people were eager to see her run again on dirt to see if she wasn't just some West Coast fluke insulating herself with California's synthetic tracks. Rachel Alexandra, on the other hand, found her wheels spinning more slowly.

A rain-dampened December in Louisiana—a record twenty-six inches of precipitation—kept Rachel Alexandra confined to the barn, thus she missed several days of training. This would be a haunting specter.

Rachel Alexandra came back to the track at Fairgrounds in Louisiana on January 31, 2010, just two days after her fourth calendar birthday (all thoroughbreds turn a year older on January 1). It was her first work since her thunderclap win against older males in the Woodward Stakes nearly five months earlier. It was an easy half-mile move in fifty-two seconds. Exercise rider Dominic Terry kept her in the middle of the track and felt she went perfectly, galloping out nicely. Assistant trainer Scott Blasi thought highly of the horse's work as well, noting that one had to trick her into going more slowly, which is "physically impossible for her."

Meanwhile, Oaklawn Park kept working on a "Race for the Ages." Zenyatta was, at one time, retired, yet curiously she remained in training after her Classic win. Prior to the Eclipse Awards, her owners announced that she would race in 2010. A meeting between the two seemed inevitable. Charles Cella, Oaklawn Park president, announced that the $500,000 Apple Blossom Handicap, to be run on April 3, 2010, at one and one-sixteenth miles, would be changed to the $5 million Apple Blossom Invitational at one and one-eighth miles—only if Zenyatta and Rachel Alexandra entered the starting gate.

Both parties were pleased. However, Rachel Alexandra's trainer, Steve Asmussen, was quick to say, "It's great to see how much interest there is in the mares, and hopefully it will come together. From a timing standpoint, it's less than optimum." In other words, you can't bake a cake in half the time at twice the heat.

On February 6 Rachel Alexandra picked up the pace with a four-furlong drill in 50.60 seconds—seven lengths faster than her inaugural move. In the meantime, Fairgrounds wrote a race specifically for her to make her 2010 debut—a cushy spot for her to stretch her legs, get an easy win, and be on her way to Arkansas for the Apple Blossom. The race would be the New Orleans Ladies Handicap, run at one and one-sixteenth miles.

Before the dust settled on her last workout, Asmussen announced on February 10 that Rachel Alexandra would not be ready to take on a horse of Zenyatta's caliber with the Apple Blossom just two months away. He said, "Out of respect for the level of competition and the importance of this race, I have told Mr. Jackson it was not in the best interest of the horse to race on April 3. Getting to this level of fitness after a six-month layoff takes time. If all goes according to schedule, and we don't have any further weather delays, the earliest we could have a prep race would be the middle of March. It is then not fair to Rachel to ask her to race again three weeks later."

Jackson added, "Everyone wants see to Rachel race against Zenyatta—including me. In fact I want it to happen several times this year."

Cella then moved the date of the race back six days, to Friday, April 9, 2010, in an attempt to ensure that Rachel Alexandra would be ready and to give her the time that her handlers said she needed.

"I've never had so much trouble giving $5 million away," said Cella.

So Rachel Alexandra's workouts zipped through February. With the date of the Apple Blossom pushed back, the "students" had more time to study for the exam, so to speak. Rachel Alexandra's debut race at Fairgrounds—the New Orleans Ladies Handicap—waited. All was well. If Rachel Alexandra made quick work of this small field, a field that included the John Shirreffs-trained Zardana, then a meeting with Zenyatta would follow.

Rachel Alexandra's strides became smoother, and her fitness crept back. The long layoff had taken its toll, however; her inertia was similar to a cruise ship. She was schooled in the paddock on March 6, 2010, as she always is before a big race. "She was relaxed for her not having run in six months," according to Asmussen.

Four challengers were set for the New Orleans Ladies Handicap. As a precautionary measure, Asmussen had said that Rachel Alexandra wasn't quite fit yet, almost as if to say that it was within the realm of possibility for his Horse of the Year to suffer defeat.

And that's what happened.

Jockey Calvin Borel tracked the leader early in a comfortable spot just off the rail. Borel and Rachel Alexandra plowed into the wind. On the turn, Borel let Rachel Alexandra loose, and she took the lead. Zardana loomed and surged to Rachel Alexandra's flank. The two exchanged the lead. First Zardana went by, and Rachel Alexandra—having never been passed once on the lead—battled back. But Zardana grinded and edged to a three-quarter-length victory.

After going 8 for 8 in 2009, embarrassing her own sex and smashing the boys three times, Rachel Alexandra lost a race written for her on her terms, to trainer John Shirreffs's second-string mare in Zardana.

On the same day out, March 13, 2010, West, Zenyatta took care of her business, upping her record to a perfect 15–0 in the $250,000 Santa Margarita Stakes. What would happen when Zenyatta came back East?

The following day Rachel Alexandra's owner, Jess Jackson, said, "I decided today she will not be going to the Oaklawn Invitational on April 9." The accelerated nature of training had created too much pressure, like trying to hammer a square peg into a round hole.

And with that, North America's two most popular horses—and females at that—missed the runway. The hope remained, however, that with eight months of racing ahead of them, Rachel Alexandra and Zenyatta would meet on dirt, on an oval, where it mattered.

It was only March, but the two would never meet.

∽

The year wasn't over. The ultimate goal was the Breeders' Cup, more specifically, the Breeders' Cup Classic. So Rachel Alexandra's handlers turned the screws and brought her to her favorite track and the site of her most visibly awesome triumph: Churchill Downs.

Rachel Alexandra registered swift workouts: a five-furlong breeze in 1:00 1/5 seconds, a six furlong, a twelve-clip drill in 1:12 flat, and another six-furlong move in 1:11 1/5 seconds. Her next race would be the $400,000 La Troienne Stakes on Kentucky Oaks Day, run at one and one-sixteenth miles.

The expectations were no less dampened. After all, she was back at Churchill Downs, where she won the Kentucky Oaks by 20¼ lengths. As the 1–9 favorite, Rachel Alexandra ran into the eventual 2010 Breeders' Cup Ladies Classic winner, Unrivaled Belle, and lost by a head after rumbling down the homestretch. Rachel Alexandra was 0 for 2.

Calvin Borel, again, kept Rachel Alexandra in a strong hold before letting her loose. And again she lacked the kick to bury her rival. "She finished second," said Asmussen, "and the excuses are obvious when you go to searching."

She'd stay at Churchill Downs and train under the twin spires, putting in her fourth consecutive Monday workout—this one a six furlong in 1:11 1/5 seconds. Asmussen slipped her name into the entry box for the Grade 2 Fleur de Lis Handicap in an effort to get her first win in 2010.

At last Rachel Alexandra provided relief for her connections on Saturday, June 12, 2010, when she romped to a 10½-length win. Steve Asmussen gave

Scott Blasi a smashing hug, as if squeezing juice out of him. Even Borel was happy: "She stepped it up today. She did the impossible last year."

So it was on to Saratoga Springs.

⌒

She returned to Barn 65 and to Stall No. 1, where she had lived during her memorable summer a year earlier. Blasi said she looked fabulous.

Rachel Alexandra drilled in the fog and whispered over that Oklahoma Training Track dirt. As she had done last summer, she would race down on the Jersey Shore at Monmouth Park, yet another race created just for her—the $400,000 Lady's Secret Stakes, run at nine furlongs, on July 24.

Columnists and reporters argued that Zenyatta lacked prestige, because her handlers insulated her in California, with its synthetic tracks and soft competition. However, Rachel Alexandra, in her four-year-old year, was certainly the beneficiary of special treatment. The New Orleans Ladies Handicap was written for her. The Lady's Secret was also created for her—its original distance one and one-sixteenth miles for $150,000, to be run a week later on the Haskell Invitational undercard. Monmouth moved the date to better capitalize on Rachel Alexandra, but also to keep her on her prescribed racing schedule.

Monmouth Park was the scene of Rachel Alexandra's most explosive triumph of 2009 in the Haskell Invitational, where she toyed with the boys before unleashing a neck-cracking six-length win over eventual Champion Three-Year-Old Male Summer Bird. It was hot and humid, the heat index 100. People who expected that same turn of foot didn't get it—they *did* get a win from her: a three-length score.

Back at Saratoga it was quickly decided that Rachel Alexandra would stretch out to ten furlongs, the coveted one and one-quarter miles, in the Grade 1 $300,000 Personal Ensign Stakes. Zenyatta had proven that she could handle the distance. Now it was time for Rachel Alexandra to prove it. If she could, then it would be a matter of fine-tuning, and then that meeting, that star in sky, a clash between the undefeated mare Zenyatta and the 2009 Horse of the Year, would percolate.

The Saratoga main track was the scene of her greatest triumph, and she would be the 2–5 favorite breaking from Post 2. She'd face the nifty five-year-old mare Life At Ten coming in off a six-race winning streak, including the Grade 1 Ogden Phipps and the ten-furlong Delaware Handicap. Life At Ten would, undoubtedly, be sent to the front.

Only five horses broke from the starting gate, and Rachel Alexandra sprinted to the lead heading into Saratoga's clubhouse turn. With Life At Ten at her right flank, Calvin Borel drew Rachel wide into the turn. He had no intention of relinquishing the lead. What was startling to jockey John Velazquez was that he was joined by Calvin Borel and Rachel Alexandra on the front end. "That was a speed duel," said Velazquez. "I thought my filly would be on the lead and Rachel would rate in second, but he sent her out and got in the lead, and all that did was create more problems for my horse because now she was engaged. But I wasn't going to take her back; I just left her alone. I wasn't going to go back either, so I just held my position and left it alone."

The two swept around the turn sizzling a quarter mile in 23.66 seconds. They blitzed ahead of the field by ten lengths, then fifteen lengths as the half-mile fraction shot up in 47.73 seconds—over a second slower than Rachel Alexandra's half-mile jaunt in the Woodward Stakes a year earlier. Three-quarters of a mile went in 1:12.02.

Alan Garcia, aboard Persistently, began to uncoil her stride after a mile was run in 1:37.54. Rachel Alexandra kicked clear by daylight from the Grade 1-winning mare Life At Ten. Rachel Alexandra's bubblegum-colored tongue flopped out of her mouth as Borel urged her for more run. She straightened out for the wire, still an eighth of a mile away, still in front by daylight. The ground gave out from under her. She seemed to be running on a treadmill: churning so hard but covering zero ground. Persistently came up to her. Borel whipped Rachel Alexandra right-handed. Rachel Alexandra's tongue lashed. Her ears splayed against her head, her fire-ringed eyes extinguished.

Persistently skipped by to win by a length in a time of 2:04.49. Rachel Alexandra came home in a pedestrian 25+ seconds. "She just got outrun," Borel said. "I had everything my way, and she just got outrun. After we put away Life At Ten at the quarter pole, I didn't feel any acceleration and I got worried. She wasn't really there. I knew if anyone was running behind us, we were in trouble. If you can't take the losing with the winning, you can't be in the game."

It was Rachel Alexandra's third loss of the year, and after this race it was clear that ten furlongs would be out of the question. If she couldn't hold off Persistently, then how could she hold off Zenyatta? Or the 2010 Stephen Foster and Whitney champion Blame? Or the 2010 Donn and Woodward champion Quality Road? If Rachel Alexandra went to the Breeders' Cup on the weekend of November 5 and 6, she certainly would run in the Ladies Classic at one and one-eighth miles—the distance she relished as a three-year-old to win the Kentucky Oaks, the Mother Goose Stakes, the Haskell Invitational, and, finally, the Woodward Stakes.

The night of the Personal Ensign, trainer Steve Asmussen and owner Jess Jackson didn't discuss retirement. Asmussen, however, sounded defeated: "We'll talk to Jess and decide what's next. Still trying to absorb Sunday. If I'd ever went to sleep last night I would have woke up saying, 'You're lying.'"

Rachel Alexandra went back to the work tab two weeks later with a swift five-eighths move in 1:00.65. She drilled a week later, three-quarters of a mile in 1:12.05, and then a week later, on September 27, she fired a bullet half-mile work in 48.45—the fastest of all thirty-eight times that day. It looked as though she was sharp and ready to take on a competitive field of fillies and mares in the Grade 1 Beldame Invitational in five days.

Then it happened. No turn signal. Nothing. Jess Jackson pulled the emergency brake and retired Rachel Alexandra on September 28.

As much as the racing world wanted her to regain the thunder of 2009, it simply would never happen. She endured, quite possibly, the most aggressive three-year-old campaign a filly had ever tried, certainly since Winning Colors in 1988. And she came out of it 8–0 while beating the boys not once, not twice, but three times.

For 2010's entirety, Calvin Borel took Rachel Alexandra back off the pace, that was, until her final race. But in that race she was pressed. It prompted a review of Rachel Alexandra's notes from her past performances leading up to the 2009 Kentucky Oaks:

> . . . has won from slightly off the pace, but is 4-for-4 lifetime when she is the leader at 1st call; obviously is not as effective when she takes back off the engine . . . is obviously the filly to beat.

That was on May 1, 2009, and it seemed every bit as true today that she, when relaxed, was best on the front end and, most certainly, always the filly to beat.

Perhaps it was too painful to see her struggle to win, and in so doing, to come up shy by a length. Maybe it was like leaving a prizefighter in the ring a few punches too long. And maybe they wanted to pay her back with the rest she deserved.

Rachel Alexandra was vanned to Lane's End Farm, where she was bred to two-time Horse of the Year Curlin on February 21, 2011. She now lives at Jess Jackson's Stonestreet Farm on Old Frankfort Pike in Lexington, Kentucky, where Jackson seeks to "reward her with a less stressful life." Racing, after all, is only half of racehorse.

She ran circles with the best over her three-year career, covering 153.5 furlongs—19.1875 miles—at eight different tracks across North America. And as the tide recedes from her athletic career, other images return. There'd always be the morning of her fog-cloaked eruption; the dozens of heads watching; the swiveling necks; the jaw-dropping velocity; the deafening silence of her winged cadence; that most memorable breeze three weeks before the 2009 Woodward Stakes.

She appeared and, no sooner, she bent around the turn, fading from sight, where the headlines would soon read "Where to?" She pierced that seam of fog and slipped through with the mist clapping back onto itself, closing the curtain.

References

About.com, "Hayward named NYRA President," November 5, 2004.

Associated Press, "Commentator wins again in Whitney," July 27, 2008.

Araton, Harvey, "Thoroughbred racing wrestles with its reputation," *New York Times*, May 2, 2009.

Affruniti, Anthony, "Nassau OTB, NYRA continue their feud," *New York Post*, July 24, 2009.

Affrunti, Anthony, "'Rachel' on track for showdown," *New York Post*, July 29, 2009.

Amedio, Steve, "The Many Faces of John Morrissey," *Jaybel's Saratoga Summer Magazine*, Summer 2000.

Angst, Frank, "Addition of slots helped bring Derby winner to Chester," *Charleston Gazette*, July 25, 2009.

Beyer, Andrew, "Again, Borel's tactics turn out brilliant," *Washington Post*, May 17, 2009.

Beyer, Andrew, "Rachel Alexandra crashes through the glass ceiling," *The Washington Post*, September 4, 2009.

Blasi, Scott, interview with Karen Johnson, http://www.ntra.com/blogprint.aspx?blogi d=25&year=2009&month=6&day=25, June 25, 2009

Blood-Horse, "Nassau Regional OTB to show Saratoga racing," July 29, 2009.

Borel, Calvin, "What is it like to ride Rachel Alexandra?" *Facebook.com*, January 23, 2010.

Bossert, Jerry, "Saratoga's success in 141st season is up to Rachel Alexandra, Mother Nature," *New York Daily News*, July 29, 2009.

Boston Globe, "Rachel acting like a pro after Woodward win," September 6, 2009.

Bouyea, Brien, "Of shear will and brawn." *Spirit of Saratoga*, August 2007.

Business Review, "Post time: An interview with NYRA CEO Charles Hayward," July 27, 2007.

Conley, Kevin, "Black beauty." *Vogue*, May 2009.

Courier-journal.com, "Wiggins left to watch Rachel from a distance," May 17, 2009.

Courier-Journal, "Alexandra the Great outruns boys again," August 3, 2009.

Crist, Steven, "New York's offtrack betting setup a fine mess," *Daily Racing Form*, July 30, 2009.

Crist, Steven, "Rachel's agenda a perfect fit." *Daily Racing Form*, September 3, 2009.

Curry, Mike, "Smith back on Mine That Bird for West Virginia Derby," *Thoroughbred Times*, July 5, 2009.

Daily Freeman, "His generosity—How he helped a poor church in Saratoga," May 2, 1878.

Daily Racing Form, "Rachel Alexandra bound for Haskell," July 14, 2009.

Daily Saratogian, "Mr. Morrissey performs a kind act," August 9, 1871.

Daily Saratogian, "Hon. John Morrissey purchases the Pavilion Property," August 26, 1871.

Daily Saratogian, "His condition precarious—An attack of paralysis," April 29, 1878.

Daily Saratogian, "His condition a trifle, easier this afternoon," April 30, 1878.

Daily Saratogian, "False statements—His condition today—The return of his disease," May 1, 1878.

Daily Saratogian, "A sketch of his career," May 2, 1878.

Daily Saratogian, "The Remains of the Senator viewed by a large number of people—Singing of a quartette—Remains taken to Troy," May 2, 1878.

Daily Saratogian, "Senator's Morrissey's death," May 2, 1878.

Daily Saratogian, "The death of Senator Morrissey—Eulogies by Senators Harris, Jacobs, Pomeroy, Hughes, McCarthy and Ecclesine," May 3, 1878.

Daily Saratogian, "An immense concourse, and an imposing funeral—The last respects to Senator Morrissey," May 4, 1878.

Diamos, Jason, "HORSE RACING; This time, Krone gets plaudits from Zito," *New York Times*, June 11, 1995.

Diamos, Jason, "HORSE RACING; Squabble has added an edge to Travers," *New York Times*, August 25, 2000.

Diamos, Jason, "Birdstone has shot at upsetting Smarty Jones again," *New York Times*, September 4, 2004.

Diamos, Jason, "Z stands for zero so far for Zito in Triple Crown," *New York Times*, June 11, 2005.

Drape, Joe, "HORSE RACING; Zito seeks top-grade efforts in Gold Cup," *New York Times*, October 5, 2001.

Drape, Joe, "HORSE RACING; The odd couple of the backstretch," *New York Times*, July 28, 2003.

Drape, Joe, "What are the odds? A trainer with 5 shots to win the Derby," *New York Times,* May 4, 2005.

Drape, Joe, "HORSE RACING; Trainers, bettors, horses and officials on edge at Saratoga," *New York Times*, July 28, 2005.

Drape, Joe, "Commentator fulfills a Christmas wish by winning the Whitney Stakes," *New York Times*, August 7, 2005.

Drape, Joe, "Racing Hall of Fame inducts Zito," *New York Times*, August 9, 2005.

Drape, Joe, "Bellamy Road likely to run in the Travers," *New York Times*, August 24, 2005.

Drape, Joe, "Two New York trainers linked by long odds," *New York Times*, May 19, 2006.

Drape, Joe, "Kudos for Zito, and questions about Big Brown," *New York Times*, June 9, 2008.

Drape, Joe, "Shaking off long odds at the Derby," *New York Times*, May 2, 2009.

Drape, Joe, "2 entries at Saratoga's opener: hope and gloom," *New York Times*, July 30, 2009.

Drape, Joe, "Quick trip to the Shore for Rachel Alexandra," *The New York Times*, August 2, 2009.

Durso, Joseph, "HORSE RACING; Around Barn 42, lots of buzzing," *New York Times*, May 1, 1991.

Durso, Joseph, "ON HORSE RACING; The Blue Grass Factor in winning the Derby," *New York Times*, May 7, 1991.

Durso, Joseph, "HORSE RACING; Zito makes inner peace his priority at the Derby," *New York Times*, April 29, 1998.

Durso, Joseph, "HORSE RACING; Zito takes a double shot at an upset in Belmont," *New York Times*, June 1, 1999.

Durso, Joseph, "HORSE RACING; Early test in Florida for Derby hopefuls," *New York Times*, February 18, 2000.

Durso, Joseph, "HORSE RACING; Zito's hopes for Derby are fading after loss," *New York Times*, April 23, 2000.

Durso, Joseph, "HORSE RACING; Albert the Great is Zito's ticket to the 3-year-old race," *New York Times* July 5, 2000.

Durso, Joseph, "HORSE RACING; Zito seeks late-season lightning in Breeders' Cup," *New York Times*, November 1, 2000.

Ehalt, Bob, "Next stop: The Woodward." http://www.ntra.com/blogprint.aspx?blogid=14&year=2009&month=8&day=27, August, 27, 2009.

Ehalt, Bob, "The rivalry that never was," September 29, 2010, http://ntra.com/blog/index/print?id=1125&type=blog.

Elia, Lewis, "John Morrissey left his mark on Saratoga Springs," *Saratogian*, June 26, 2007.

Eskenazi, Gerald, "HORSE RACING; Zito and Strike the Gold: Winners for New York," *New York Times,* June 7, 1992.

Eskenazi, Gerald, "Zito, Strike the Gold Trainer, is accused of hitting writer," *New York Times*, June 10, 1992.

Farrell, Mike, "Lady's Secret next for Rachel," *Daily Racing Form*, July 1, 2010.

Farrell, Mike, "Rachel gallops, ready for Lady's Secret," *Daily Racing Form*, July 23, 2010.

Farrell, Mike, "Rachel Alexandra takes care of business," *Daily Racing Form*, July 24, 2010.

Finley, Bill, "HORSE RACING; Zito is too familiar with finishing second," *New York Times*, June 10, 2001.

Finley, Bill, "HORSE RACING; After two-year absence, Zito is back in the race," *New York Times*, April 28, 2004.

Finley, Bill, "HORSE RACING; Zito ends his drought with 'greatest' victory," *New York Times*, June 6, 2004.

Finley, Bill, "Racing; N.Y.R.A. shakes up its staff," *New York Times*, July 15, 2005.

Finley, Bill, "Prospects of Florida Derby Finally looking brighter for Zito," *New York Times*, March 31, 2005.

Finley, Bill, "In road to Derby, Zito finds it's all coming up roses," *New York Times*, April 16, 2005.

Finley, Bill, "A winner for Zito: The Hall of Fame," *New York Times*, June 1, 2005.

Finley, Bill, "Zito looks to 2-year-old to rekindle his success," *New York Times*, October 27, 2007.

Finley, Bill, "Once again, Zito plays the role of spoiler," *New York Times*, June 8, 2008.

Finley, Bill, "Filly is a champ, and may not be finished," *The New York Times*, May 27, 2009.

Finley, Bill, "Munnings hot going into Haskell," *ESPN.com*, July 31, 2009.

Finley, Bill, "'Rachel' beating the best," *ESPN.com*, September 2, 2009.

Finley, Bill, "Woodward victory would solidify Rachel Alexandra's spot in history," *The New York Times*, September 5, 2009.

Finley, Bill, "Rachel Alexandra is tested but wins the Woodward," *New York Times*, September 6, 2009.

Fitz-Gerald, Charles, "Old Smoke and the Benicia Boy," *New York Alive*, November/ December, 1989.

Forde, Pat, "How a common man rode to greatness," *ESPN.com*, May 4, 2007.

Forde, Pat, "This Kentucky Derby offers chills, thrills," *ESPN.com*, May 2, 2009.

Fountaine, Ed, "'Rachel' waits at Spa," *New York Post*, August 4, 2009.

Fountaine, Ed, "'Rachel' gets nod for Woodward run," *New York Post*, August 24, 2009.

Fountaine, Ed, "Alexandra 'heavy' favorite vs. lighter field in Woodward," *New York Post*, September 5, 2009.

Futterman, Matthew, "Where Calvin Borel learned to ride," *Wall Street Journal*, June 5, 2009.

Grening, David, "Ice's small stable has a big future," *Daily Racing Form*, June 6, 2009.

Grening, David, "Haskell pivotal to Rachel's ultimate goal," *Daily Racing Form*, July 31, 2009.

Grening, David, "Rachel blows away colts in the Haskell," *Daily Racing Form*, August 2, 2009.

Grening, David, "Borel tunes up Warrior's Reward for Travers," *Daily Racing Form*, August 23, 2009.

Grening, David, "Borel back on Mine That Bird," *Daily Racing Form*, August 31, 2009.

Grening, David, "Taking stock of Commentator," *Daily Racing Form*, August 6, 2009.

Grening, David, "Rachel Alexandra, Mine That bird work," Daily Racing Form, August 17, 2009.

Grening, David, "Decision on Rachel expected next week," *Daily Racing Form*, August 19, 2009.

Grening, David, "Rachel Alexandra enters Woodward," *Daily Racing Form*, August 24, 2009.

Grening, David, "'Rachel' morning chauffeur," *Daily Racing Form*, September 2, 2009.

Grening, David, "Wooward: Old Pros take shot at Rachel," *Daily Racing Form*, September 3, 2009.

Grening, David, "Rachel 'not likely' to again this year," *Daily Racing Form*, September 6, 2009.

Grening, David, "Rachel Alexandra arrives in Saratoga," *Daily Racing Form*, June 30, 2010.

Grening, David, "Rachel Alexandra rolls into Monmouth," *Daily Racing Form*, July 20, 2010.

Grening, David, "Rachel's timing just right," *Daily Racing Form*, July 22, 2010.

Grening, David, "Rachel likely to stay home next time," *Daily Racing Form*, July 25, 2010.

Grening, David, "Rachel Alexandra looks strong in Spa work," *Daily Racing Form*, August 2, 2010.

Grening, David, "Rachel Alexandra comes home quick in six-furlong work," *Daily Racing Form*, August 9, 2010.

Grening, David, "Rachel works toward Personal Ensign," *Daily Racing Form*, August 16, 2010.

Grening, David, "Rachel Alexandra 2-5 for Personal Ensign," *Daily Racing Form*, August 26, 2010.

Grening, David, "Rachel goes longer than ever before in Personal Ensign," *Daily Racing Form*, August 28, 2010.

Grening, David, "Rachel's camp takes moment to regroup," *Daily Racing Form*, August 30, 2010.

Grening, David, "Rachel Alexandra sharp in Saratoga drill," *Daily Racing Form*, September 13, 2010.

Grening, David, "Rachel Alexandra works; no confirmed plans," *Daily Racing Form*, September 20, 2010.

Grening, David, "Rachel Alexandra, 2009 Horse of the Year, is retired," *Daily Racing Form*, September 28, 2010.

Guthrie, Julian, "Jess Jackson took fast road to winner's circle," *San Francisco Chronicle*, July 4, 2009.

Haskin, Steve, "Big assist: Assistant trainers are the glue that holds big stables together," www.grayson-jockeyclub.org/newsimages/bigassist.pdf.

Haskin, Steve, "Rachel 'doing great,' ships to Ky. Tuesday," *Blood-Horse*, September 30, 2009.

Hanson, Vance, "The Woodward solution," Brisnet http://www.brisnet.com/cgi-bin/editorial/news/article.cgi?print=yes&id=15828, August 4, 2009.

Hersh, Marcus, "Rachel out of Apple Blossom," *Daily Racing Form*, March 14, 2010.

Hersh, Marcus, "Six-furlong breeze for 'Rachel,' " *Daily Racing Form*, February, 25, 2010.

Hersh, Marcus, "Tight schedule adds a hurdle for Rachel," *Daily Racing Form*, March 10, 2010.

Hersh, Marcus, "Rachel visits gate, gallops in fog," *Daily Racing Form*, March 11, 2010.

Hersh, Marcus, "Rachel may need this one," *Daily Racing Form*, March 11, 2010.

Hersh, Marcus, "Zardana spoils Rachel's comeback," *Daily Racing Form*, March 13, 2010.

Hersh, Marcus, "Rachel out of Apple Blossom," *Daily Racing Form*, March 14, 2010.

Hersh, Marcus, "Apple Blossom returns to Earth," *Daily Racing Form*, March 15, 2010.

Hersh, Marcus, "Rachel works half-mile right on schedule," *Daily Racing Form*, March 22, 2010.

Hersh, Marcus, "Rachel works before hitting the road," *Daily Racing Form*, March 29, 2010.

Hersh, Marcus, "Fair Grounds renames stakes for Rachel Alexandra," *Daily Racing Form*, September 29, 2010.

Hersh, Marcus, "Reflecting on Rachel Alexandra's next chapter," *Daily Racing Form*, October 1, 2010.

Himelstein, Abram, "Rachel schools in Fair Grounds paddock," *Daily Racing Form*, March 6, 2010.

Himelstein, Abram, "Rachel will face four foes in return," *Daily Racing Form*, March 8, 2010.

Himelstein, Abram, "Rachel cruises through final workout," *Daily Racing Form*, March 8, 2010.

Himelstein, Abram, "All systems go following Rachel's final work," *Daily Racing Form*, March 9, 2010.

Himelstein, Abram, "Rachel Alexandra gallops," *Daily Racing Form*, March 19, 2010.

Kane, Mike, "NYRA officials meet with horsemen," *Blood-Horse*, August 18, 2005.

Kane, Mike, "Saratoga girl," *Saratoga Living*, Winter 2009/2010.

Karmel, Terese, "Good job, Charlie," *The Blood-Horse*, April 25, 2009.

Kercheval, Nancy. "Rachel Alexandra holds on to lead to win Preakness." *Bloomberg*, May 16, 2009.

Kerrison, Ray, "Girl's got game," *New York Post*, August 3, 2009.

Kerrison, Ray, "Rachel is giving '70s legend run for money," *New York Post*, August 8, 2009.

Kerrison, Ray, "Rachel, beware!" *New York Post*, September 5, 2009.

King, Byron, "Unrivaled Belle beats Rachel Alexandra," *Daily Racing Form*, April 30, 2010.

King, Byron, "Rachel Alexandra back in winner's circle," *Daily Racing Form*, June 12, 2010.

Lambert, Craig, "Horseplayer extraordinaire," *Harvard Magazine*, March–April, 2010, p. 60–62.

LaMarra, Tom, "Hayward: NYRA has big plans, wary eye," *Blood-Horse*, December 9, 2008.

Layden, Tim, "Did that really happen?" *Sports Illustrated*, May 11, 2009.

Layden, Tim, "Lady's first," *Sports Illustrated*, May 25, 2009.

Layden, Tim, "Rachel reigns," *Sports Illustrated*, September 14, 2009.

Layden, Tim, "The Gossip Girl," *Sports Illustrated*, December 7, 2009.

Law, Tom, "Festival links venerable institutions," *Thoroughbred Times*, July 18, 2009.

Levinson, Mason, "Belmont has $3 million riding in Preakness on Mine That Bird," *Bloomberg*, May 15, 2009.

Lifton, Dave, "Rachel works six furlongs in Saratoga fog," *Daily Racing Form*, July 12, 2010.

Liftin, Dave, "Rachel 'nice, loose and happy" in work," *Daily Racing Form*, July 29, 2010.

Manning, Landon, "Did Saratogian deserve heavyweight title?" *Saratogian*, March 10, 1971.

Marr, Esther, "Lotta heaven," *The Blood-Horse*, August 8, 2009, 32.

McAdam, Mike, "Getting their bearings," *Daily Gazette*, August 5, 2009.

McKee, John, "John Morrissey brings high-stakes gambling to Saratoga Springs," *Chips: News from the Historical Society of Saratoga Springs*, Spring 1998.

McGee, Marty, "A day in the life: Calvin Borel," *Daily Racing Form*, June 6, 2009.

McGee, Marty, "Borel taken off Mine That Bird," *Daily Racing Form*, July 1, 2009.

McGee, Marty, "Rachel Alexandra has first Churchill workout," *Daily Racing Form*, April 5, 2010.

McGee, Marty, "'Very good work' for Rachel Alexandra," *Daily Racing Form*, April 12, 2010.

McGee, Marty, "Rachel Alexandra fires off fast work," *Daily Racing Form*, April 10, 2010.

McGee, Marty, "Rachel much fitter for rematch," *Daily Racing Form*, April 28, 2010.

McGee, Marty, "Rachel works for fourth straight Monday," *Daily Racing Form*, May 31, 2010.

McGee, Marty, "'Very smooth work for Rachel Alexandra," *Daily Racing Form*, June 7, 2010.

McGee, Mary. "Rachel will face just four in Fleur de Lis," *Daily Racing Form*, June 9, 2010.

McGee, Marty, "Rachel not first champ to run out of gas," *Daily Racing Form*, June 10, 2010.

McMurray, Jeffrey, "Despite safety reforms, racing fatalities continue," *Associated Press*, September 7, 2009.

Moran, Paul, "NYRA changes original plan," *Newsday*, June 6, 2005.

Moran, Paul, "The Inside Track," *Newsday*, June 28, 2005.

Moran, Paul, "Time has come for NYRA to hand over reins," *ESPN.com*, May 31, 2009.

Moran, Paul, "Defining greatness," *ESPN.com*, September 2, 2009.

Morrissey, John, letter to the editor, *Daily Saratogian*, June 17, 1871.

Munson, John, "Belmont winner Summer Bird just didn't have enough to beat Rachel Alexandra," *Star-Ledger*, August 2, 2009.

Murray, Ken, "Rachel Alexandra wins Preakness," *Baltimore Sun*, May 17, 2009.

National Thoroughbred Racing Association, "Rachel has first work." http://www.ntra.com/blog/index/print?id=44644&type=news.

National Thoroughbred Racing Association, "Oaklawn talking "Race for the Ages." February, 4, 2010, http://www.ntra.com/blog/index/print?id=44665&type=news.

National Thoroughbred Racing Association, "Zenyatta, Rachel matchup worth $5 million," February 4, 2010, http://www.ntra.com/blog/index/print?id=44680&type=news.

National Thoroughbred Racing Association, "Rachel Alexandra picks up the pace," February 6, 2010, http://www.ntra.com/blog/index/print?id=44732&type=news.

National Thoroughbred Racing Association, "Rachel won't make Apple Blossom," February 10, 2010, http://www.ntra.com/blog/index/print?id=44767&type=news.

National Thoroughbred Racing Association, "Rachel to make 2010 debut at Fair Grounds," February 11, 2010, http://www.ntra.com/blog/idnex/print?id=44802&type=news

National Thoroughbred Racing Association, "Apple Blossom showdown back on," February 11, 2010, http://www.ntra.com/blog/inex/print?id=44788type=news.=

National Thoroughbred Racing Association, "Rachel Alexanddra looks strong at Fair Grounds," March 21, 2010, http://www.ntra.com/blog/index/print?id=45103&type=news.

National Thoroughbred Racing Association, "Personal Ensign next for Rachel Alexandra," July 31, 2010, http://www.ntra.com/blog/index/print?id=46173&type=news.

National Thoroughbred Racing Association, "Rachel Alexandra fires bullet at Saratoga," September 27, 2010, http://www.ntra.com/blog/index/print?id=46557&type=news.

New York Times, "John Morrissey's burial," May 4, 1878.

New York Times, "Brophy drops Zito as trainer," January 23, 1992.

New York Times, "Zito tells his side to police," June 11, 1992.

New York Times, "HORSE RACING; Perfect run for Zito except for the finish," May 22, 1994.

New York Times, "New Pastime for Mattingly," May 3, 1996.

New York Times, "HORSE RACING; 15-day suspension of Zito reported," Jun 24, 2001.

Nobles, Charlie, "With victory, High Fly course for Derby," *New York Times*, April 3, 2005.

O'Brien, Maureen, "Turmoil at Time," *New York Post*, June 27, 2006.

Odato, James, "Ante rises for VLTs," *Times Union*, August 18, 2009.

Paulick, Ray, "In a league of her own," *ESPN.com*, September 6, 2009.

Pedulla, Tom, "Rachel Alexadra beats boys again, gallops to Haskell crown," *USA Today*, August 3, 2009.

Plonk, Jeremy, "Racing's legendary ladies," *ESPN.com*, September 2, 2009.

Post, Paul, "NYRA reveals '09 giveaways," *Saratogian*, June 30, 2009.

Post, Paul, "Big names spur racing excitement," *Saratogian*, July 22, 2009.

Post, Paul, "NYRA shuts out Nassau Regional OTB," *Thoroughbred Times*, July 24, 2009.

Post, Paul, "NYRA to sue Nassau OTB," *Saratogian*, August 5, 2009.

Powers, John, "Filly fanatics will turn out to watch 'Rachel' at Woodward," *Boston Globe*, September 5, 2009.

Powers, John, "'Rachel' makes historic run in Woodward," *Boston Globe*, September 6, 2009.

Precious, Tom, "Hayward officially name CEO of NYRA," *Blood-Horse*, November 4, 2004.

Privman, Jay, "HORSE RACING; Two trainers with Triple Vision," *New York Times*, Jne 3, 1996.

Privman, Jay, "Who's Borel riding now?" *Daily Racing Form*, May 18, 2009.

Privman, Jay, "Mine That Bird can give Borel a personal sweep," *Daily Racing Form*, June 6, 2009.

Privman, Jay. "Rachel Alexandra wins Horse of the Year," *Daily Racing Form*, January 18, 2010.

Privman, Jay, "Rachel confirmed for Friday's La Troienne." *Daily Racing Form*, April 24, 2010.

Rampellini, Mary. "Apple Blossom preparations gathering stream." *Daily Racing Form*, March 2, 2010.

Rees, Jennie, "Derby winner Mine That bird a star in West Virginia," *Courier-Journal*, July 31, 2009.

Rees, Jennie, "Stretch duel wowed trainers," *Courier-Journal*, May 18, 2009.

Rees, Jennie, "Macho Again's camp isn't afraid of Rachel," *Courier-Journal*, September 3, 2009.

Rees, Jennie, "Alexandra the great dazzles in Woodward," *Courier-Journal*, September 5, 2009.

Rosenblatt, Richard, "Rachel Alexandra dominates boys in Haskell," *Lexington Herald-Leader*, August 2, 2009.

Rosenblatt, Richard, "Travers still compelling despite missing 2 stars," *Associated Press*, August 29, 2009.

Rowe, Howard, "Saratoga's sponsor," *American TURF Monthly*, August, 1986.

Scheinman, John, "Zito's key to success: Training the owner," *Washington Post*, May 3, 2005.

Scott, Jeff, "Why not Saratoga?" *Saratogian*, June 30, 2009.

Singelais, Mark, "'Bird' is Saratoga's latest star," *Times Union*, July 2, 2009.

Thoroughbred Times, "Gross rises 45.6% at Saratoga sale," August 12, 2009.

Vecsey, George, "Holding her own for her new team," *The New York Times*, May 17, 2009.

Veitch, Michael, "Zito's Travers Edge," *Saratogian*, July 22, 2009.

Welsch, Mike, "Rachel looks like old self in Churchill breeze," *Daily Racing Form*, April 26, 2010.

Welsch, Mike, "Asmussen: Rachel ran fine, looks good," *Daily Racing Form*, May 1, 2010.

Welsch, Mike, "Rachel Alexandra has final drill for Personal Ensign," *Daily Racing Form*, August 23, 2010.

Welch, Mike, "Persistently stuns Rachel in Personal Ensign," *Daily Racing Form*, August 29, 2010.

West, Gary, "Rachel Alexandra is as close to greatness as we will see," *Star-Telegram*, September 5, 2009.

Wheeler, Lydia, "Racing toward a new meet," *Post Star*, July 26, 2009.

Wilkin, Tim, "Already talking about dream race," *Times Union*, June 30, 2009.

Wilkin, Tim, "Rachel going for greatness," *Times Union*, September 4, 2009.

Wilkin, Tim, "Rachel shows she's best," *Times Union*, September 6, 2009.

Wilkin, Tim, "Rachel roars; so do we," *Times Union*, September 6, 2009.

Wilkin, Tim, "Rachel could rest till 2010," *Times Union*, September 7, 2009.

Yusko, Dennis, "Uncertainty as post time nears," *Times Union*, July 26, 2009.

Books

Life of John Morrissey, The Great Publishing House, 1878.

Manning, Landon. *The Noble Animals, A Look into the Past of Events of the Turf at Saratoga, New York*, Landon Manning First Printing, 1973.

Hotaling, Edward. *They're Off! Horse Racing at Saratoga*, Syracuse University Press, 1995.

Johnson, Karen, M. *The Training Game, An Inside Look at American Racing's Top Trainers*. New York, DRF Press, 2008.